SUCCESSFUL COMMUNICATION
FOR
BUSINESS DEVELOPMENT

Successful Communication for Business Development

—

Edited By

ANGELA WADIA

KANISHKA PUBLISHERS, DISTRIBUTORS
NEW DELHI-110 002

KANISHKA PUBLISHERS, DISTRIBUTORS
4697/5-21A, Ansari Road, Darya Ganj
New Delhi-110 002
Phones: 327 0497, 328 8285
Fax: 91-328 8285

First Published 2000

ISBN 81-7391-324-2

PRINTED IN INDIA

Published by Madan Sachdeva for Kanishka Publishers, Distributors, 4697/5-21A, Ansari Road, Darya Ganj, New Delhi-110 002; Typeset by Laserdot, Noida-201301, and Printed at Nice Printing Press, Delhi.

Preface

We live in a world driven by communication. The information explosion that has taken place in the past two decades comprises three basic elements: the computer, representing the electronics revolution; the telecommunication upsurge which has made possible the fact of globalisation and the global village; and the technological revolution that has helped realise the advances in industry, manufacturing, services and consumer goods. Rising aspirations have led to the phenomenon of consumerism and surplus purchasing power has resulted in a marketing boom that would appear to be unprecedented in the history of mankind and his world of trade and commerce. The great driving forces in this revolution of the millennium have been the spirit of innovation in business enterprises, the miracle of the computer software industry, and last, but not the least, the insatiable market fuelled by ever-new marketing techniques. The result in its totality has been stunning.

Communication is the golden key that opens the lock of successful marketing. Whether the entrepreneur communicates with his customer—either interpersonally, through mail and promotional literatures, or through advertising—or communicates with his distributor or with his suppliers and vendors, the purpose is to elicit the right response and promote one's business. Successful communication for business development stresses the very cornerstone of corporate and entrepreneurial growth. The guidelines profile presented in the present publication encompass such vital areas as, information gathering and analysis for decision-making, information systems for business control and resource management, written and oral communication for business development, the value and interpretation of market intelligence, the meaning of in-house communication, and the strategic applications in areas such as marketing, accounting and critical administration. Collectively, the materials point to the need for information that is correct and timely, analysis that is appropriate and company-oriented, and communication that is effective, positive and comprehensive. The publication will be of much use to all students and teachers of business administration, management executives, aware entrepreneurs and marketing specialists.

ANGELA WADIA

Contents

CHAPTER 1

Process and Patterns of Communication: An Introduction

Perspective

The world has opened up for the enterprising individual. The age of globalisation and free market economies has brought about a sea change in the interaction of people across countries, even continents. The age of information is a gift of science to the thinking and doing people of the world. This chapter provides a profile of the dynamics of the age.

In 1980, when the demand for a New International Information and Communication Order brought into focus the sharp divergence of views between a group of Western countries led by the United States, and the rest of the world, a meeting of the Inter-Governmental Council of the Non-Aligned Movement (NAM) in Baghdad adopted a Declaration according to which the New Information and Communication Order should be based on:

(a) The fundamental principles of international law, notably self-determination, sovereignty and non-interference;
(b) The right of people and individuals to an objective picture of reality by means of accurate and comprehensive information;
(c) The right of every nation to develop its own independent information system, in particular by regulating the activities of transnational corporations;
(d) The right of every nation to make known worldwide its interests, aspirations and its political, moral and cultural values;
(e) The right of every nation to resist, within constitutional limits, the distribution of the false or distorted information;

(*f*) The right of every nation to participate at governmental and non-governmental level in international exchange of information under favourable conditions.

As a further extension of these principles, the Baghdad Declaration also underlined that the New Information Order was intended to contribute to the establishment of a New International Economic Order and to promote human rights through intensified efforts to consolidate social, economic and cultural development. As a part of this objective, hunger, disease, illiteracy and unemployment which are the bane of developing countries should be countered through communication. Of international importance were the other two stipulations in the Declaration. First, the New Information Order should strengthen peace and international understanding, safeguarding detente and promoting disarmament. Secondly, the New Order should effectively contribute to the struggle against imperialism, colonialism, neo-colonialism, racism, Zionism and apartheid and all forms of foreign aggression, occupation, domination and interference. In the international context this was a most significant formulation.

Surfeit of Images

These principles came into focus at the General Conference of UNESCO (Belgrade, November 1980) and were reflected in such documents as the MacBride report and the New Information and Communication Order Resolution, as accepted by UNESCO. While it is not necessary to discuss, in this chapter, the developments which followed and ultimately inflicted a serious blow on UNESCO and the university of its character, it needs to be stated that the principles of the Baghdad Declaration reflect the genuine concerns of a large part of the world. The challenge of colonialism, Zionism, apartheid, for example, has still to be met through the information media and communication systems. Similarly, the role of communication for 'strengthening peace and international understanding' can also not be overestimated. Clearly, international communication (media flow across countries and continents) has been both the cause and effect of the prevailing state of international relations. Whether it is through the contents of messages in international broadcasting (including news which is expected to be factual), or through the exchange of such material as films, books, newspapers, etc., the level of understanding between any two countries has been a most important indicator in determining direction as well as trends.

In 1966, the UN General Assembly adopted a Covenant on Civil and Political Rights, Article 19 of which stated that:

1. Everyone shall have the right to hold opinions without interference;
2. Everyone shall have the right to freedom of expression; this right shall include freedom to seek, receive and impart information and ideas of all kinds, regardless of frontiers, either orally, in writing or in print, in the form of art, or through the media of his choice.

Of course, another paragraph in this article makes a reference to "respect for the rights or reputation of others" and "protection of national security or of public order or of public health or morals." On these grounds, it is stated that a nation can restrict the flow of information from outside its borders. The fact, however, remains that flow of information across the borders has been subjected to all kinds of restrictions including jamming of broadcasting, distortion of facts or misrepresenting the aspirations of the peoples, besides misinformation and disinformation.

Stipulations similar to the ones provided in Article 19 of the Covenant have been adopted by several countries in their own policy documents but their observance has been uneven, to put it mildly. Often, prejudices of governments or of individuals in the media and the dominance of interest of certain organisations like the multinationals on the media have exerted pressures, outside the declared policies.

The role of a communicator or a journalist needs to be discussed against this background. Of course, the role of a communicator has defied any clear definition but a few principles, primarily in the Indian context, may be mentioned at this forum.

In his autobiography, Mahatma Gandhi mentioned three objectives of a newspaper. One, to understand the popular feeling and give expression to it. Second, to arouse among the people certain desirable sentiments. And three, to fearlessly expose popular defects. These principles, irrespective of the terminology, are universal in character and are subscribed to by media professionals anywhere in the world. Of course, Gandhi had a mission which in his own words was "to teach by example and percept under severe restraint the use of the matchless weapon of *satyagraha* which is a direct corollary of non-violence and truth." To further clarify his point Gandhi said that he tried not to write in anger or with malice and not to write merely to excite passion. All these principles, even today, provide philosophy for the various kinds of media guidelines.

Since then, some major changes in communication media, particularly in their formats, have taken place and access to high technology has introduced several new factors. These changes have invested the media with tremendous power to influence and to mould opinion in whatever direction. Even so, we in India have reaffirmed our faith in free flow of information and ideas. Article 19 of the Indian Constitution guarantees freedom of speech and expression. India's first Prime Minister, Jawaharlal Nehru, who was one of the most passionate defenders of liberty, once said:

> "I do think that basically it is dangerous to suppress thought and the expression of thought in any way, because this may, besides suppressing a particular good thing, produce many kinds of evil which stunt the growth of a social group." This statement may appear as a somewhat qualified acceptance of total freedom of the media and raise the question whether free expression ought to be unlimited. But Nehru believed that words alone may produce grave international situations. On another occasion, he said: "We cannot imperil the safety of the whole nation in the name of some fancied freedom which puts an end to all freedoms."

The point to be underlined, as we believe, is that the freedom of media professionals cannot be without responsibility.

Only Educate and Inform

What then is the role of a communicator or journalist? There is a world-wide acceptance that his or her responsibility is to inform and educate. This is achieved through "the news on the news page and editorials on the editorial page." Whether the journalist has also a responsibility to "organise" is a point for discussion.

Prof. Yassen Zassuraskly, Dean of the Moscow State University School of Journalism, holds the view that information must provide for the "objective needs of the reader." Since any information or commentary contributes to behaviour and actions, the role of the journalist as an "organiser" is implied in the behaviour and actions of the people.

This concept has come under some severe criticism in the Western media. But do the journalists in the West function under complete freedom and with total "objectivity"? How do they respond to the pressures of the governments, particularly in international relations, or even of multinationals who have vested interests in serious matters of war and peace?

We believe that a journalist while enjoying freedom to report and comment has a social responsibility. He can perform this role without compromising his role as an "investigator" or as a "watch-dog." In other words, while the journalist is not to be contented with a "stand and watch" role he cannot disregard ethics of communication including such international obligations which concern basic questions of peace and war. This fact has become particularly sensitive because of access to high communication technology which, as I have said, invests the media with formidable power.

The New Information Age

Technologists and Western communications scholars would have us believe that we shall soon enter what is called the Information Age. Sophisticated telecommunications networks, use of computers not only for collaborative industrial, commercial or public service functions but by individuals in their own homes, and access to satellites for mass communication will, in the foreseeable future, usher in a communication revolution the impact of which will not spare any part of the globe. The concept of a "global village" which Marshall McLuhan propounded will be a reality. They would also assure us that world communications networks will benefit both developing and industrial countries. While for the developed countries the revolution will create a major market for equipment, in developing countries a more comprehensive world system will increase international traffic to the advantage of the operator. Besides, it is claimed, the new information technology will augment trade and commerce which, in turn, will increase understanding leading to "a better and safer world." This, obviously, is a vision of a "happy world."

There are two points to be made in this scenario of induction of modern communication technology in developing societies. First, it is not a "normal" process, *i.e.*, it does not admit of people's familiarity with and acceptance of the new tools in a society which has only a small percentage of well-to-do urban and literate people. Even if and when the opportunities are extended to the rural population, where is the guarantee that they will not be grabbed by the rural rich alone? And secondly, which is a much more important human factor in developing societies, the total concern about economic growth misses the social and cultural consequences. The development of mediated communications, warns the MacBride report (1977), may be a threat to the quality and values of culture. It may also indiscriminately open doors to new experiences and impressions by the media which will alienate people from their own culture.

Let me relate this point to our own experience. India today has acquired access to the principal tool of communication technology, *i.e.*, satellite, computer and telecommunications. But whether it is the telecast of programmes through satellite, introduction of computers in public utility services or even in schools, or of extension of telecommunications, the social and cultural issues thus arising have not been comprehended. The plans of communication technology and their implementation have, by and large, been left to policy makers and technocrats.

Some such questions were discussed by us recently, perhaps for the first time, in a national seminar on "Technology and Communication Development" organised by the Indian Institute of Mass Communication and NAMEDIA Foundation.

The seminar brought together some highly committed technologists, dedicated media professionals, social scientists and policy makers including the Minister of State for Science and Technology, Advisor to the Prime Minister on Technology Missions and the Secretary, Ministry of Information and Broadcasting. The views expressed at the seminar are, therefore, of considerable importance.

The fact that the process of modernisation in communication had been initiated, broadly, within the country's own resources and with a view to achieve certain national objectives, it was noted, was a significant development. But a fear was also expressed that communication technology will benefit a small section of the metropolitan towns thus widening, rather than narrowing, the existing gap in access to information and its utilisation. Similarly, unless technology is demystified and diverse sections of society are made familiar with its potential and attitudinal changes envisaged as part of the communication process, technology will alienate the bulk of the community rather than bringing the people together. More importantly, the modernisation of communication cannot be divorced from ethical and social considerations, which in our society involve a synthesis of national, regional and local diversities. In this context two related factors mentioned were: first, traditional modes of communication which have been found effective in all situations including the freedom struggle cannot be marginalised. And, secondly, folk and traditional media are a part of our cultural heritage; therefore, they must be preserved as an expression of the national ethos. Modern media can trample on traditions and cause serious damage to centuries-old socio-economic patterns.

Using Indian Idiom

While India needs to adopt a new communication order making a shift with modern technology, the order has to be Indian in its character. It has to be related to "the complex and compelling needs of national integration, economic development and social emancipation in a multi-regional, multilingual and multi-religious society." The recommendation, therefore, was for evolving a policy framework in order to broadbase access to and utilisation of technology and its tools. In our state of development and in view of our economic, social and cultural diversities, this cannot be left to the market forces. Communication technologies, unlike other technologies, affect us all. Moreover, it is a powerful instrument for better or for worse.

We have referred to the views expressed at our national seminar in some detail because they have a great relevance in the international flow of media tools and contents. This has to be seen in the context of what is called a "one-way flow." I do not propose to give statistics but the fact is that exported media contents have far-reaching consequences—political as well as cultural and social.

Technology itself is not always neutral. Of a more serious consequence is the transmission of material through satellite. Direct broadcasting of TV programmes in the foreseeable future will substantially alter the situation. Will it help the national and international cause? What should then be the role of a communicator journalist.

Scenario in Developing Countries

Developing countries striving to put together an infrastructure for a news exchange system are up against two major obstacles. They are:

1. poor telecommunications
2. paucity of professionally trained journalists to man the system.

We, from the non-aligned and developing countries, therefore, look forward to the deliberations of this seminar, which is devoted exclusively to these two problems confronting us. And I have no doubt we would greatly benefit from the discussions and outcome of this seminar.

Since its inception, non-aligned news pool has been struggling to resolve the aforementioned two obstacles which stand in the way of smooth and successful functioning of this unique experiment in international news exchange, embracing four continents and connecting countries at varying levels of technological development and widely dispersed from each other.

At one end, there are countries which still depend upon the primitive manual-operated apparatus on which you tap out the Morse code. At the other end, you have countries advanced enough to utilise the facility of the satellite for transmission of news and information. In between a very large number of countries depend upon a wholly undependable and expensive wireless system for transmitting their news and information to each other.

Those amongst us who have established ground stations are switching to satellite channels for transmission of news. Some of them like India and Sri Lanka and Indonesia, have already introduced the concessional PBS for Press messages. More countries are expected to follow the example.

Several of the major non-aligned countries have availed of the facility offered by the Inter Press Service as a carrier over the latter's widespread computerised satellite network that links up with a large number of non-aligned countries in the Arab world, Latin America and some countries in Africa.

An integrated telecommunication system that dovetails terrestrial system with the satellite channels would appear to be the answer. And that is what we are trying to achieve.

The other obstacle, the paucity of professionally trained journalists is also being vigorously tackled. A crash programme of special training in news agency journalism has been launched in five centres in five different non-aligned countries, with English, French, Spanish and Arabic as the medium of instruction.

In India, this course is being conducted by the Indian Institute of Mass Communication, New Delhi. The first batch of trainees from 15 different non-aligned countries including India have already gone through the course, which began in December 1978 and concluded in May 1979. The second batch began their course on 1 September 1979.

There are of course other communication problems confronting the developing countries, which need to be tackled scientifically and systematically. Many of these countries, like India or Indonesia, have vast rural hinterland; much of it is inaccessible by road or telecommunication, and have largely to depend upon the transistor radio for news, information and instruction as well as entertainment. They are beyond the reach of the Press, which is largely urban-oriented. Nor are they within the reach of the television, as of now.

This creates a situation where even though the majority of the country's population live in the rural region, very little news of the rural areas reaches the cities. It is in the villages that significant social change occur, and yet it often goes unnoticed and unreported by the media. Here is indeed a local version of one-way flow of news, from urban to rural areas, and with urban bias, nearly as bad a one-way as from the developed to the developing countries. Whereas, our aim and effort should be to generate a two-way flow of information between the countryside and the city. Then alone we will know what is really happening in the country, as overwhelming majority of the people live in the villages, and that is where the news about the country is.

We at this seminar should find a remedy for this anomaly. Basing part time correspondents in villages is no satisfactory solution. My own suggestion of a remedy is that the urban newspapers should maintain a specialised staff, well-versed in rural developmental and agrarian and agricultural problems, who should from time to time tour the rural areas and come back and report on the social, economic and developmental aspects of the village life, so as to establish a two-way flow of news between rural and urban areas and provide the valuable feedback to the government on what the people think and do.

There is also a great need to establish periodical newspapers, weeklies and monthlies, to meet the reading requirements of the rural population—periodicals exclusively devoted to the reading needs of the rural population, covering such subjects as agrarian reform and agricultural reform and progress and which provide incentive for social change. Here the state has a role to play, by subsiding and encouraging rural journalism and journals.

One of the problems of the rural regions is the lapse into illiteracy among adults, which can be best averted by the kind of periodicals I have mentioned earlier as well as cheap reading material through paperbacks sold at such popular resorts as the post offices and highway petrol pumps.

The problem of rural neglect by the media could also be tackled by more intensive, imaginative and purposeful use of radio so as to produce a two-way exchange and feedback.

Taming Television

Indiscriminate introduction of television in countries which do not command either the hardware and software to make it worthwhile leading to another hazard in the developing countries. A clever salesman from Western industrialised countries palms off on a backward country a television set-up. Television being a status symbol among new nations, the governments swallow the bait and gets television installed in the country, made available to it on easy financial terms.

Once TV is installed, the realisation comes that the country concerned commands neither the software nor even adequate repairs and maintenance facilities for the hardware. That only leads to greater dependence on the industrialised nation that sold the TV apparatus to the government of the developing country. It means importing, on a large scale, of Western mostly American TV programmes. There are developing countries where 65 to 80 per cent of the TV programmes are American or West European. That amounts to a cultural invasion through the media, culturally detrimental to the country which is the victim of such invasion. As evening after evening the young people of the country watch TV programmes presenting American way of life, entirely divorced from the realities and values surrounding them, the country faces the danger of cultural subversion and other evils of cultural disorientation. This is a hazard confronting most developing countries which are snowed under not only by alien and inimical TV image but also by the one-way free flow international news disseminated by the monopolist Western news agencies.

In New Delhi, as you enter the hexagonal foyer of the headquarters building of All India Radio, the following lines, etched in golden letters hold your attention:

> I do not want my house to be walled in on all sides and my windows to be stuffed. I want the cultures of all lands to be blown about my house as freely as possible. But I refuse to be blown off my feet by any. Mine is not a religion of the prison house.

These words from Mahatma Gandhi, father of the Indian nation, not only symbolise the affirmation of India's faith in freedom, but focus the light on the dilemma confronting the developing countries.

We do want to enrich our own culture from the freely blowing winds of other cultures. But we do not want to be blown off our feet by the sheer velocity of alien cultural winds.

It has been the experience of many developing countries that despite the vogue of modern electronic mass media, the traditional and interpersonal media continue to be the most effective in certain areas such as family planning or agricultural propaganda. We would do well here to devote some time and attention to this aspect of communication, particularly in the area of nation-building tasks. I have no doubt that it is possible to plan a judicious mix of the two kinds of media to derive the maximum benefit.

I would like to say a few words about the functioning of the Non-Aligned News Pool, which has been a target of attack and considerable misconception among its Western critics.

Non-Aligned News Pool is today several years old—and very much alive and kicking, despite the gloomy prophecies of its enemies.

Since 1976, when the Pool was launched amid much controversy and hostility from the West as well as some quarters in the non-aligned world, we have travelled a significant distance. Many who came to scoff and jeer, stayed on to cheer and are now reconciled to the institution of a news exchange system among the non-aligned countries. They realised we meant business.

By way of building its infrastructure, the Pool has established redistribution centres in the various regions of the non-aligned world. Most of these centres are functioning effectively. The volume of news exchange has increased more than five times. Today, approximately 40,000 words of news is being exchanged everyday among the non-aligned nations.

As stated earlier by me, we have achieved a breakthrough in regard to two major obstacles in the effective function of the Pool. Both the telecommunication problem and the problem of paucity of trained journalistic personnel are being vigorously tackled.

In addition, efforts are being made to persuade those non-aligned countries who do not yet have news agencies of their own, to set them up. They have been offered technical and financial assistance—the financial assistance is sought to be obtained from UNESCO. Mauritius and Seychelles have already applied for such assistance, and their applications are now being processed. Sierra Leone is in correspondence with me exploring possibilities of launching a news agency of its own.

Seminars and workshops are being held among journalists from non-aligned countries at which practical problems of handling non-aligned news are analysed and discussed and remedies sought and experiences exchanged. We held such a seminar in Baghdad in October 1978 and a workshop at Kinshasa alongside the meeting of co-ordination committee in March 1979.

Our charge of imbalance and one-way flow in the pattern of international news, initially indignantly denied by the Western media, has now been conceded by them. Our complaint of bias, and of distortion, in the Western coverage of news from the developing countries too has been acquiesced in. Indeed, there have been protestations from the West that they were not at all opposed to developing countries setting up their own news agencies, and that they indeed welcomed a multiplicity of sources of information. They have even preferred technical aid and professional assistance to the developing countries in building up infrastructures for setting up their national news agencies.

We are of course appreciative of their offers of technical and financial aid and training facilities. But we are naturally anxious not to repeat our past mistakes, which were responsible for the perpetuation of the colonial pattern of news flow in the developing world. We are committed to a decolonisation of news.

We would, therefore, want to be very careful and choosy in accepting their offers so as to ensure that the news services we evolve are not once again based on alien Western values but conform to our realities and media needs and our concept of the role of media in the developing society.

Hence our insistence that all external aid should be routed through UNESCO, and not given bilaterally, and that we should determine the manner and pattern of the utilisation of that aid, particularly in the field of training.

Emerging News Scenario

But make no mistake. The battle is not ended yet. Hostility, suspicion and distrust persist on the part of the Western media against non-aligned countries' efforts to build their own news sources and media. These legitimate efforts at self-reliance by the developing countries continue to be dubbed as disguised attempts to control news and shut out Western mediamen from the developing countries, as if it is a crime to start our own national news agencies.

We regret to note a tendency on the part of Western mediamen to retract from the commitments undertaken by the Western governments in subscribing to the Declaration on mass media, unanimously adopted by the UNESCO, in Paris, and to the very concept of a new and more balanced World Information Order to which the West committed themselves. They now seem to reject even the concept of responsibilities of journalists and a code of ethics evolved by the journalistic profession itself, to which the historic media Declaration of UNESCO commits them.

They accept at the domestic level a code of ethics and self-regulation through a Press Council and ombudsman. But they, in the same breath, refuse to countenance them at the international level, where a code and some constraints seem imperative, particularly in the present electronic era and nuclear age of instant messages and images, where a slip of misinformation could start a nuclear war, without any time available to rectify the misinformation.

In the hazardous times we live in, it is but right that we should look around for some device whereby international media are made more responsible and accountable to the international community.

CHAPTER 2

Basics of Effective Communication

Communication is a two-way process. One person sends the message and another receives it. But what happens when I send a message and the other person doesn't receive it fully? Is it still communication?

Of course it is. After all, it does have a person who is transmitting a message and who wants to share it with someone else. Only it isn't *effective communication.*

We have heard innumerable jokes about the consequences of miscommunication. For instance, suppose you heard somebody say, "Genes cause cancer." Wouldn't you throw your Levis out of the house? And all because you thought he meant "jeans" instead of "genes!"

So where does that lead us? It leads us to the fact that communication is effective only when it gets the desired action or response (see Fig. 2.1).

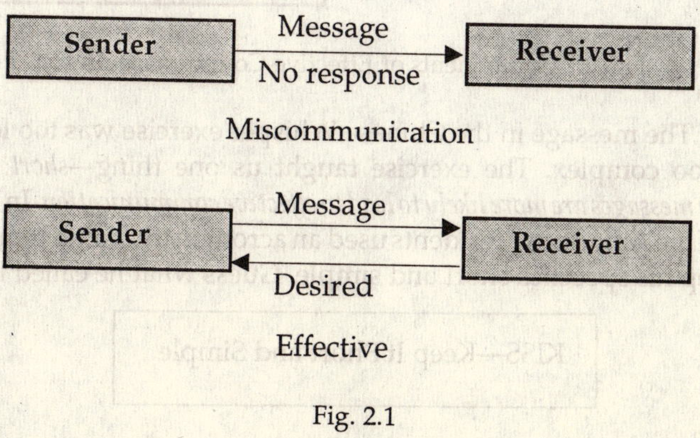

Fig. 2.1

Suppose you tell the watchman—"Please move that car in front of the gate, I want to take out my scooter." Later you find that the car which was parked just outside the gate has now been moved inside, but you still can't take out your scooter. Obviously your communication to the watchman has not got you the desired response.

Let us summarise. We know now that communication:

— is a two-way process
— involves a sender and a receiver
— is most effective only when it gets the desired response from the receiver

Now let's take a look at what could make communication more effective (see Fig. 2.2). Do you recall the exercise done in class? What was it that led to the sad state of communication?

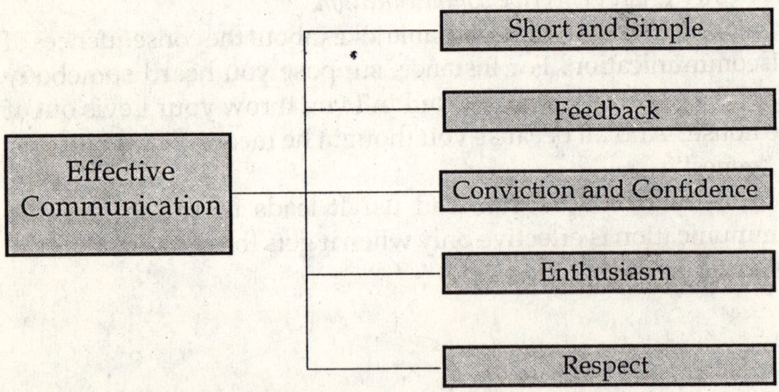

Fig. 2.2 Components of Effective Communication

The message in the Chinese Whisper exercise was too long and too complex. The exercise taught us one thing—*short and simple messages are more likely to lead to effective communication.* In fact one of the American Presidents used an acronym to remind himself to keep his speeches short and simple. Guess what he called it?

KISS—Keep It Short and Simple

What else did we learn from the exercise? We learnt that one-way communication can make the message go awry. It is very essential to get *feedback* from the receiver to ensure that he has received the message we sent.

Take the case of the carpenter and his assistant—very eager but definitely low on IQ. The carpenter picked up a large nail and said, "When I hold this nail in position and nod my head, hit it hard with the hammer." We all know that the poor carpenter died instantaneously (God bless his soul!). But couldn't it have been avoided? If only he had asked his assistant for feedback he would have discovered that by "it" the assistant understood "my head" and not "the nail." A classic example of poor communication, easily avoidable if only feedback had taken place.

Remember, everyone will have his own perception of what he thinks you said. So why not clear it up by using feedback together with *clarity, simplicity and brevity.*

There is a lot more to effective communication. Look at people who have been universally acknowledged as great communicators. Look at Indira Gandhi, Winston Churchill, John F. Kennedy, Atal Bihari Vajpayee. Why do we call them good communicators? Is it only because they keep their messages simple and take regular feedback. Surely there is something more to it!

In simple terms, one would call it style. But what is a good style or a bad style?

All these famous orators had certain traits in common. Their posture for example. They had a very *alert, attentive and enthusiastic posture.* They never had a lazy look about them. The way they stood, the way they held their head, the way they made gestures, the way they looked at the audience everything about them signified action and enthusiasm. Next time you get an opportunity to hear a good speaker, observe these things.

It is not just the contents of a speech but also the way it is put across that makes the difference.

Another great thing about good communicators is their projection of confidence and conviction. Recall any of Kennedy's speeches. You will find his tone extremely compelling and forceful. You can almost physically feel the force of conviction in his speeches. It is amazing, the way you feel after listening to one of these good speeches. You feel like going out and doing something about it straightaway. Why do you feel this way? Because you have been convinced that this is the thing to do.

And this is true of any communication between any two people. If you talk to somebody with conviction, he is likely to believe you and may be spurred into action. If on the other hand the other person thinks that you lack conviction, he will definitely not be convinced by you. Imagine this happening in a selling situation. Imagine the salesman in a shop selling music systems. If the salesman sounds bored, keeps yawning, and appears thoroughly unconvinced about his own product, would you ever buy from him? Of course not! He does not seem to believe in his own product so how can you?

Why don't you try this simple exercise.

Stand in front of a mirror and talk to your mirror image. Try to convince your mirror-image about something you yourself are not convinced about.

Now straighten yourself up, and try to convince your image about something you believe in very strongly.

Did you notice the difference?

Didn't you feel better after the second attempt? That is exactly the point. *Confidence and conviction are crucial to any communication activity.*

Respect for the Other Person

Recall an incident where someone was rude to you. It may have been someone rudely pushing you aside when you were standing in a queue for tickets. Or it may have been a motorist shouting at you to get out of his way. Or it may just have been a clerk in a government department, firing you for not having all twenty-two documents that you were supposed to have, complete, and in triplicate.

How did you feel in such cases? Upset? Unhappy? Hurt? Probably all of these and more. Would you like to deal with these people again? Obviously not—you would much rather deal with someone who gave you respect.

Remember, every human being has a certain self-esteem. And he certainly wants to be treated with courtesy, politeness, and respect. If not, your communication will break down because he simply does not want to talk to you any more.

Can you see how crucial this is in a selling situation? If your customer does not want to talk to you any more, how can you sell to him? Conversely, some of the best salespeople in existence are those who give their customers due respect. "Yes Sir! I quite understand your problem, Sir. However, would you mind if I check with my Head Office," is a far better approach than "Who told you that? Never! I'll check with my Head Office, but you are just wasting your time—and mine!"

What goes into respect? Many, many things. For instance, speaking to your customers politely. Not interrupting him while he is speaking. Appreciating his point of view. And remember, it is not just the Managing Director who deserves your respect. Even a *paan-wallah*, if he happens to be your customer, deserves the same respect. After all, if you rise to become the General Manager (Sales), the very same *paan-wallah* is at least partly responsible, isn't he?

Communication Hierarchy*

In order to make upward communication meaningful, the management may take the following steps. These may be called the methods of upward communication also.

Opportunity to Make Suggestions

Employees should be invited not only to make suggestions but to sell suggestions. Some of them are capable of making suggestions on the basis of their long experience and personalised skill on the job. They may make suggestions for improving the method of work, equipment, working conditions or the efficiency of work by reducing wastages.

Usually suggestion boxes are fitted at every conspicuous place—usually one box for each 25 to 30 employees; the suggestions are secured by a committee and they are approved for implementation. If the suggestions are result-oriented the employees are rewarded in two ways:

(i) they are given merit and recognition award, and
(ii) cash or tangible value award.

---

* This part of the chapter is based on discussion paper on Corporate Communication published by the American Management Association, Detroit Chapter.

In order to make the method as an effective system of upward communication, it becomes necessary that all suggestions received should periodically be scanned and speedily disposed of on merit. Those which can be implemented should be done immediately and those which require further clarification should be referred to the concerned employee.

Opinion Surveys

On certain issues the employee will not like to express his opinion openly for fear of retaliation by his superiors. Opinion surveys provide anonymity to employees besides giving them the instrument of free and frank expression of their opinions. Such surveys are undertaken to assess the reaction of employees on such issues as "working conditions, pay, employee benefits, co-operation of fellow employees, employee-supervisor relations, confidence in management, competence of supervision, effectiveness of administration, communication, job security, status, recognition, opportunity for growth and advancement and identification with the company." Opinions so collected should not be locked in cold storage otherwise it will do more harm than good to the company. These opinions should be systematically classified to identify the issue which may be taken for action either unilaterally by the management or in consultation with employees' representatives.

Grievance Meetings

This forum provides an opportunity of upward communication. The employee either personally or through his union may represent his grievance for redressal by management. The grievance may be put either orally or in writing.

Reports and Documents

Report is a factual document which contains the information meant for the superiors. The middle level management may make a report for the top management or the non-managers may report to the managers. The fundamental object of preparing the reports is to inform the superiors of the progress made, the idea about the future performance, the causes responsible for any deviation from the set course and suggestions made to remove the causes for the difference between planning and performance.

Meetings and De-briefing

Meetings between the superior and the subordinates may also provide an opportunity for upward communication. Meetings are regularly organised to exchange information between the superior and subordinates. Whereas the superiors will try to educate the subordinates regarding policies, programmes and problems facing the enterprise, the subordinates may be motivated to give suggestions regarding improving the policies and programmes of the enterprise. They may also be encouraged to give suggestions to improve the operability of the enterprise by removing the problems confronting it.

"Hotline Telephones"

In times of emergency or under the condition of indispensability, the employee may pick up such telephone lines which are located at strategic places. The employees may inform management about a particular incident in a plant or the work place.

The communication percolating downward is of a directive nature. The object of the communication is to initiate subordinate to work. This will require a package of instructions, guidelines, a manual of Do's and Don'ts. They may take the form of rules and orders.

Terry states rule as "a specific guide for action, established authoritatively and utilised in order to inform employees of conditions under which designated activities are to be performed." Such of the examples of the rules may be "Smoking when other fellow passengers do not object," or "the factory time is 8 a.m. to 4 p.m."

An order tells what is to be done? How is it to be done? When to be done? Where to be done?

The downward communication also includes instructions and reports as already pointed out.

The barriers in downward communication are as follows which has been described by Dr. Leonard Sayles.

1. The same word means different things to different people.
2. The speaker and listener may differ in background and experience.
3. We may pass on information which the employee is not prepared to grasp.
4. An employee may not believe his superior because what he hears may have been contradicted by previous actions.
5. An employee's emotional state of mind colours what he hears.
6. Stereotypes and beliefs influence what a man wants to hear.
7. A person may be dead set against a message because he suspects his superiors' motivation.

Lateral Communication

Lateral communication or horizontal communication comes into existence to effect co-ordination. In a state of departmentation whether by process, functions or product, the departmental heads having different organisational sub-goals have to co-ordinate their activities with a view to achieve the organisation's main goal. Such co-ordination cannot be possible at the lower echelons of organisational framework. It may only be possible to achieve at the higher level where the persons occupying higher positions could co-ordinate each other's functions and activities through horizontal communication. Landsberger emphasises that horizontal relationships come to exist consequent to the holding of different positions but having different organisational sub-goals. In spite of their independent positions, their activities are generally inter-dependent.

In such a situation, the disagreements and conflicts are too frequent and inevitable but they may be averted through the pattern of horizontal communication. The horizontal communication is followed by vertical communication.

Barriers of Communication

The object of communication is to effect change by influencing others to action. The communication may prevent or provoke a person to action only when the communication basically not controversial, is understood by the communicatee in its proper perspective and he has the capacity to respond to action as desired in addition to the existence of necessary means to effect the desired change. More often the communication channel is defective, the message ambiguous, defect in transmission and a host of other barriers. Under the following circumstances the communication fails to evoke the desired results:

Unacceptable Change

When the communicator tries to effect unacceptable change in the behaviour pattern of the communicatee it will go unheeded by persons in spite of best efforts by the communicator. Unless the communicatee has a desire to respond, it will evoke no change. For instance, if the communicator intends to make the employees accept the principles and doctrines upheld by the employers, the employees will not take any notice of such communication. Similarly, any communication designing to effect the doctrine of division among the employees will not be acceptable to them. It becomes imperative that unless the communicatees are convinced of the legitimacy and efficiency of the manager they will not respond. In other words the communication will go without response due to the barrier of unacceptability.

Organisational Constraints

The organisational structure if designed to adhere strictly to hierarchical approach in the channel of communication, it may lead to frustration to the persons operating at different levels. If an employee confronts problems in the execution of work, he should have the needed liberty to consult and get enlightened from the persons not falling in the hierarchical structure. Such a regimented approach denying consultations *inter alia* among persons not directly related to him either in capacity of a superior or subordinate may provide organisational block in the system of communication which may in addition to vitiating the object to be achieved provide a good deal of setback to the employee to the point of being hurt in his sentiments. Edmund P. Learned, David N. Ulrich, and Donald R. Booz support the thesis of progressive attitude towards communication which may have increasing acceptance of the majority in industry.

Freedom of consultation does not mean infringement of organisational discipline. It may be allowed with the express or implied consent of the supervisor. At no point of time a subordinate should consult others above or around him, if such act puts his superior in an embarrassing position. Conversely, he should inform or seek permission of his superior if he has to deviate from the normal channel of consultation.

Semanticism

Semaniticism provides barriers to communication. Some of the abstract concepts of democracy, labour, management connote different meanings to different persons. Everyone is expected to interpret these terms within the framework of his own experience and environments in which he has been brought up. The concept of democracy to an Indian or an American is different from a Nepali or even a Pakistani.

Semantics convey different meanings to the word. Suppose a boss is very much angry with one Mr. X. He asks his peon to throw him out of the room. It does not mean that the peon should physically lift him and throw him out. The experienced peon knows it what his boss means. In other words, "it is not only words but actions, implications and the entire situational context that produce misunderstandings."

Text of the Message

The text of the message also creates the problems. The words used in the message, the composition of the message, the emphasis given in communicating the message and sometimes faulty translations convey wrong meaning to a communication. Lack of clarity and precision sometimes result in blunders having far reaching implications. Sometimes the faulty words, defective sentence formation, inadequate vocabulary and the reliance on jargonism more often result in conveying different meaning to the text of the message.

Faulty interpretation is either due to lack of understanding of the message or defective emphasis on the message communicated. For instance, the following message is an example of defective emphasis.

"Appoint him not reject him."

This message may be interpreted differently if the communicatee does not get clear indication as to the emphasis in the subject matter. He may interpret it in any of the following two ways:

(i) "Appoint him, not reject him" or
(ii) "Appoint him not, reject him."

It becomes essential for the communicator to communicate correctly the emphasis contained in the message if he wants a correct response from the communicatee.

Status as a Barrier

Sometimes, status acts as a barrier in upward communication. Subordinates are hesitant to report their shortcomings and mistakes to their superiors because they feel that a happy and ignorant boss is much better than an informed boss. Once the boss comes to know of the mistakes of subordinates it may upset him to the point of penalising the subordinate. The subordinate may lose all chances of promotion and push because his elevation is directly the result of boss's satisfaction.

Subordinates sometimes are so much status conscious that they will not report even the genuine and legitimate grievances and problems on which they have absolutely no control.

Status becomes a barrier primarily due to the behaviour pattern of the superior. If the superior has always tried to maintain distance with his subordinates which creates a void in confidence between the two, the subordinates will never venture to communicate with the boss. However, if the boss practises different style of functioning, status may not provide any impediment in the way of communication.

Elaborating the point of status consciousness prevailing among the subordinates further, it may be stated that the status becomes a formidable impediment in the communication process because the subordinates do not dare to talk to their boss because they do not have the necessary manners or even language to communicate. Whatever language they possess it is lost at the first sight of person-to-person contact. Under such circumstances it is the superior who should try to understand the feelings of the subordinates more by their actions and behaviour rather than words, language or expression.

Faulty Transmission

Faulty transmission vitiates the very purpose of communication. Let us give an example of our own. We received the following telegram from the Registrar, Pune University.

"FIXED AT BANGALORE (.) KINDLY CONDUCT."

This message did not convey anything. We went to the telegraph office. They informed that about eight words were missing. They took three days to get the complete message from Pune telegraph office.

"CANDIDATES VIVA FIXED FOR SECOND APRIL AT BANGALORE (.) KINDLY CONDUCT."

We could not conduct the viva on the said date because by the time we received the message the date was already over.

It was detected that it was purely the transmission defect which jeopardised the very object for which the communication was transmitted.

Loss in Transmission

It has been observed that there are chances of loss of communication in the process of transmission. Experiments conducted in this connection reveal that about 30 per cent of the information is lost in each transmission. Consequently it is the practice in big enterprises not to rely on oral communication which is apt to be incomplete. More often even the written communication duly accompanied by interpretations are subject to loss in the process of transmission.

The loss in transmission may be on account of two factors: one—poor retention capacity of the communicator and two—defect in the process of communication.

Communication does not end in the desired result sometimes due to the communicatee remaining mentally absent while receiving communication from the communicator. The communicator transmits physically the message to the communicatee and the communicatee though physically receiving cannot resort to the desired action due to his mental occupation with other thought or idea. There is non-listening in the midst of physical listening. This may be attributed either due to "self-centredness or anxiety or plain contempt for another's viewpoint."

Implied assumptions more often provide barrier to communication. It is difficult for the listener to understand implied assumptions because it is not clear between the communicator and the communicatee as to what are such assumptions. The communicatee when goes by the face of communication fails to execute the desired action. For instance, it is known about the way of working of a former Chief Minister, where subordinates implemented only those orders which were written in red ink and ignored those written in blue ink. It was only known to the concerned secretaries of government departments.

Every communication to be implemented into actual practice requires some gestation period. If the gestation period falls short of requisite limit we may call it as a barrier to communication. For instance, a communication received from the head office by the branch office to the effect that the training of Mr. X be completed within two weeks' time. Conversely, since the training cannot be completed within two weeks, the communication directing action remains unexecuted due to lack of gestation period.

Superiors who are in the habit of changing commands till the last moment act as barriers to communication. The subordinates will not initiate any action because they apprehend that by the time they initiate the work of execution, the orders will change and all their efforts may prove to be an exercise in futility.

Rogers and Roethlisberger have rightly expressed that the element of hasty evaluation of communication may prove to be an impediment in the communication process. The communicator should not be in undue hurry to evaluate results immediately after the message is communicated. Every response to communication requires time and patience on the part of communicator because the communicatee will first listen, understand and then respond accordingly. This involves the time factor which has to be given due place in the communication system.

Principles for Effective Communication

Effectiveness of communication is judged by the response from the communicatee. If the communication results in desired action, the communication is effective; if it does not within the reasonable time limit, there is something wrong either with the message or the communication technique or with the listener. Accordingly the check list of principles which make communication effective is given as follows:

Need for Clarity

Every communicator should evoke response from the listeners if the communication possesses clarity in expression and flawlessness in transmission. The communication if comprehended by the receiver properly, there is no reason why it should not respond according to the letter and spirit of communication. Further, the receiver of communication should be fully conversant with the language, the inherent assumptions, if any, and the mechanics of communication. "This requires a literate approach to language and familiarity with language pattern of subordinates, peers and superiors." This requires concentration by the listeners also.

Fundamental Integrity

The fundamental object of managerial communication is to motivate the subordinates to take action as agreed upon. In this process, the subordinates should be relied upon and their integrity upheld by the superiors. They should not be bypassed by the superiors in quest of contacting the ultimate employee whether advertently or inadvertently. To be specific, the integrity of the enterprise is related to the level of integrity possessed by the subordinates. No communication may evoke response from subordinates if their actions and behaviour are doubted by the superiors. The superiors should establish the reputation of believing the subordinates, accepting their viewpoints and never doubting their intentions in executing the tasks entrusted to them. Once the executives repose confidence in them, they will also respond accordingly.

Integrity is an essential ingredient of communication. What has been communicated by the executive to his subordinates may result in action only when the subordinates possess integrity to the point of implementing the command both in letter and spirit.

Use of Informal Organisation

Ordinarily, the superiors give orders and the subordinates respond to implement them into practice. This is the established formal channel of communication through which all messages are transmitted. Sometimes the formal channels of organisation may prove to be ineffective to evoke the needed response from the subordinates. If the superiors continue to rely only on formal organisation and its channels of communication, the very purpose of command will be forfeited. The subordinates may manage to evade the authority on one pretext or the other. To ward off such a contingency the executives should adopt the strategy of making use of informal organisation. They may contact the subordinates themselves or through someone else and persuade them to implement their orders into action. Informal organisation at times proves far more effective than formal organisation.

Communication Process

Prof. Lawrence Appley has pointed out the following steps in communication process:

1. Clarify the idea or the problem
2. Getting participation in developing a solution to the problem
3. Transmitting ideas or decisions
4. Motivating others to take action agreed upon
5. Measuring the effectiveness of the communication

Clarify the Idea

John Dewy has rightly pointed out that "a problem well stated is half solved." The transmitter before transmitting communication should have full comprehension of the problem. He should know the scope and the limitations of the problems before he asks his subordinates to perform the desired task. In the process of acquiring full knowledge about the problem, the superior may have to gather facts from different sources and evaluate them to find out the missing links. He may then proceed with developing alternate solutions and then finally ask his subordinates to execute the desired action.

Generally, the efforts made in obtaining desired results fail to provide the requisite results primarily due to communicational defects. The busy executives due to their heavy occupation just transmit information to subordinates to implement them into action without providing the background information and even the needed clarification to the subordinates which are relevant to the execution of the desired task. The executive may satisfy his subordinates only when he himself is crystal clear regarding the scope, details and methodology of executing the task entrusted to his subordinates.

Participation of Others

The executive tries to draw others in the development of the solution to the problem owing to three important considerations:

- *(a)* To clarify and test his own thinking by sharing his ideas with others.
- *(b)* To gather the ideas and suggestions of others in a position to contribute to the solution of the problem.
- *(c)* By inviting their participation, to motivate those responsible for carrying out the decisions.

The executives who are even brilliant and mature some time fail to evoke legitimate enthusiasm among subordinates to put their orders into action. This necessitates participation of not only the subordinates but all those who are capable of contributing towards the solution of problems. "Productive participation demands careful preparation, a permissive climate, sensitive listening, and the willingness to credit others for their contribution." However, it requires that the persons drawn into problem have the capacity to contribute because their mere enrolment will serve no purpose.

This step helps the executive to arrive at a definite decision to accomplish results. The participation crystallises the issue properly which may now be executed by the subordinates.

Transmission

The next step in the process is to transmit the command to subordinates to achieve the desired object. Before doing this the executive has to make sure that whatever he communicates is received in letter and spirit by subordinates because it is on such communication depends successful execution by subordinates. He has accordingly to plan carefully:

- *(i)* what to communicate?
- *(ii)* to whom to communicate? and
- *(iii)* how best to communicate?

While transmitting the message he has to take into account a number of factors: what is the level of attainment of the subordinate? the nature of person with whom he is communicating; the organisational and psychological barriers that may come in the way of communication and a host of other factors such as language, relationship between the superior and subordinate etc. which are likely to influence the communication process.

Motivation

The fundamental object of communication is to motivate the subordinates to resort to the execution of the desired task. Mere command or status of the executive is not sufficient to provoke the subordinates to action. It amounts to dragging an unwilling horse to water. It is not sufficient. More important is that the horse drinks water. The subordinate accordingly cannot be forced to resort to action by coercion. He should be encouraged or enthused to respond to the orders of superior.

The subordinates will feel motivated if there is effective communication both ways. The subordinates should have the right to communicate to superior either to seek clarification or guidance or even to give suggestions to make amends in the procedure adopted to accomplish the desired objective. Participation of subordinates to the point of suggesting changes in the methodology of implementing the tasks may encourage them to implement the commands of their superiors.

Measuring Effectiveness

To what extent communication has been effective may be an important step towards making communication result-oriented. The touchstone of effective communication is the desired response from the subordinates. If the response is inadequate then the causes have to be found out and the measures taken to rectify the situation accordingly. The requirements of effective communication may be divided under two broad heads: one—Basic and two—Regulatory.

Basic Requirements

The basic requirements revolve round the executive:

(i) his faith in communication, and
(ii) ability to improve communication through guidance and exposure to the technique of communication.

The communication systems cannot be effective to achieve the desired results unless the executive is convinced of the role of communication in his organisation. He should be prepared to have communication both ways. The subordinates should be drawn in communication process in as much the same manner as the superior himself. Mere communicating commands to subordinates is not sufficient to accomplish the desired results; more important is the clarification and the guidance provided to the subordinates in solving their problems.

Truly speaking, communication depends on the will, competence and the attitude of the executive towards communication. The executive may nourish or stifle the communication process. It carries an indelible mark of the leader.

The other basic requirement of communication is the ability of the leader to acquire proficiency in communication technique. His ability of decision-making or his competence to perform the task entrusted to him may not be enough for communication. Communication is a technique which has to be acquired through guidance from somebody or even training. The executive should have no inhibition to undergo even a programme of training because it is the communication skill which becomes an indispensable component of decision-making process. An executive cannot accomplish desired results without the help and co-operation of his subordinates. Subordinates cannot function properly unless they have been communicated proper message to make it intelligible to them to implement into action. Further, the communication should be motivating to encourage the subordinates to respond to the commands of his superiors. Both these functions depend on the nature and technique of communication which may be acquired through proper training.

Checklist of Basics: Nature of Organisational Communication

Nature of organisation revealing the character and the needs of organisation is an important variable to make communication effective. If the policy of organisation is authoritarian or centralised in decision-making, it will obstruct free flow of communication both ways. Authoritarianism believes in the principle of "rule of thumb;" it considers participation of subordinates in communication process as irrelevant or even undesirable. Under such conditions, the communication system will prove ineffective.

Spontaneous response from subordinate depends on the climate of trust and confidence and reciprocity existing between the superior and the subordinate. It is in this climate that the superior is sure of legitimate response to his command from the subordinate and the subordinate is equally convinced of the rationality and reciprocity of his superior regarding proper consideration of the suggestions put forth by him.

Communication should be pursued in all directions as a continuous process. It should not end with the completion of a transaction, otherwise it will become weak to respond to desired expectations. If one medium fails, the other should be tried; this exercise should continue till success is achieved. Communication should be practised not merely to achieve immediate goals but to create climate conducive to achieving bigger organisational goals.

The text of the communication and the mechanics thereof should not develop indifference, apathy or even allergy in the communicatee. If the listener becomes deliberately inattentive or careless towards communication, it may be due either to the defect in the text of communication or the method adopted by the communicator. Under such circumstances, the communicator shall have to mend himself in such a manner that whatever he communicates is stimulating to help achieve the desired objective.

Purposive Communication

Communication of a general nature is not very responsive. The communication should, therefore, satisfy the instincts of individuality and self-respect of the people. Hence all communications should be directed to the individual employee as far as possible with the flavour of personal touch in official decorum. This idea has been expressed candidly by Alexandar Heron in the following words:

> "The foundation for any programme for understanding between us and our employees is a complete respect on our part for the personality and the individuality of the employee. When there may be a hundred or a hundred thousand employees on our pay roll, and while we may bargain collectively with them through their chosen representatives, our relations are not with a mass of men; our relations are with each one of a hundred or a hundred thousand individual persons. We cannot share information with an abstract, imaginary entity such as "the public," "labour," or the "union" or the "rank and file." We can share information with (each) . . . who work with us and receive their income in wages which we deliver to them."

Two-way Communication

Communication is a two-way traffic; if forced to be only one way, it is bound to collapse. The management should be prepared to listen, interpret, amend and implement in the same manner as to ask, command and direct his employees to implement. Communication will acquire greater effectiveness if the executive encourages the subordinate to participate in the mechanics of achieving the desired object. This will provide confidence, will to implement and the inspiration to respond to the will of the supervisor.

Supervisors are the most effective chain between the management and the operating force. It is the supervisors who may interpret and misinterpret the communication from management meant for the employees. Similarly, they are the persons who know intimately the pulse of people and it is through them the management may know the attitude and the thinking of people to make necessary amends in their commands which could be implemented without opposition.

Under the circumstances, the selection and training of supervisor is very vital to the functioning of an enterprise. The supervisor may be trained not only as a post office to communicate the commands of management received by him to the subordinates but to act as a vital chain between the management and employees. He should have the capacity to receive communication and communicate in the same spirit to the subordinates. He should also have the competence to put communication in the manner that it stimulates employees to respond quickly to command of supervisors.

Communication is apt to be diluted or even distorted when it passes through different levels of management. It has already been pointed out that communication is interpreted differently at each level according to the attitude and thinking of persons. In this process it is possible that by the time the communication reaches the implementing stage it is completely changed both in letter and spirit. To ward off such an exigency the communication should be as direct as possible.

Employees with the passage of time are not merely influenced by what management states but what management does. They become conversant with the way of functioning with the result that they execute many tasks without reference to the superiors. It means effective communication is not what is said but what is done. In other words, "it is not what people are *told* but what they *accept*."

PRINCIPLES OF GOOD COMMUNICATION

Following are the principles which seek to improve the efficiency of communication:

Clarify the Ideas Before Communication

The problem to be communicated to the subordinates should be clear in all its perspective to the executive himself. The entire problem should be studied in depth, analysed and stated in such a manner that it is intelligible to the subordinates. For this purpose the competence and skills of subordinates, their attitudes and aspirations and their environments of work have to be taken into account before they are asked to respond. Further, if some queries are made by the subordinates, the executive should answer each of them besides providing the needed guidance for implementing the tasks into actual practice.

Object of Communication

The object of communication should be crystal clear to the communicator. What object he proposes to achieve by transmitting a message to the communicatee? Whether he wants certain information or initiate certain action or change the attitude of the subordinate? The object is related to the mechanics of communication. It is the object which will determine the language, tone, the style of communication. Such object should be clear for each communication.

Environmental Factor

Environments in which the communicator and the communicatee have to interact influence the process of communication. Environments within the organisation will determine the attitudes and aspirations of superiors and subordinates and the environments without it, *i.e.*, social and political, influence the psychology of the superiors and the subordinates. Whether the environments *inter se* permit communication both ways? To what extent are subordinates permitted to participate in the communication process? Whether the subordinates are responsive to commands of superiors? All these variables depend on environmental factors. Even the socio-political environments determining the behaviour pattern of unions are ultimately related to effectiveness or otherwise of the communication system.

Consultation with Others

Before actually communicating the message it is better to draw others in developing a plan for communication. The consultation will be helpful in crystallising the problem and the methodology for its execution. Persons consulted if asked to execute will feel motivated owing to satisfaction of their ego need.

Tone and the Contents of the Message

The contents of the message and the tone, *i.e.*, the language used, the manner in which the message to be communicated, are the other important elements of effective communication. The language used should be such that it does not offend the sentiments and self-respect of the listeners. It should be stimulating to evoke response from the listeners. "Similarly, your choice of language—particularly your awareness of the words you use pre-determines the reaction of the listeners." Someone has rightly said that the word of mouth may turn the best friend into an enemy.

Convey Things of Help and Value to Listeners

While conveying messages to others, it will be better to know the interests and needs of the people with whom you communicate. If the message relates directly or indirectly to such interests and needs it will certainly evoke response from the communicatees.

Follow-up Communication

Follow-up action helps communication to be effective. The communicator may ensure the success of communication by asking questions regarding the efficiency of communication. The receiver of communication may also be encouraged to respond to communication. If need be, the communication process may be improved by the feedback received to make it more responsive.

Communication for Present and Future

Generally communication is needed to meet the existing commitments. To maintain consistency the communication should aim at future goal of the enterprise. For instance, if you postpone pointing out shortcomings to loyal subordinates, it will create problems in future. The subordinates will not only feel embarrassed but insulted if such shortcomings are pointed out in future. The enterprise on the other hand will get setback in its plan of action. Hence it will be consistent to long-term goals that the subordinates should be properly educated as to their shortcomings immediately when they are noticed.

Correlation Between Action and Communication

There should be no contradiction between action and communication. The effective communication is not merely what you say but more importantly what you do. This requires good supervision, clear assignment of authority and responsibility, proper reward system and the enforcement of sound policies.

Be a Good Listener

Communication depends not only on commands but the ingenuity of patient listening. Subordinates may experience problems of understanding, execution and co-ordination. These problems could be removed if you could listen to the queries of the subordinates with patience and then render necessary advice and guidance if needed.

CHAPTER 3

Business Information Design and Development

The strategy of experimental assurance in development of information system applications may be achieved by an evolutionary design method commonly called *prototyping*. Prototyping is used when requirements are difficult to specify in advance or when requirements may change significantly during development. The prototyping methodology is based on the simple proposition that people can express what they like or do not like about an existing application system more easily than they can express what they think they would like in an imagined, future system. A prototyping methodology is initiated by a user who conceives of a problem or an opportunity to be solved by an information system. The user seeks assistance from a professional system designer who is competent in the prototyping methodology.

Prototyping Process

Prototyping an application system is basically a four-step process, as described below and depicted in. There are two significant roles: the user and the system designer.

Step 1: Identify the user's basic information requirements: In this stage, the user articulates his or her basic needs in terms of output from the system. The designer's responsibility is to establish realistic user expectations and to estimate the cost of developing an operational prototype. The data elements required are defined and their availability determined. The basic models to be computerised are kept as simple as possible.

Step 2: Develop the initial prototype system: The objective of this step is to build a functional interactive application system that meets the user's basic stated information requirements. The system designer has the responsibility for building the system using very high level development languages or other application development tools. Emphasis is placed on speed of building rather than efficiency of operation. The initial prototype responds only to the user's basic requirements; it is understood to be incomplete. The early prototype is delivered to the user.

Step 3: Use of the prototype systems to refine the user's requirements: This step allows the user to gain hands-on experience with the system in order to understand his or her information needs and what the system does and does not do to meet those needs. It is expected that the user will find problems with the first version. The user rather than the designer decides when changes are necessary and thus controls the overall development time.

Step 4: Revise and enhance the prototype system: The designer makes requested changes using the same principles as stated in step 2. Only the changes the user requests are made. Speed in modifying the system and returning it to the user is emphasised.

All illustrated in step 3 and 4 are iterative. The number of iterations may vary considerably. There may be one or two reasons that iterative modification is ceased. First, the user determines that the prototype is not useful and the working prototype is discarded. Second, the user is satisfied with the system and it becomes an "operational prototype." It may be modified at a later stage, but at this point it is considered usable any may be distributed to other users. Alternatively, it may "seed" the idea of a new major application and be used to provide initial specifications for the application development effort.

The prototyping methodology, as outlined above, has several significant advantages in development of applications having high uncertainty as to requirements:

- Ability to "try out" ideas without incurring large costs
- Lower overall development costs when requirements change frequently

- The ability to get a functioning system into the hands of the user quickly
- Effective division of labour between the user professional and the MIS professional
- Reduced application development time to achieve a functioning system
- Effective utilisation of scarce resources

A major difficulty with prototyping is management of the development process because of frequent changes. Also, there may be a tendency to accept a prototype as the final product when it should only be the basis for a fully-specified design. For example, a prototype may no handle all exceptions or be complete as to controls. It "works," but it is not complete.

Variations on Standard Model

The model described above assumes only two participants: a user who is a functional expert and a system designer who is expert at the development of prototypes. The prototyping methodology may be modified to accommodate a greater number of participants.

Multiple users may be involved in prototype development when the application is useful across a broad area with many different user, or when it is so complex as to require input from several specialists. Both situations require added time for communications and negotiation among users. They do not significantly affect the designer's time required to build the prototype. If an application requires complex technical or analytical skills, it may be necessary to have more than one designer, and this may add time to the prototype-building process.

As users become more familiar with very high level development languages and gain experience with the use of prototype, it will become more common for the user to also function as the system designer. In such cases, it is important that the user have access to computing resources. One approach is a service organisation such as an information centre.

Life Cycle Approach to Application System Development

Although there are a growing number of applications that should be developed using an experimental process strategy such as prototyping, a significant amount of new development work continues to involve major operational applications of broad scope. The application systems are large and highly structured. User task comprehension and developer task proficiency are usually high. These factors suggest a linear or iterative assurance strategy. The most common method for this large class of problems is a *system development life cycle model* in which each stage of development is well defined and has straightforward requirements for deliverables, feedback, and sign-off. The system development life cycle is described in detail since it continues to be an appropriate methodology for a significant part of new development work.

The basic idea of the system development life cycle is that there is a well-defined process by which an application is conceived, developed, and implemented. The life cycle gives structure to a creative process. In order to manage and control the development effort, it is necessary to know what should have been done, what has been done, and what has yet to be accomplished. The phases in the system development life cycle provide a basis for management and control because they define segments of the flow of work which can be identified for managerial purposes and specify the documents or other deliverables to be produced in each phase.

The phases in the life cycle for information system development are described differently by different writers, but the differences are primarily in amount of detail and manner of categorisation. There is general agreement on the flow of development steps and the necessity for control procedures at each stage.

The information system development cycle for an application consists of three major stages:

- Definition
- Development
- Installation and operation

The first stage is the process which defines the information requirements for a feasible cost-effective system. The requirements are then translated into a physical system of forms, procedures, programmes, etc., by system design, computer programming, and procedure development. The resulting system is tested and put into operation. No system is perfect, so there is always a need for maintenance changes. To complete the cycle, there should be a post-audit of the system to evaluate how well it performs and how well it meets cost and performance specifications. The three stages of definition, development. And installation and operation can, therefore, be divided into smaller steps or phases as follows:

Stages in Life Cycle	*Phases in life cycle*	*Comments*
	Proposal definition	Definition assessment
	Feasibility	
	Information requirements analysis	
	Conceptual design	
	Physical system design	
Development		
	Physical database design	
	Programme development	
	Procedure development	
	Conversion	
Installation and operation	Operation and maintenance	
	Post audit	

At completion of each phase, formal approval sign-offs are required from the users as well as from the manager of project development. Each phase also results in formal documentation. The information system development cycle can follow an iterative assurance strategy. For example, the review after the physical design phase may result in cancellation or continuation, but it may also result in going back to prepare a new conceptual design.

It is instructive to note that upon completion of coding of programmes and beginning of programme testing, the application is probably only about 60 per cent complete. For example systems involving much testing, completion of coding may mark about the halfway point. Many errors in estimation of project completion dates can be attributed to failure to allocate adequate time to programme testing and conversion.

The Life Cycle Definition Stage

Ideally, a major system development project is conceived as a component of the information systems planning process, but a proposal may come from other sources such as users and data processing personnel. After a project is proposed, the next step in the definition stage is feasibility assessment, which is discussed briefly here. Once a proposed alternative is approved, the next phase is information requirements analysis. Following requirements analysis, a conceptual design phase produces a high-level design emphasising the application as seen by its users. Upon completion of the definition stage most of the key decisions that affect the user have been made. The definition stage is, therefore, critical in making sure the application will meet user needs. Although perhaps only 25 per cent of total efforts has been expended, the important decisions that shape the remainder of the effort are in place. The definition stage must, therefore, not be neglected if applications are to satisfy the users. In a study by McKeen, it was found that projects which spend more time in the definition phase were more successful regardless of the outcome measure used. Both user satisfaction and ability to develop the application within budget were enhanced.

Design Specifics

The proposal definition phase is not necessary if the application was defined as part of information system planning. Otherwise, a simple procedure may be used for proposal of an application. Proposals may be for entirely new applications or for enhancements to existing applications. The proposal should not be complex but in a short one- or two-page document should provide sufficient justification to support a decision to proceed with a feasibility analysis. Examples of items that may be included are the following:

- Identification of those proposing the project and others who have an interest in the application;
- The organisational need for or benefit from the application (the business reason);
- Organisational support (budget, sponsor, management support, etc.);

- Schedule considerations (date needed, availability of user personnel, etc.).

Following user management approval, the proposal is reviewed by the management authority responsible for allocating information system development resources (user management, a steering committee, or the information systems executive).

Feasibility Study

When a new application is proposed, it normally goes through a feasibility study before it is approved for development. If the application is part of the predefined MIS master plan, it still should go through the feasibility assessment phase in order to evaluate alternative approaches to its development, even though the general idea has been approved with the rest of the plan. If a proposal is submitted outside of the plan, the feasibility study includes whether it is consistent with the existing plan and whether it should override the priorities of other applications already planned.

Five types of feasibility are addressed in the study. They result in recognition of both the benefits and risks inherent in the development and implementation of the proposed application system:

1. *Technical feasibility*: Can the proposed application be implemented with existing technology? Analysis of project risk relative to technical feasibility includes not only whether the technology is available on the market but also its "state of the art" both in absolute terms and relative to the company's current technical sophistication.
2. *Economic feasibility*: Will the system provide benefits greater than the costs? The feasibility study presents intangible as well as tangible benefits in a formal way. A relatively detailed analysis of the costs of both development and operations of the various alternatives is also presented.
3. *Motivational feasibility*: The probability that the organisation is sufficiently motivate to support the development and implementation of the application with necessary user participation, resources, training

time, etc. This motivation is usually demonstrated by an owner or champion for the application who has sufficient organisational power to provide the resources and motivate others to assist and co-operate.

4. *Schedule feasibility*: The probability that the organisation can complete the development process in the time allowed for development. Adding development resources does not always reduce the development time; in fact, adding staff who cannot be used effectively may impede development because of time spent in communication.
5. *Operational feasibility*: Will it work when installed? This analysis may involve a subjective assessment of the political and managerial environment in which the system will be implemented. In general, the greater the requirements for change in the user environment in which the system will be installed, the greater the risk of implementation failure.

The feasibility study may be staffed in different ways. Some alternatives are:

1. Evaluation group with representatives from users, information systems, and other groups affected by the system. The head of the study group may be user or from information systems.
2. Evaluation person or group from information systems.
3. Evaluation person or group from users.

Each of the alternatives has advantages and disadvantages, and the selection of the staff for evaluation may depend on the type of the project and the organisational culture with respect to responsibility. For example, an evaluation group with many representatives has advantages when the application will have significant impact on several groups or on the fundamental operations of the organisation. The evaluation by information systems may be appropriate for highly centralised organisations in which the evaluation is primarily technical. The feasibility evaluation by users is consistent with user responsibility for information system resources. It establishes user commitment to the new system, and requires that user management be "sold" by the user evaluators.

The feasibility report covers items such as the following:

- General description of the application
- Expected development schedule
- Schedule of resources and budget required for development
- Schedule of expected cost and benefits from operations
- Summary of evaluation with respect to technical, motivational, schedule, and operational feasibility

If the feasibility study includes several alternatives, the report should present the budget, expected benefits, schedule of resources required, etc., for each (including the alternative of "do nothing"). The choice of alternative is based on the relative feasibility of each of the alternatives. For instance, the following alternatives were considered for an accounts receivable system for one division of a large multidivisional company (after rejecting "do nothing"):

1. Dedicated minicomputer system with modification of a purchased software package.
2. A minicomputer system for data entry with processing on the central computer using a generalised transaction processing package.
3. Online data entry to the central computer using an accounts receivable system developed by another division and modified as required.

The feasibility report is reviewed by the management of information systems and by the requesting department. If not part of the master plan, it may also be reviewed by the information systems steering committee. Once the feasibility study has been accepted and an alternative is approved, information requirements analysis can begin.

Information Requirements Analysis

A contingency approach to selecting one or more methods for determining information requirements was outlined. In order to effectively obtain a complete and correct set of requirements, it is necessary to use a method or methods that take into account the extent to which requirements are already known *versus* their needing to be searched out or discovered.

The result of the information requirements analysis or requirements determination phase of the application development life cycle is a report detailing the requirements for the application. The requirements consist of items such as the following:

- Reports (including the data items on the reports)
- Queries (both regular and *ad hoc*)
- Conceptual schema for database (From data modelling or other analysis)
- Functional requirements (including operational characteristics)
- User interface requirements

Conceptual Design

In the proposal definition, some user needs were specified; in the feasibility assessment phase, additional requirements were identified and some fairly general design alternative were evaluated. The information requirements analysis phase elicited and documented a more detailed set of requirements. The conceptual design phase establishes a more complete user-oriented design for the application.

It is useful to divide application design into a conceptual design phase and a physical design phase. These two phases can also be characterised as external design and internal design or general design and detailed design. The conceptual design emphasises the application as seen by those who will operate or use the outputs of the system; the physical design translates those requirements into specifications for implementing the system. The conceptual design establishes the inputs and outputs, functions to be performed by the application, and audits and controls. In general terms, conceptual design treats the actual processing functions as "black boxes" physical design specifies the actual processing given in conceptual design. Conceptual *versus* physical designs in application development are loosely analogous conceptual *versus* physical modelling in database development.

Typical contents of a conceptual design reports are the following:

- User-oriented application description. Documents the flow of the application activities through the organisational units providing inputs and using outputs.
- Distinguishes manual operations from automated operations performed by the application system.
- Inputs for the application with general description of each (visual display screens, source documents, forms, queries, etc.).
- Outputs produced by the application with general description of each (visual display screens, query responses, printed outputs, reports etc.).
- Functions to be performed by the application system.
- General flow of processing with relationships of major programmes, files, inputs, and outputs.
- Outlines of operating manuals, user manuals, and training materials needed for the application.
- Audit and control processes and procedures for ensuring appropriate quality in the use and operation of the application.

The Life Cycle Development Stage

The development stage of the system development life cycle consists of four classes of activity which may occur somewhat concurrently: physical system design, physical database design, programme development, and procedure development.

Physical System Design

The physical system design phase, also called internal or detailed design, consists of activities to prepare the detailed technical design of the application system. The physical system design is based on the information requirements and the conceptual design. In turn, it provides the basis for physical database design, programme development, and procedure development. Testing is sometimes defined as a separate phase, but testing is really part of each phase. Some life cycles include physical database design in the physical system design phase; however, since the trend is toward more independence between programmes and data and specialised skills are often required for physical database design, it is considered a separate design phase in this explanation. The results of the physical system design phase are specifications and designs for the following:

- System design showing flow of work, programmes, and user functions
- Control design showing controls to be implemented at various points in the flow of processing
- Hardware specifications for the applications if new hardware is required
- Data communications requirements and specifications
- The overall structure of programmes required by the application with procedural specifications on functions to be performed by each
- Security and backup provisions
- An application test quality assurance plan for the remainder of the development.

The physical system design work is performed by systems analysts and other technical personnel. Users may participate in this phase, but much of the work requires data processing expertise instead of user function expertise.

The work of the physical system design phase is to take the fairly high level, user-oriented requirements of the conceptual design phase and produce a specific technical design. This process is generally one of defining the "black boxes" that will produce the required outputs based on the inputs defined in conceptual design. There are a number of different methods an analyst may employ. By supporting the systematic process of expanding the level of detail and documenting the results, the methods aid in reducing the complexity and cost of developing application systems and in improving the reliability and modifiability of the designs.

Generally, physical system design techniques achieve simplicity by subdividing the application system into small, relatively self-contained modules. System modules can be programmes or procedures which are subsections of programmes. System complexity is reduced because each module can be developed, coded, and tested relatively independently of the others. Reliability and modifiability are enhanced because a change can be made to a system module with minimal, well-understood effects on the rest of the system. The techniques are thus based on well-understood principles of systems theory.

Some of the available techniques are summarised below:

Techniques	*Description*
Top-down design	A processing unit is defined by a general statement of its purpose then broken down into smaller and smaller refinements. The design is depicted as a hierarchy chart with general control modules at the top and detailed modules at the bottom. The resulting programme is also structured.
Structured design	Each, module of a programme is defined by the specific function it performs. Emphasis is on decoupling or minimising the integration between modules; each module is highly cohesive, meaning all the statements within it are functionally related. Structure charts, similar to hierarchy charts, show module definition. The transformation of data is represented by data flow diagrams.
SADT	Systems Analysis and Design Technique is a proprietary system utilising a graphical modelling language to describe, in a top-down fashion, the functions of the system and the data utilised.
HIPO	Hierarchy-Input-Process-Output is a documentation technique which can also be used to communicate system specifications to project participants throughout the design process. The three types of charts, each depicting a finer level of detail.
Warnier-Orr	The methodology was originally developed in France by Warnier; it has been adapted and expanded by Orr. The methodology assists in defining the hierarchical structure of systems. It can be used in defining the logical structure of the processing system, data structures, and control structures and flow of control in programmes. Nested braces are used in documenting the hierarchical structure.

The objectives of these examples of techniques for detailed design are similar, but each has unique features for defining and communicating system specifications. They can be used in communicating the design specifications to users, although they are not necessarily easy to understand for a person untrained in the technique. Another advantage of these physical design approaches is that they support the use of *structured programming*, to be described later in this chapter. One problem with all of the techniques is that they require a large investment in training analysts and converting to the new procedures. Each requires a rather complete commitment and changeover; it is not easy to "borrow" elements from each and combine them.

Since the early 1960s there has been ongoing experimental work in techniques for automating the system design process. The intent of these efforts has been to provide a means for specifying the information requirements of a system and automatically generating programme code and database specifications. The problem is to develop a requirements language which is rich enough to provide the necessary information yet easy to understand. Another problem is developing adequate tools to generate code and organise data structures automatically.

The most comprehensive research project to date has been ISDOS at the University of Michigan. The ISDOS approach begins with a problem definer who defines the information needed, specifies timing and volume requirements, and provides algorithms and logic to produce output. The requirements are written in a Problem Statement Language. The software system analyses the problem statements and in a limited sense performs system design, complies programmes, organises files, and directs execution of the resulting application system. In other words, information requirements statements. The ISDOS system thus performs tasks associated with physical system design, physical database design, programme development, some procedure development, conversion, and operation phases of the system development life cycle. The system is in limited experimental use.

Physical Database Design

The approach to physical database design for an application depends on the existing database and the approach followed for database requirements determination. There are three major approaches to meeting the data requirements for an application.

1. *Create a new physical life or database*: This is appropriate if no database is used or a database is dedicated to the application; in either case the application "owns" the data and objectives of a database are violated. New data may be required and the files or database must be designed and created from data collected specifically for the application.
2. *Using and modifying an existing database*: This method is appropriate if an evolutionary strategy for database development is followed. It may require special functions to be evoked by the database administrator for restructuring the existing database as well as adding necessary data.
3. *Access an existing database by means of a user schema*: This approach is possible if a complete conceptual model of the enterprise, anticipating new application needs, was used as the basis for physical database design. New data may need to be added to the database, but the connection between the logical description of the data needed by the application and the physical database is easily made through the database management software.

The third alternative assumes that a complete data model of the enterprise will anticipate further application requirements. The second alternative is more likely even if a data modelling approach to database definition was followed. Fortunately, one of the advantages of database management systems is that the database can be restructured to accommodate evolutionary application requirements.

Programme Development

A primary output of the physical design process is a set of specifications that define programming tasks. The goal of the programme development phase is to code and test programmes required for the application. Testing of each module is performed on test data representing a fairly complete set of variations in input data in the user environment.

Problems encountered during the programming phase are typically a result of lack of complete specifications provided during conceptual or physical design. This often results in extensive reprogramming efforts when specifications are changed. The techniques for formalising the conceptual and physical design process are aimed at alleviating this problem. Another problem in this phase is inadequate programme testing prior to system test and conversion. A number of programme development techniques reduce programme complexity and aid in achieving programme correctness. Important examples are modularity, structured programming, application generators, and tailoring of application packages.

The concept of *modularity* has already been discussed. The practice of subdividing a programme into small, relatively well defined modules is generally accepted. Modularity aids in reducing programme complexity and in enhancing reliability and modifiability. In most programming languages, modules can be programmed as subprogrammes with well-defined procedures for passing data values between them. Each module can be coded and tested by itself before begin integrated and tested with other modules.

In *structured programming*, a small set of basic coding structures is used for all programme code, which generally results in programmes that are straightforward in flow of logic. Structured programming is related to modularity in that use of the coding structures ensures well-defined modules. Structured programming is often termed "GOTO-less" programming because GOTO statements are discouraged or prohibited. The reason is that use of GOTOs can introduce unnecessary complexity. However, structures results in code which does not require GOTOs.

Testing represents a critical factor in application development. It can take up from 15 to 50 per cent of the total development effort depending on the size and complexity of the application. Formal approaches to system testing involve a discipline which begins early in the programme development phase. There are three distinct phases of programme testing:

1. *Module testing*: Each individual programme module is tested using dummy routines for calls to other modules.
2. *Integration testing*: Group of programme modules are tested together to determine if they interface properly.

This may be done incrementally as they are developed until the entire programme system is tested.

3. *System testing*: This involves testing of the complete set of application programmes.

There is debate over what constitutes a correct or adequately tested programme. Some errors will be revealed only after the system is in production; however, a system that is put into production with too many errors can be disastrous in terms of corrective activity required and organisational acceptance of the application. Criteria for programme correctness vary widely and tend to be related to the method of generating test data.

It is useful to distinguish between reliability and correctness for programmes. A *correct* programme meets specification; a *reliable* programme operates in an acceptable manner under both intended and unintended input data and operating conditions. In other words, a reliable programme will perform satisfactorily under a wide range of correct and incorrect inputs; a correct programme need only perform satisfactorily as long as the inputs are as specified.

An alternative approach to application development with high potential payoff in productivity is to purchase generalised software packages and modify them to meet the unique needs of the organisation. Many applications, such as payroll, have similarities across organisations and across industries, suggesting the possibility of using generalised software instead of writing unique application software. There are two alternative approaches to the use of generalised application software packages:

1. *Have organisation adapt to the package*: The application software producers are fixed and the operating procedures of the organisation are modified to conform to the software. This alternative may be desirable for an organisation with applications where there are no significant unique organisational requirements or internal training is less expensive than modifying the software. Another situation is when cost limits or the urgency for the system to be implemented offsets the benefits of unique requirements that can be obtained only through delay and extra cost associated with unique application development. Small business, for example, can frequently

afford the cost of conforming to a package but not the cost of unique development.

2. *Adapt package to organisational needs*: Recent trends, accepted by software vendors and purchasers, have been to provide general packages that can be easily modified because of modular design to fit unique organisation requirements. The increasing cost of software development relative to packages makes it cost-justifiable to purchase a package and spend the same amount as the acquisition cost to modify it. Some vendors "tailor" packages themselves; others provide the source code for their clients to modify. The tailoring alternative is suited for situations in which the essential features are found in a package, but the purchasing organisation desires unique features.

When the choice is made to purchase a software package rather than to develop in-house, it is still important to have complete, accurate system design specifications. The specifications provide the guidelines for evaluating different software packages and choosing the one that most closely meets the specifications. They also dictate how the chosen package should be modified, providing a basis for estimating the cost of modifications and assuring that it is done adequately.

Procedure Development

Procedure development can take place concurrently with programme development. Procedures should be written for all personnel who have contact with the system. This includes the following:

1. *Primary users*: This includes instructions for how to interpret a report, how to select different options for a report, etc. If the user can execute the system directly, as in online queries, it includes detailed instructions for accessing the system and formulating different types of queries.
2. *Secondary users*: This includes detailed instructions on how to enter each kind of input. It is more oriented to "how to" and less to "what" for different inputs.

3. *Computer operating personnel*: There are generally maintenance procedures to be performed by computer operators and/or control personnel. Procedures include instructions for quality assurance, backing up system files, maintaining programme documentation, etc.
4. *Training procedures*: In some cases, a separate training manual or set of training screens is developed for the implementation stage and subsequent training.

One of two groups may be responsible for writing procedures: analysts or users. The advantages of analyst-written procedures are technical accuracy, project control over completion, and conformance to the overall documentation; disadvantages are the tendency of analysts to write in technical jargon or technical abbreviations and to assume users have knowledge of the technical environment. The advantages of user-written procedures are an appropriate level of technical description and instructions that are understandable; disadvantages are the difficulty of assuring clear, complete instruction. A mixed strategy is one in which analysts and users work together to produce a technically correct, understandable manual.

An effective procedures manual, one that communicates well and can be referenced easily, must be well designed. Several alternative layouts are shown. Conditions under which are most appropriate are the following:

Format	*Conditions for use*
Conventional	Sequenced set of instructions for one job title or unit. Possible use for policy statements.
Playscript	Sequenced set of instructions involving several job titles or units.
Caption	Unsequenced procedures or policies.
Matrix	Two conditions determine a procedure or an action.
Decision	Several conditions and one or more procedures or actions.
Live specimen	Supplement for all of above.
Flowchart	Supplement to playscript, matrix, or decision table.

It is important that procedures be kept current to coincide with changes to the information system. A document numbering system that ties procedures to particular programmes, modules, or data files is useful for this purpose.

The Life Cycle Installation and Operation Stage

The third stage of the information system development life cycle begins with conversion to the new application system. The rest of the system development life cycle refers to the life of the system in use. After the system is in production, changes and enhancements are made during the operation and maintenance phase of the system. Periodically, a post audit of the system is conducted; based on this activity, the system may be modified, enhanced, or replaced.

Conversion

Conversion to the new application system begins after all programmes and procedures have been prepared and individually tested. Three major activities prepare for actual conversion: acceptance testing, file building, and user training.

Acceptance testing is testing of the completed application and comparing it to specifications. It verifies to the user that the system meets performance criteria and operation requirements. The testing includes user inputs, operating and control procedures, and outputs. Differences between what users expected and what the system delivers are identified and resolved. The acceptance test was developed as part of the planning for the system.

File building refers to the collection and conversion to machine-readable form of all new data required by the application. File building can be a long and tedious process, and careful planning is important. *Ad hoc* file conversion programmes may be employed if the required data is already in computer-readable form. If not, the data must be gathered, coded, and entered into the database. Sufficient time and human resources should be provided to "clean up" the data, that is, remove inaccuracies and inconsistencies and make the data complete.

User training may be relatively straightforward or a critical effort, depending on the degree to which the new application system affects existing jobs. If techniques such as job design are used, training will involve substantial reorientation of the users to their jobs. Proper user training is an important factor in overcoming user resistance to new systems. In a later section of this chapter, training as a subset of the implementation or change process will be discussed.

Conversion from the old system to the new takes place after acceptance testing, file building, and user training are complete. Conversion can be accomplished in several ways. The most careful method is to run the old and new systems in parallel; the new system is run under actual conditions and the results are compared with the old system for reliability and accuracy. After the new system has shown consistent results for a reasonable period of time it becomes operational and the old system is dropped. The drawback to this method is that it is expensive; both machines and employees work double time. Machine time can be costly if new hardware is replacing old and both must be maintained. More important, employees are required to perform essentially two full-time jobs, one of them being new and unfamiliar. Moreover, if the system has not been sufficiently tested and errors are detected during conversion, costly delays and employee frustration can cause serious problems.

If parallel processing of the old and new systems is not feasible, the new system should be tested under simulated conditions of full volume before cutting over from the old. Complete cutover is often referred to as "burning the bridges" because it is usually impossible to return operations to the old system once cutover takes place. Problems with the new system are corrected by "brute force" since no alternative is available. This is frequently a risky strategy, especially for systems such as payroll where very little delay can be tolerated. If possible, conversion should take place gradually, one portion of the system at a time.

Conversion Hazard

A shoe manufacturer and importer, a division of a large company, waned a computer. The company hired a consultant to recommend computer hardware, prepare programmes, and convert company records. The invoicing and inventory systems were to be the first applications, followed by accounts receivable and accounts payable.

The first computerised invoices resulted in customer complaints. The inventory reports could not be compared with the parent company reports. The consultant was terminated, and he filed a lawsuit for fees due.

Some errors in development were highlighted in pre-trial discovery:

1. The company had no experience with computers but still decided to implement all major applications at one time.
2. The manual system of inventory control had been developed by employees without formal training, resulting in somewhat unique features. The consultant never fully understood the existing system.
3. Live data items were used in the testing. This produced huge test outputs which could not be checked adequately.
4. The parent company system and the company's new system were not compatible, so the parent company inventory files were not copied. Instead, temporary input clerks were brought in to prepare data, but no programmes were available to validate this input. The input data quality was poor.
5. No audit trails were included to identify corrections. No one knew what has changed or who made the changes.
6. No company personnel were assigned to the project. Lower-level employees were afraid to contradict the consultant; high-level employees refused to participate at all.

Operation and Maintenance

When the system appears to be operating without difficulty it is turned over to the information processing production function. This often requires not only approval by the user stating that the system meets predefined acceptance criteria, but also approval of the system operations and maintenance groups stating that it meets standards for documentation and maintainability.

Any subsequent changes in the application are handled as maintenance. Maintenance of an application can be classified as repairs or enhancements. Repairs are required when incomplete or incorrect coding renders the application defective. Enhancements are additions or improvements. Repairs dominate the maintenance activity for the first few months of operation. Later, most of the maintenance is enhancement. Sometimes maintenance is performed by the system developers, but often it is the responsibility of a separate maintenance group.

Post-Audit

A desirable part of the system development life cycle is a review of the application after it has been in operation for a period, such as a year. An audit team with representatives from users, development, maintenance, operations, and perhaps internal audit review the operation, use, cost, and benefits of the application. Recommendations from a post-application and suggestions for improving the development process on subsequent applications.

Project Management

When an information system project is approved, its consequences are not certain; there are risks associated with it. The anticipated benefits may not be achieved, costs may be higher than planned, time for implementation may be greater than estimated, or performance of the hardware and software may be lower than anticipated. There are three factors, recognisable prior to implementation, that affect the inherent risk in a project: size, the degree of structure of tasks to be automated, and the level of technology of the project relative to the organisation. Note that the first two are similar to the factors contributing to uncertainty of information requirements. The level of company-relatively technology introducers risk in system implementation but is relatively independent of requirements definition. Using combinations of high and low for these three factors, there are eight possible risk estimates for projects.

Relatively level of technology used	*Structure*	*Size*	*Risk*
Low	High	Large	Low
		Small	Very low
	Low	Large	Low
		Small	Very low
High	High	Large	Medium
		Small	Medium-low
	Low	Large	Very high
		Small	High

In other words, a large project using high technology for an application having low structure for the tasks to be automated has a very high risk. A small project using a low relative technology and high structure for tasks has a very low risk.

The contingency approach to project management is to organise and manage a project according to the level of risk in the project. Four types of tools and techniques are applied to obtain appropriate project management.

1. External integration tools and techniques to link the project with users. Examples are user project managers, users on project team, and user steering committee.
2. Internal integration tools and techniques to keep the project team working as a unit. Examples are project review meetings, minutes, and team participation in decisions.
3. Formal planning tools and techniques to structure and sequence tasks. Examples are critical path scheduling, milestones and project approval processes.
4. Formal control tools and techniques to evaluate progress. An example is a series of formal status reports with variance analysis.

In general, the lower the structure of the tasks to be automated, the greater the need for high levels of external integration with user involvement. High level of technology relative to the organisation generally is aided by high internal project integration and fairly low formal planning and control. High formal planning and control tend to be most useful for large projects with low technology.

Recording and Data Collection

An organisation's performance of a transaction is generally recorded on a document or a form. The form may direct a transaction to take place, or record its performance, or confirm its performance. The capture of data is a necessary first step in processing a transaction. The initial recording of the transaction is critical. The design of the recording procedure has a substantial impact on speed and accuracy of recording and on subsequent efforts to detect and correct errors.

Accuracy, completeness, and authenticity of the input transaction data affect all subsequent processing and, therefore, warrant particular consideration. Furthermore, the volume of data collected can reach staggering proportions. The cost of data collection is often one of the largest single components of operating an information system. It follows, then, that the choice of data collection device is one of the most important design characteristics of an information system. There is a large variety of data collection devices. These differ in means of recording and sensing information, degree of automation, speed, portability, cost accuracy, and the like. The form on which each transaction is recorded can be filled in manually, electronically, typewritten, or be partially pre-printed. Some coding may take place, such as assigning a standard and compressed representation of data recorded in the source document; for example, sex may be signed a one-letter code. *Pre-printed forms* and coding reduce the probability of erroneous recording.

Data Conversion and Verification

Data conversion is the process of transforming data from a human-readable medium to a computer-readable medium. Recorded transactions go through a data entry process that converts the data into a computer input medium, such as a diskette, or magnetic disk. The converted records then become the transaction file.

A typical system may use different types of devices to meet a variety of requirements and data sources. These include key transcription devices, optical font typewriters, bar-code readers, and online terminals. The converted computer-readable result of these devices comprises magnetic disk documents that can be read by optical readers, and the lime. If the fields in a transaction record are known in advance, there is greater incentive to covert by a medium that reads prepared documents rather than by a medium that requires initial recording on a form. Remote terminals are now extensively used for direct entry of transaction data into the computer system. In such cases actual source documents are not prepared, and the stages of recording and data conversion are thus integrated: the original recording is computer-readable. Examples are automatic tellers in banks and point-of-sale terminals in retail businesses. You have to watch, though, that controls are properly devised in such systems, for the absence of a source document may cause control problems.

The data conversion activities may introduce errors. It is, therefore, necessary to check the conversion into computer-readable form. The process of insuring that the data recorded on a source document has been accurately transcribed to a computer-readable form is called verification. Verification can be performed by either re-keying the source document or sight proof-reading. Typically, not all the data in a record is verified, in order to save cost. Where complete accuracy of data fields is necessary, 100 per cent verification is usually the only answer. With current intelligent key-transcription devices and terminals, verification can be handled by a programme stored in the memory element of the device, that immediately detects errors, displays them on a screen, and initiates rekeying of the source document.

Data Validation

The boundary separating data verification and data validation was quite clear in the old days of off-line keying. With current data entry devices, the boundary is fuzzy. In many cases the stages of recording, data entry and validation. However, we can still make the following logical distinction. Verification refers to the accuracy, completeness, and authenticity of converted source documents. It can be handled manually or by a computer programme, and does not require a comparison against master file records. Validation, on the other hand is always a computerised process involving a transaction file having records already verified and a check of relations between transaction records and master file records.

Data validation is thus the process of screening transaction records against a set of validation criteria designed to detect certain types of inaccuracy, unreasonableness, or incompleteness. Validation checks are usually applied to individual characters and fields and / or to combinations of several fields from the transaction record, either alone or in conjunction with the content of one or more master files.

Data validation tests should normally be made at the earliest possible point in the transaction processing cycle in order to reject, suspend, and correct invalid records.

A computer programme, usually labelled *edit programme*, reads in the transaction records and tests for all detectable errors.

The edit programme may, for instance, determine that each customer number in the transaction record matches a currently active customer. The edit programme produces a new *transaction file* containing only valid records.

It also produces a list of records rejected for errors. The rejected records are then corrected and re-entered through the edit programme. This process is continued until the input transactions are free of error.

The rejected records represent potentially valid transactions. It is essential to ensure that they are either correctly re-entered into the system or discarded as erroneously prepared transactions. A sound control technique is to write the rejected transactions onto a separate "suspense file" together with a code of the edit criteria that led to the rejection. By holding rejected records in suspense, the edit programme ensures that they will be correct and not lost or unduly delayed.

To recapitulate, the stages of data verification and validation are intended to correct erroneous transactions before they reach the processing stage of the transaction processing cycle. At this stage computer programmes perform file update, computation, and retrieval. Errors can result from an erroneous recording of a transaction or from a faulty conversion of the data to a computer-readable form. In most batch information systems, the verification and validity checks take place prior to the processing stage for the following two reasons:

1. The update and retrieval programmes are usually too complex to contain the extra validity checks.
2. The processing programmes are normally executed in fixed time intervals in one or several computer sites. Input preparation, on the other hand, is a continuous process throughout a certain time period and is distributed in many locations. Error corrections will be more efficient if done close in time and distance to the transaction occurrence.

Modern technology makes it possible for the recording, data verification, and data validation stages to be integrated by direct recording of data into a microcomputer or an intelligent data entry device. The separation between the stages is determined by the technological and economic alternatives available to a specific organisation. Generally speaking, the more sophisticated the data entry devices are, the more integrated the stages can be.

File Processing and Updating

When the input transaction file has been edited, corrected, and cleared for use, *file processing* occurs. Processing the transaction file may take various forms and involve this file alone or this file in conjunction with one or more master files.

Sorting is a common example of processing the transaction file alone. Sorting is the arrangement of records into some predetermined order, using a field in the record as a sorting key. There are many ways to sort records, depending upon the file media and equipment used. Sorting is an important data processing activity, requiring a significant part of the information processing effort. If it is performed prior to *input editing*, the purpose is to detect duplicate transaction file in the same order as the master file to which it applies. Sorting may also be performed prior to printing output in order to have the data in a form that is convenient for distribution—for example, arranging a customer bills output file by zip codes before printing it. Processing the transaction file may involve other master files, from which data is retrieved only. One example is the processing of sale transactions for billing. Such transactions may contain a customer's number only; the customer's name and address are then obtained from the customer name-and-address file. Another example is the processing of a batch of inquiry transactions, such as requests to print various student records. For each transaction of this type, the student master file is accessed and a record retrieved for painting.

Updating is an example of processing the transaction file in conjunction with one or more master files. The *master files* are the permanent files of the organisation and are maintained on a regular basis. Examples are the personnel file, the accounts payable file, and the general ledger file. The format of fields in master file records usually remain constant even though the field contents may change frequently. Master files must be kept accurate by updating fields in the records, by adding new records, and by deleting old ones. For example, students are deleted from a student file once they graduate, and incoming students are added to the file periodically.

The procedure for updating the master file depends on the type of file organisation, and the processing methods.

In general, the record in the master file to be updated is read, updated, and then written onto an update file. In a sequential processing system, we usually assume that processed sequentially. Updating a file essentially involves reading of each master file record. If there is no transaction that applies to the record, the record is rewritten without change. If there is a transaction that applies to the record, the record is updated with changes; transactions reflecting new entities are used to add records to the file. If there is a transaction that indicates that the relevant record should be deleted, then the record is simply not rewritten onto the updated file. In essence, the current master file is rewritten to produce a new, updated file. This approach of sequential batch processing of a salesperson master file.

Inputs to the monthly salespeople update and analysis computer application consist of keyed receipts of gasoline and room and board expenditures incurred by the salespeople, as well as adjustments. The keyed receipts represent transaction records that update or add to variable fields in sales people's records. They do not alter fundamental information stored in master files. For instance, they alter the year-to-date expenditure field in the salespeople's record, but not the address field. The keyed adjustments represent change or addition records, which are used to alter data fields considered constant in the master file, such as salespeople's names and addresses, or to add a new salesperson. This type of record adds to file contents, alters contents, and/or adjusts for errors.

After keyed data is edited, the transactions are sorted by salespeople's numbers and processed by the analysis and update programme. This processing entails totalling and posting expenditures to master file records, adding and deleting salespeople records, and printing a report. The previous salespeople master file was produced as output from the last monthly process. The salespeople master file output from this month's process will, in turn, become the input to next month's process. Batch processes normally produce other output files, which can be used in other applications. For instance, the salespeople update programme can produce a check file that will be used by a check programme to print checks for reimbursing the salespeople.

The sequential process may seem cumbersome and somewhat archaic. You are right; however, in many organisational applications that do not require online update and retrieval of data, this process is still the backbone of data processing.

Note that batch processing is also applicable when direct access storage devices are in use. In such cases some sorting and rewriting operations can be skipped, provided that the master files are not sequentially organised. However, the basic principle of operating in batches is not changed so long as the orientation of the TPS as a whole is not online.

Reporting

The reporting stage provides the interface between the TPS and the users of its output. Effective reporting that aids the user in his or her perception of relevant information can substantially contribute to the usefulness of the system. Not all outputs from the system are reported. A large proportion of outputs may be stored in the data base without being reported in detailed form. Other outputs are stored for future processing. A payroll TPS, for example, can produce several outputs, including files, printed reports, documents and microfilmed reports.

The TPS produce three major types of output: preplanned reports, preplanned responses to inquiries, and transaction documents. *Preplanned reports* are preplanned as to content and format. They cover a predetermined time period and report either a status at a point in time or a flow during the period. *Preplanned responses* to inquiries are generally associated with limited output, usually with respect to part of the records in a master file.

A *transaction document* is an item such as an invoice, pay-check, bill or purchase order. Transaction documents can initiate some action, such as a purchase order, and they can be used to report a confirmation of a completed action. A documented designed for return and use in processing the completion of a transaction is known as a *turnaround document*. Examples are optically readable forms sent with customer billings with the request that they be returned with the payment. Transaction documents can also provide background information to the recipient and be used for reference purposes. For example, copies of student's grade cards do not initiate action by the teacher; they are both a confirmation that grades were assigned and reference documents, should inquiries arise.

The various reporting techniques and reporting media are each associated with costs and benefits. Some of these are:

- Preprinted paper forms
- Computer generated paper forms
- Optically readable forms
- Computer output microfilm (COM)
- Hard-copy terminal output
- Soft-copy (Visual display) terminal output

The form of displayed output can vary. An alphanumeric display uses only a limited number of characters (the alphabet, numerals, special characters). Alphanumeric output is almost always a *tabular display*; only rarely in narrative form. *Graphic display* present information by means of graphs and patterns. Compared to tabular reports, graphic reports are not used very widely by transaction processing systems.

Local and Remote Input/Output

The various stages of the transaction processing cycle can take place in physically adjacent locations or in locations far apart. Also, the transactions and the computer can by physically separate. Similarly, there are various means of moving the transaction inputs to be processed and moving the output back to the users. Local processing is the term used when the transactions and the processing are physically adjacent; remote processing is the term when they are physically separate.

Remote processing may rely on mail, couriers, and transportation facilities to move inputs and outputs. In most cases, however, it relies on data communication facilities and on remote data entry devices to send transaction records in batches and to receive reports and documents. So long as processing and updating of files (including validation of transactions against master file) are not involved, this remote job processing should be classified as part of a batch transaction processing system. It does not merit any special discussion, since conceptually it was covered in the preceding sections. In other words, the only change that we now introduce into the transaction processing cycle is that data and information moving from one stage to another, or from one location to another, are transmitted electrically and not physically.

Facilities that are dependent on a distant data processing system linked by communication lines are thus equipped to perform part of the transaction processing cycle. Typically, they have data entry equipment that enables them to convert *source documents* into computer-readable input transactions, and they may also have printing equipment that can produce reports and documents.

In other cases, such equipment may include a microcomputer. This approach allowed the remote facility to handle data verification also. Transaction inputs is then verified and corrected at the point of entry, before it is communicated to the data processing centre for processing. When data collection has an immediate effect on existing master files, the discussion applies to online transaction processing systems, to which we now turn.

Online Transaction Processing Systems

In contrast to the delay inherent in periodic batch processing, online transaction processing can provide immediate data validation, or immediate updating and processing, or immediate reporting, or all these stages combined. In an online environment, the user is actually provided with direct access to files and computer programmes *via* remote terminals and communication lines. The user can enjoy an immediate, real-time response.

One of the main characteristics of an online processing system is that the sequence in which transactions are received is random, and each terminal may be treated as a separate transaction input source. Transactions are processed continuously rather than periodically. Files are online and available to the system at all times for data validation and file updating. Errors in transactions may be detected immediately and corrected by the person making the data entry, rather than left for periodic processing, where erroneous transactions are returned to the source individual. The master files are continuously up to date and, thus, almost immediately reflect the occurrence of all events (provided that the transactions are immediately entered).

These advantages of online transaction processing are not gained without substantial costs. Extra computer time is required for processing and use of terminals; the application software and the system software are more complex than for batch processing; and a relatively heavy investment in acquisition and operation of terminals, communication lines and devices, direct access storage devices, mainframe computers, and additional control features is necessary.

Often online processing entails only part of the transaction processing cycle. This has to do mainly with the stages of data collection and data conversion and verification: transactions may be entered directly through terminals, immediately verified for correctness, then batched and processed at a subsequent time, as with batch processing. The advantages of this mode of delayed batch processing over conventional batch processing are the immediate capture of transactions in a computer-readable form and the immediate feedback for error correction

Imagine a central warehouse connected online to a computer. The warehouse receives stocks from suppliers and issues stock items to manufacturing units. These transactions have to be entered and the inventory master file has to be updated immediately to constantly reflect quantities on hand.

A warehouse clerk, equipped with a computer terminal, enters each transaction into the system as it occurs. At the end of the data transmission, the system sends an acknowledgement to the terminal. This technique assures the clerk that the computer correctly received the transaction.

As soon as the transaction is received at the computer, the following tasks are performed:

1. The transaction (including date and time) is recorded onto a file called the *transaction log*. The transaction log is used for recovery from an error or a malfunction.
2. The transaction is verified and validated (including comparison against a master file record) to make certain it is acceptable. This task is under the control of an edit programme that can directly access the master inventory file.
3. If the transaction is erroneous, the system rejects, it, displaying the reason for rejection on the screen with an error message. The erroneous transaction is entered as an error records into a *suspense file* stored on a direct

access device. The error record includes a code that indicates the error type, date and time, transaction type, and the content of the transaction. The error record is maintained until the corrected transaction is entered from the terminal.

4. An *update programme* makes the master file record current. There are four types of transactions in our warehouse example, each requiring its own unique handling. Each type is identified by a transaction code:

   ADD—Add a new master record for a new stock item
   DEL—Delete an existing master record for an item that will not be stocked any more
   ISS—Quantity of an item issued
   REC—Quantity of an item received

At the end of each working day the following batch system functions are performed:

1. The transaction log is terminated, dumped on a tape, removed from the computer, and stored in a safe place.
2. The inventory file and the suspense file are copied onto tapes, and the copies are stored in a safe place for backup and recovery purpose.
3. The system sends and prints on the terminal a list of all stock items that have reached predetermined safety levels. This is done under the control of a print programme.

Sometimes a failure destroys the current inventory and suspense files or makes them inaccessible to the system. When this occurs, it is impossible to proceed until the master files has been restored to their prefailure status. Therefore, the warehouse clerk is not allowed to access the system until it is operating with correct information. The restoration of service is accomplished by executing a computer programme that recovers all the necessary information. The copies of the master files and the transaction log as of the beginning of the day are inputs to the recovery programme. This recovery programme repeats all the transaction processing upto the point of failure. The output of the recovery programme is the reconstructed master files, which allow the system to be restarted at the point of failure. Once again, the warehouse clerk can access the system.

Structured Decision Systems

The files maintained by the various transaction processing systems serve both the operations and management modules of the information system. The difference between the modules is revealed in the various computer programmes, not in the data files. We, therefore, distinguish between the data base and the model base of an information system. The *model base* is the collection of application programmes using the *data base*.

The term *structured decision system* refers to information systems that make structured decision. While the TPS supports the activities of the operations level, the SDS makes decisions that are within the realm of operational and management control levels. The various SDSs cannot develop before the applicable TPSs are developed, since the automatic decisions made by an SDS are the result of processing data maintained by a TPS. For example, an SDS that determines stock reorder quantities cannot function without a inventory TPS, which collects inventory transactions and updates an inventory master file. Such an SDS can operate as and independent application, triggered by manual intervention, or as an application that is part of the processing stage of the inventory transaction processing cycle.

Any SDS incorporates programmes that instruct the computer to process some relevant data by employing one or more decision models. A decision model represents a human decision-making process that is completely structured, and hence, programmable. The SDSs can be developed by one of two complementary approaches. First, as more and more transactions are collected and can use this data. Second, the organisation can adopt known models or develop custom-made models, then use them to process either currently stored data or new data that was not collected before due to the lack of models.

Suppose a wholesale business has an inventory TPS that updates an inventory master file. The business uses a model to determine the quantity of each item to order from vendors. The model expresses the quantity to order as:

Quantity to order = (quantity to be sold + safety stock + customer back order) - (balance on hand + quantity on order).

This model is admittedly simplistic. It assumes that material will be ordered without regard for purchase order costs and inventory costs, that the order frequency is known, and that the safety stock of watch item is predetermined.

A simple batch-mode SDS that determines reorder quantities based on this model. This SDS is activated at predetermined time intervals. Its input is a customer orders file that is one of the outputs of the customer orders TPS. This file is first sorted by stock item number of facilities more efficient processing. The records in this file contain the quantities of each item to be sold. The reorder programme accesses the updated inventory master file. Each item record in this file contains the safety stock, customers' back orders for the item, balance on hand, and quantity on order. For each item that has customer orders, the reorder programme uses the relevant fields in both files and computes the new quantity to order. It then updates the inventory item master record with the new quantity on order and prints a line for each item that needs reordering.

What does this contrived SDS do? It makes reorder decisions that were once made by the firm's buyer, and it makes them in a faster and more accurate way. It uses data that was captured and processed by the customer orders TPS and by the inventory TPS. We may add that the safety stock for each stock item was predetermined by another SDS that employed the following model:

Safety stock = (maximum less normal demand for item) X (vendor lead time + order frequency).

Decision Support System

This safety stock model accepts an inputs the data about demand for inventory items, the vendor lead times, and the order frequencies. It processes this data and produces an automatic decision. What happens if the demand is subject to extreme fluctuations and dependent on many variables, not all of which can be easily quantified (for instance, consumer tastes, the business cycle, competitive firms, political considerations, and the like)? The demand forecasting then becomes an unstructured decision that cannot be converted to a computer programme. It requires assumptions review the resulting forecast, change some more, and so on. He or she will finally select one of the forecasts and establish it as the figure used by the safety stock model. There are several implications in this short example, including the following:

1. Many decisions at the senior management level are unstructured or semi-structured.
2. The decision makers at this level must resort to assumptions, intuition, and experience when making such decisions.
3. The decision-making process is an interactive human-machine process. The machine supports the decision maker by evaluating various alternative solutions, and the decision maker selects one alternative and, thus, culminates the decision-making process.
4. The computer system provides supporting information to the decision maker by accessing the data base and using one or more models from the model base.
5. The interactive process takes place in a relatively short time. The senior manager cannot wait hours for the results of his or her processed assumptions. The process, therefore, normally requires an online mode of system operation.
6. The internal data base may have to be augmented by external data, such as those relating to business cycles. This data is not routinely captured by the TPS.
7. A prerequisite for the success of the interactive decision-making process is a convenient interface between the decision maker and the model base and between the decision maker and the data base.

These implications indicate, in effect, the necessary components and tools of a decision support system. Unlike TPSs and SDSs, DSSs are used to help solve the semistructured problems typical of the senior manager's world. They rely on the decision maker's insights and judgment at all stages of problems solving—from problem formulation, to choosing relevant data, to selecting the alternative solutions, and on to evaluating the solutions.

Office Information System/Definition and Attributes of a DSS

The term *decision support system* (also referred to as "management decision system," "management support system," or "strategic planning system") has been subject to a wide range of definitions. At one end is the narrow, specific definition of the DSS as "an interactive, computer-based system which supports managers in making unstructured decisions." At the other end is the more global assessment that a DSS is an aid in decision-making and implementation; succinctly put, the DSS serves as an "executive mind-support system." It is one of the many tools a manager can choose to aid in daily decision-making activities. The decision support system is not an "automated manager," but rather a "right-hand person," standing ready to support, not replace the manager. The hallmark of a good decision support system is not its sophistication or efficiency, but its ability to increase the effectiveness of the manager who employs it.

Another definition, which clearly distinguishes a DSS from an SDS, asserts that "a DSS is a computer-based information system used to support decision-making activities in situation where it is not possible or not desirable to have an automated system perform the entire decision process."

Regardless of how a decision support system is defined, conceptually it must possess four essential components: data, decision models, a user-system interface, and decision maker(s).

A DSS supports a semistructured decision; it is designed to support a decision maker in any stage of the decision-making process. The decision maker can choose those functions of the DSS that support some stage while not using other functions. For instance, a decision maker may require the use of data but not models. The key to successful human-machine co-operation is this principle of specified DSS support.

Early DSS literature defined DSS-appropriate problems as those that are semistructured. The degree of problem structure is, indeed, central to DSS. At one extreme, if a decision problem can be completely structured then an SDS can replace the human decision maker. At the other extreme, if no structure can be imposed on the problem, decision support is impossible. It is only between these extremes that DSS is relevant.

Ginzberg and Stohr stated that a problem is semistructured when it is possible to impose some structure on the problem, such as when a decision maker is willing to accept a certain data set or certain models as relevant to the problem situation. Thus, DSS can be defined as systems applicable to problems that can be at least partially, but not completely, structured.

It does not matter to which stage of the decision-making process the structure is applied. Indeed, DSS literature has examples of support for all phases—intelligence, design of alternative solutions, evaluation of and choice among alternatives, as well as monitoring the implementation of the chosen solution. Of course, the type of support will vary from stage to stage since the nature of the activities varies. For instance, relatively few DSSs support the design stage, which typically requires the system to have more problem domain knowledge than is the case for other stages.

Before delineating the typical components of a DSS, we wish to remind you of the fundamental premise of the systems approach. Systems, regardless of their specific contexts, share a common set of elements. A DSS, being system, has a specific *environment*, mainly the users and their decision situation; the system impacts the user by providing some *outputs*; the system consumes some *resources*; and, the system has some *internal structure*, comprising *components* and their *interrelationship*.

The purpose of a DSS is to support a decision-making process. DSS can support decision makers in many ways, including the following:

- Retrieving single items of information
- Providing a mechanism, for *ad hoc* data analysis
- Providing prespecified aggregations of data
- Estimating the consequences of proposed decisions (*i.e.* sensitivity analysis, causal models)
- Proposing solutions

Providing each of these types of support is likely to require different DSS capabilities. This, in turn, will lead to different components and arrangements. DSS literature seems to agree about three generic components of a DSS. These hardware/software components correspond to the conceptual components specified.

The Dialogue Management Subsystem

The dialogue management subsystem provides and manages the framework in which outputs are presented to the user and in which inputs are specified by the user. The dialogue between the user and the system is two-way: output representations define the context for and prompt subsequent user inputs. An ideal dialogue management subsystem has three elements.

1. *User interface*: Concerned with the syntactic aspects of the interaction, the interfacing with specific input and output devices and issues relating to the style of interaction. The specific design of the user interface element depends on the proficiency of users and the frequency of use.
2. *Request constructor*: Provides the two-way transformations between users' requests and the specific modelling and data access repertory. In one direction, it translates users' requests for data to valid data base *queries*, and users' model references to corresponding model-invoking commands. In the opposite direction, it translates requests issued by the model base subsystem for the incorporation of user-supplied parameters in a specific mode. The specific design of this element reflects the vocabulary of the element, and the constraints imposed by the data base and model base subsystems of the DSS.
3. *Control element*: Guarantees the smooth operation of the dialogue management subsystem; determines the mode of system's use, which can vary between "system-prompted" mode and completely "user-driven" mode. This reflects the structure level of the supported decision situation (system-prompted mode for highly structured situation; user-driven mode where no predefined sequence of activities can be provided by the system).

Data Management Subsystem

The intelligence phase of the decision-making process involves scanning the environment in search of problems or opportunities. These problems or opportunities are recognised by accessing relevant data. In the case of a marketing decision, for instance, data must be accessed on each of the company's products as a first step in determining which products are to be phased out. This data might include such items as dollar sales, physical volume, total unit cost, and price per unit. Data such as this will normally be systematically collected from the internal environment as part of a routine TPS. However, a DSS, as distinguished from a TPS, will often require collection of data concerning other environments. This may include data concerning competitors' actions, general societal trends, customer demand, or legal and/or governmental constraints. This type of data may be collected routinely or on an *ad hoc* basis. This relevant data is collected and stored in a data base to await the scanning stage.

A manger armed with the objectives of the firm begins the ongoing search for problems or opportunities. This search can take one of three forms, depending upon the type decision to be made and the level of the decision maker. A structured continuous search is usually performed in order to make decisions that are well defined and regular. The user may extract isolated data in order to perform such functions as monitoring the work flow and scheduling operations of a production department, or he or she may receive prespecified standard reports that act as input to the design stage of the decision-making process.

Data may also be retrieved by a structured, but *ad hoc*, search in order to make infrequent decisions. Plant location is such a decision since it will normally occur infrequently. Yet the necessary intelligence gathering activities can be clearly structured. The output from such a search usually suggests the process to be used to analyse the situation, but it can also indicate the need for human intervention before the process can begin.

Finally, there are problems and opportunities for which the search must be done heuristically through examination of data by the manager. This type of decision is usually made by senior management. The intelligence phase primarily provides the managers with easy access to the data base. The data retrieval capabilities of the DSS must, therefore, be rapid. This, of course, has many implications for the design of a DSS. The output from such a search generally identifies the situation but leaves the rest of the decision process to the manager. Sometimes the manager employs some programmed models to manipulate the relevant data and come up with alternative solutions.

The management of data—the ability to store, retrieve, and manipulate—is thus fundamental to a DSS. These activities are performed by the *data management subsystem*, which contains four generic elements. These four elements are:

1. *The data base management system*: provides an access mechanism, to data in the data base. The DBMS provides such services as data sharing and integration, data definitions, data manipulation, and data integrity. The DBMS also shields the other subsystems of the DSS from physical aspects of access to the data base.
2. *The query facility*: Serves as the front-end element of the data management subsystem and as the subsystem's interface to the model management and dialogue management subsystems. It accepts requests for data from these subsystems, determines how these requests can be filed, translates the requests to DBMS-specific commands, and finally returns the requested data to the issuing subsystem.
3. *The data directory*: Provides the basis for answering preliminary questions submitted by the query facility concerning availability and source of data, or their exact meaning. This element contain *meta-data*. It is much needed in *ad hoc* DSSs, the directory's function is internal to the DBMS element and might then disappear as an independent element.
4. *The staging element*: Provides access to sources of data that are external to the DSS. It is an interface between the DBMS element and its DSS-specific data base and other organisational data bases or remote data bases. Its structure reflects the nature of external data sources from which data is extracted. For instance, if remote data bases are to be accessed, some data communications facility is included in the staging element.

Office information systems are the combination of hardware, software and people are in information systems that process office transactions and support office activities at all levels of the organisation. It is basically the lack of office information technologies in the past that made the office one of the least efficient segments of contemporary organisations. The most unproductive workers in many organisations are office employees and executives. Between 1972 and 1977 blue-collar productivity in the United States grew by more than 2 per cent annually, while white-collar efficiency increases by only 0.4 per cent a year. In the American oriented economy, 25 per cent of the national work force in 1980 was tied up in offices; the figure is projected to rise to 40 per cent by 1990. While the average American worker was aided by about $2,000 in capital investments. In the mid-1950s, companies first started the era of data processing. The second part of the 1970s saw the growing role of information technology in processing numeric data and, thus, the revolutionising of office work. This led initially to the emergence of office work processing to complement DP in organisations.

Other developments in information technologies in the 1980s have led to the convergence of office information systems and conventional DP systems into a comprehensive organisational information system, where both office and non-office systems are closely linked and structured along the TPS, SDS, and DSS layers.

Office information system is thus a concept involving a number of current and future technologies that are introduced into the office to improve office productivity, to facilitate organisational communications, and also to provide more stimulating and intellectually rewarding work for people in the office. These technologies, which are briefly reviewed in the following sections, include microelectronics, telecommunications, main storage, micrographics, image and voice processing, teleconferencing, videoconferencing, facsimile, and software technologies.

Following this brief introduction to the relatively new sector of organisational information systems, we now turn to a discussion of the main issues pertinent to office information systems. After classifying office activities and information, we suggest a logical order of computerising the activities, and then note the technological components that are needed for the computerisation.

Classification of Activities and Information

The activities performed in the office can be classified into two main categories. These are:

1. Activities performed by clerical personnel (clerks, secretaries, typists, messengers)

2. Activities performed by an executive and professional personnel (managers, staff, assistants, engineers, economists, and researchers)

Obviously there is some activity overflow between the two categories. Therefore, the characteristic activities discussed here are not necessarily exclusive to one category.

The following is a list of activities typical to the clerical personnel:

- Typing
- Filing and recording of documents
- Mailing
- Message switching
- Scheduling of meetings and conferences
- Calendar keeping
- Retrieving documents and preparing materials for meetings discussions

The following is a list of activities typical to the executive and professional personnel:

- Conferencing
- Production of information (in the form of messages, memos, reports, etc.)
- Controlling performance

The information produced in the office, or that which transfers through it, can be classified into the following types:

- Text that is mainly literal
- Numeric data (DP systems)
- Graphical information (graphs, charts, histograms, etc.)
- Images (drawings, pictures)

We can safely assume that automated offices of the future will encompass most of these activities and information types. However, the computerised implementation of the various subjects will be gradual and will be dependent on several factors. Some of these factors are listed here:

- The availability of technology
- The logical ordering of computerisation of activities
- Economical feasibility
- The organisational climate and its ability to absorb and operate computerised office systems.

Stages of Office Computerisation

It is rare for an organisation to have the technological and organisational capability to simultaneously computerises the number and variety of office activities. It is, therefore, necessary to set priorities. The order of priorities presented here is based on the degree of activity complexity and on the availability of technology. We are not taking economic consideration into account, since these must be examined for each case of computerisation. The order of stages presented here assume; that since most of the work load in the office is performed by the clerical personnel, the greatest marginal savings will be obtained by computerising these activities prior to computerising activities of the executive/professional personnel.

Stage 1: Word Processing

A word processor is a configuration of hardware and software that provides typing, editing, production, reproduction, and document storage services. A work processor can operate as an independent *workstation* where the minimal configuration is a keyboard, a CPU with internal storage, a screen, a printer, and an external storage device. More complex configurations can include several workstations sharing common resources.

Since a word processor produces documents on a magnetic medium, its implementation is practically a prerequisite for computerising an office. While its advantage is that it can be independently implemented in different offices, it is necessary to retain the option to link such independent systems to a network that may be implemented in a subsequent stage.

Stage 2: Electronic Filing

Once a WP system is implemented, filing of outgoing mail on a magnetic medium is an almost immediate consequence. The implementation of this function relies on appropriate cataloguing and retrieval software. Most of the work involved concerns conventional office and procedures analysis, and not technological issues.

It should be emphasised that this immediate electronic filing pertains to outgoing mail and to other documents generated by the WP system, such as contracts and manuals. The electronic filing of incoming conventional mail and documents requires a much more complex technology.

Stage 3: Controlling Performance

Controlling performance is a managerial function pertaining to the recording of decisions and important dates in the sequence of implementing various organisational tasks. With appropriate software, the computer can be used as a memory aid to managers or other entities.

Controlling performance is not usually a high-priority computerisation function. It is noted here as stage 3 because it can be implemented on a stand-alone WP system. The functions described in the following stages require a communications network among the various offices.

Before proceeding to the next stage, note that stages, 4, 5 and 6 do not have to be implemented in sequence, but can be implemented simultaneously.

Stage 4: Electronic Mail

Electronic mail involves the transfer to letters and documents through telecommunications lines, rather than through physical facilities. It speeds up mail deliveries and reduced the cost and time of paper mail. Electronic mail relies on facsimile transmissions equipment and on communicating word processors to transfer any type of document.

An electronic mail system requires a telecommunications network and software that can identify addresses and temporarily store incoming and outgoing mail. Terminals in the office workstations are tied to a computing and telecommunications network. The workstations handle all internal correspondence by delivering letters and memos electronically; each piece is electronically read from any location and is then indexed, filed, retrieved, or disposed of automatically.

Two substage can be associated with electronic mail implementation: internal mail and external mail. It is obvious that organisations that want to correspond electronically must subscribe to a telecommunications network.

Stage 5: Message Switching

The linking of office workstations in a telecommunications network can provide for the transmission of message in the network in addition to electronic mailing. A message, as distinguished from mail, is information that is not filed or catalogued. A considerable amount of office time and a number of telephone conversations involve such memos and notes. A message keyed in form one workstation that is transmitted to another workstation reduces the load on telephone lines. It also involves a single activity—the sender and receiver of the message do not have to be in the office at the same time, since the message can be saved on an external storage device until it is retrieved by the receiver.

Stage 6: Calendar Keeping and Scheduling

Scheduling of meetings and conferences can be facilitated with electronic calendars. When several office workstations are linked in a network, calendars can be stored on a magnetic medium. A person who wants to schedule a meeting can use the automated office system to find a meeting date that is convenient for all participants. A computer programme will accept, in this case, such parameters as the duration of the meeting, the subject, and a range of dates for scheduling the meeting. The programme will review the various calendars, come up with a tentative meeting date, and display the date to the participants. If the participants approve, the programme will finalise the date, enter the data on the calendars, and then announce the meeting date to the participants. If all do not approve, the programme will come up with another tentative date and will again poll the participants.

Stage 7: Integration of Various Systems

We have already noted that the information relevant to office activities is classified into several patterns: textural data, numeric data, graphics, images, and voices. Stages 1 to 6 mainly deal with processing textual data, or with substituting a textual medium for another medium. Future office information systems will be able to process other patterns of information in an integrative way.

Currently, information patterns other than textural are processed independently using the following devices:

1. Numerical data—Processed by electronic data processing systems.
2. Graphic data—Processed manually by draftspersons or by electronic devices such as plotters, graphic monitors, computer-aided design and computer-aided manufacturing systems, photocopiers, and facsimile transmission equipment.
3. Images—Processed by photocopying devices, facsimile equipment, TV and video devices.
4. Voice-Processed by recording and playback devices, PABX systems, and dictating machines.

Current trends indicate future integration of these distinct systems. For instance, a drawing could be transmitted from one workstation to another, filed on a digital magnetic medium, and then merged into a text handled by a word processing system. Another example of such integration is a videotex system involving telephone television, and computers.

The integration of the systems will enable integrated office activities such as *teleconferencing* or *video-conferencing*. Several people in different locations can conduct a joint meeting using telephones to converse, video monitors to watch facial expressions, and computer monitors to view numerical data displayed simultaneously on all screens and retrieved from a common data base. Another example of integrated systems is a *voice message switching system*. A person wishing to send a message will not have to key it in. Instead, he or she will dictate the message to the office workstation and key in the list of addressees. The computer will store the message in a digitalized form and send it to the addressees when each switches on the workstation.

Technological Components

This section briefly presents the technological components needed to implement each stage of office system automation. While it does not deal with the technical specifications of the components or with their availability, it does specify what is needed to implement each stage listed in the previous section.

The basic workstation required for word processing comprises a microcomputer a monitor, a keyboard, a printer, and an external storage device. This hardware configuration, together with appropriate software, constitutes a stand-alone word processing system.

Electronic filing requires the same configuration, but with additional software for filing and retrieval. An office and procedures analyst is also needed to design filing and retrieval procedures.

A more complex work processing and electronic filing system can contain several microcomputer-based workstations linked in a network and accessing a common data base. Or, alternatively, a number of "dumb" workstations can be linked to a central computer, thus enabling simultaneous work by a number of persons.

The progression into controlling performance does not require a change in the hardware configuration, but does require appropriate software. Above all it requires a conceptual change since a workstation in this stage serves not only the clerical personnel but also the manager, either directly or through staff assistants.

The implementation of the next stages requires the technology of *telecommunications*. Telecommunications is the basic technology in advanced office information systems. The area of telecommunications encompasses a spectrum of topic covering optical communication, packet radio techniques, satellite communications, digital signal processing, fibre optics, and electronic switching.

Where office computing was the most significant force for change in the 1960s and 1970s, office communications will probably be the most important force in the 1980s and 1990s. By the early 1990s, many of the large offices will probably have an in-house telecommunications branch exchange that will electronically connect all types—numeric, textual, audio, and visual—of interoffice data and information flows.

Communications network technologies have led to the emergence of *value-added networks* and *information utilities*, which may incorporate various useful features into the communications network. For example, the network may provide teleconferencing, electronic mail, or computer power as basic utilities in addition to basic communications. The idea behind this is quite simple: since computers are already used for switching in communications networks, they can also be used to provide other services to the customer.

Generally we can distinguish between two types of telecommunications. These are:

1. A *local area network* that links computers or workstations in an office building, in a campus, or in a cluster of buildings where distances are measured in hundreds of yards;
2. A *remote area network* that transmits numeric data, voices, and images over long distances.

The implementation of an internal electronic mail system requires the installation of a local area network. An external electronic mail system requires subscription regular communication network. The same holds true for electronic mailing among offices of a single organisation that are geographically dispersed. In addition to the network, the various workstations must be equipped with hardware devices, such as modems and controllers, and with software programmes for controlling transmission, identifying addressees, filing, and retrieval.

Note that the progression from the first three stages to the next three stages is not a linearly gradual one, but is more a stepwise change. After installing the hardware and telecommunications infrastructure, automating the functions of electronic mail, message switching, calendar keeping, and scheduling are achieved by the acquisition and use of appropriate software. The last stage of integration requires co-ordination among computer systems, photocopying machines, facsimile equipment, telephones, video and television systems, graphical display devices, dictating machines, audio devices, and the like.

Most objective experts agree that the first half of the 1980s have not yet offered fully integrated systems. However, high-tech companies have invested considerable funds in research and development of such systems. Hence, we can fairly assume that the typical office workstation of the early 1990s will encompass the following functions:

1. All hardware and software components support local WP.
2. Linkage to a central computer for retrieving data from data processing systems, processing them at the workstation, and merging them with texts and other components of the workstation.
3. Display and drawing of graphical data.
4. Capability of entering, storing, and displaying images by linking to facsimile and photocopying equipment; also, capability of retrieving images and merging them with other components of the workstation.
5. Capability to receive and send voice data and store it in a digitalized form.

Before concluding this review of office information systems, a final note is in order. The integration and balance among automated office functions depend on the unique characteristics of each organisation. We refer here to work loads, budgets, geographical dispersion of organisational units, nature of office work, size of the organisation, organisational climate, and the like. When implementing the various stages of office automation, it makes economic sense to first automate backbone applications that could significantly raise productivity and then to automate more functions for relatively little extra cost.

DSS and Office Automation

We want to impress upon you our conviction that the various MIS, DSS, and OA systems and technologies are converging to form an integrated organisational information system. These systems should not be treated as disjointed systems, but as subentities of the comprehensive information system plan of an organisation. This plan develop from an overall corporate information system strategy, and be implemented by adherence to policies that are derived from the strategy. The policies relate to the various systems; thus an organisation may have a DSS policy and an OA policy among other policies.

Keen has made the claim that organisations have been slow in defining a real policy for OA. Plenty of promises, expectations, buzz words, and ads exist, but very few companies have evolved a coherent, organisationwide OA policy. In many ways, OA succeeded only because it came in the wake of DSS, which acted as a dry run for office automation. DSS relied on a tremendous advantage in technology—the terminal; it bypassed the formal DP channels and went directly to users; and it focused on ease of use for people having no technical background. These DSS characteristics contributed to the goals of office automation—to diffuse computerised workstations throughout to the organisation and to persuade people to use them for such key aspects of their work as text handling, communications, mail, scheduling, filing, and retrieval.

External Online Data Bases

Suppose you are managing the investment portfolio for a trust department of a bank. You are looking for a solid stock with some short-term growth possibilities, and you hear a rumour that the ABC Corporation is planning to announce a merger. It sounds interesting and you want to analyse the financial statements of ABC for the last ten years. You have a personal computer and a financial DSS based on a spreadsheet package. You are using this for sensitivity analysis of financial data retrieved from the local data base of your bank. The local data base does not have data on ABC, but you know that this data is stored on the Compustat data base. Recently you saw an advertisement in the *Wall Street Journal* by a company calling itself an information utility. Utility subscribers can access the data for which you are looking.

This is just one example of accessing to a growing number of remote data bases maintained by information service providers. By now you already know that managers in higher echelons of organisations rely considerably on external data in the decision-making process. A DSS, which is intended to support such decision makers, is improved if external data can be downloaded into the DSS data base and manipulated by DSS models.

Access to external data bases is handled by the staging element of the DSS data management component. This element connects the DSS with multiple data sources and extracts subsets of data out of large external data based for immediate and direct DSS use. Obviously, some data communications facility is part of the staging element if data is to be accessed online.

CHAPTER 4

Communication for Co-ordination

The main business of an industrial enterprise may be divided into six specialist functions—purchasing, production, marketing, development, personnel and finance. The exercise of each of these functions involves five main activities—planning, organising, directing, co-ordinating, and controlling. The task of managers is so to exercise these five activities that the operations of the six specialist functions are integrated in a total plan. Whilst the main divisions each have a definite function, they clearly do not operate in water-tight compartments. There must, therefore, be a synchronisation of effort, involving the work of every department. Without this co-ordination it is not possible to achieve a total company objective based on totally integrated operations.

Principles of Co-ordination

Mary Parker Follett (1868-1933) laid down four fundamental principles upon which any enduring, smoothly-operating organisation must rest—

1. Co-ordination as the reciprocal relating of all the factors in a situation.
2. Co-ordination by direct contact of the responsible people concerned.
3. Co-ordination in the early stages.
4. Co-ordination as a continuing process.

The first principle, co-ordination as the reciprocal relating of all the factors in a situation, shows us just what this process of co-ordination actually is. On this principle Miss Follett said—

> Think for a moment what happens between the heads of departments in a business. You cannot envisage the process

> accurately by thinking of A as adjusting himself to B and to C and to D. A adjusts himself to B and *also* to a B influenced by C and to a B influenced by D and to a B influenced by A himself. Again he adjusts himself to C and *also* to a C influenced by B and to a C influenced by D and to a C influenced by A himself—and so on. One could work it out mathematically. This sort of reciprocal relating, this interpenetration of every part by every other part, and again by every other part as it has been permeated by all, should be the goal of all attempts at co-ordination, a goal, of course, never wholly reached.
>
> You will understand that I am simplifying when I speak of A, B, C and D adjusting themselves to one another. They are of course at the same time adjusting themselves to every other factor in the situation. Or it would be more accurate to say that all the factors in the situation are going through this process of reciprocal relating.
>
> If anyone finds this principle difficult to accept, I would suggest that it is a principle which he has already accepted in regard to facts. Any fact gains its significance through its relation to all the other facts pertaining to the situation. For instance, if you have increased sales, you are not too pleased until you find out whether there has been an increased sales cost. If there has been, or one out of proportion to sales, your satisfaction disappears. Merchandising shows you this principle at work. For merchandising is not merely a bringing together of designing, engineering, manufacturing and sales departments, it is these in their total relativity.

For the second principle Miss Follett had in mind cross-relations between heads of departments instead of up and down the line through the chief executive. This seems sensible as these are the people closest to the matter in hand and it is essential for them to have the opportunity for direct contact.

The third principle means that the direct contact must begin in the earliest stages of the process—writing on this she said—

> We see how this works in the correlation of policies in a business. If the heads of departments confront each other with finished policies, agreement will be found difficult. Of

> course they then begin to "play politics," or that is often the tendency. But if these heads meet while they are forming their policies, meet and discuss the questions involved, a successful correlation is far more likely to be reached. Their thinking has not become crystallised. They can still modify one another. I should say that one of the fundamental ideas for business management is that the making of decisions and the correlating of decisions should be one process. You cannot, with the greatest degree of success for your undertaking, make policy forming and policy adjusting two separate processes. Policy adjusting cannot begin after the separate policies have been completed.

Continuing her elaboration of this principle Miss Follett stressed that the process of reciprocal relating, the interpenetration of every part by every other part, means that departmental policy should be an integral part of what is known as "general policy." She added—

> Before I leave this point, let me call particularly to your attention that this reciprocal relating, co-ordinating, unifying, is a process which does not require sacrifice on the part of the individual. The fallacy that the individual must give up his individuality for the sake of the whole is one of the most pervasive, the most insidious, fallacies I know. It crops up again and again in one place after another. In some of the businesses I have studied, I have been told that the head of a department should subordinate the good of his department to the good of the whole undertaking. But of course he should do no such thing. His departmental point of view is needed in the whole. It must indeed be reconciled with all the other points of view in the business, but it must not be abandoned.

The fourth principle, co-ordination as a continuing process, needs little comment. Clearly co-ordination should be a continuous process. It must go on all the time and not just on special occasions or when difficulties arise. If, for example, an *ad hoc* committee is set upto consider a special problem the tendency is naturally to think only of the question under discussion. But the cross-relations referred to above envisage continuing contacts in which not only immediate problems will be discussed but also the underlying principles which can serve as guides for future similar cases. In other words, there will always be an attempt to solve the immediate problem *and* an attempt to establish principles to help the collective effort in the future.

Henri Fayol suggested that in a well co-ordinated enterprise the following can be observed—

1. Each department works in harmony with the rest. Stores knows what has to be supplied and at what time; Production knows its target; Maintenance keeps equipment and tools in good order; Finance procures necessary funds; and all these activities are carried out in sure, orderly fashion.
2. In each department divisions and subdivisions are precisely informed as to the share they must take in the communal task and the reciprocal aid they are to afford one another.
3. The working schedule of the various departments and subdivisions thereof is constantly attuned to changing circumstances.

Effective Communications

The integration of the main specialist functions in a total plan involves co-ordination, and effective communications play an important part in this.

Good communications depend on clear thinking. You must first know to whom and what you want to communicate, and then decide on the best means of doing it. Sometimes circumstances will dictate the medium to be used, but often you have a choice, in which case you will be guided by one or a combination of the following considerations—

1. The time factor—is speed vital?
2. The accessibility of the person to be contacted.
3. Your knowledge of the person concerned: personal habits and inclinations.

4. The psychological aspect of the situation—the spoken word may be less dangerous than the same thing in writing, for example.

A wrong decision about what is said, the medium used, or when it is said can have disastrous results. All are important. It's not only what you say, but how you say it, and when you say it.

Whatever method is used it is important to keep in mind at all times that communication is a two-way process. Not only is there the act of sending, but also one of receiving. Communication is not complete until there is understanding and acceptance of the message, and until action results therefrom. There are many barriers to understanding. A communication can mean entirely different things, depending upon the personal background and experience of the people involved. The receiver of a communication tends to evaluate what he hears and sees in terms of his own experience, viewpoint and emotions, with the result that an accurate exchange of ideas is difficult to accomplish.

Since communication is a two-way process we must always have the receiver in mind when speaking or writing. When speaking to a child we use words that the child can understand. We do not want to treat an adult as a child, but still we must choose our language with the receiver in mind. Scientists and technicians and business men often fail to realise this. The scientist, for example, can and does make contact with his colleagues in the special vocabulary surrounding their scientific work. But outside their own department communication is much more difficult, and much more thought is necessary to convey a message. As far as possible, unfamiliar terminology must be avoided. It has been truly said that if a person really knows his subject he will discourse on it in simple, everyday terms; to the extent to which he does not know it he will take refuge in technical terminology.

The ability to impart information clearly, completely and precisely depends on these three basic qualities—concentration, discrimination, and expression. It is only when we are called upon to write or speak on a subject that we realise how vague and woolly our thoughts can be. Considerable concentrations is needed to put out nebulous idea into words and to exercise our powers of discrimination and expression.

The test of good style in any communication is: Does it do its job? Is it effective as a method of conveying exactly an idea from one mind to another *and*, at the same time, establishing a personal relationship with the other person?

Instructions and Employee Information

Clearly a communication addressed to a large number of people presents more problems than one addressed to a single individual. It has been shown by many investigators that despite the many millions spent on education a large number of people go through life without really learning to read. Many can read, haltingly, if they must, but they do not have enough skill to enjoy it and shun it if they can. They would rather look at pictures.

In the past official documents have not helped to overcome this weakness. Many have been so verbose that even well-educated people could not understand them. Fortunately in recent years there has been a move towards plainness and clarity in official communications. All whose duty it is to issue instructions must learn to write and speak so that the people concerned understand them, or better still, cannot misunderstand them. They must also be able to convey accurate information without ambiguity or resentment.

Orders and instructions should always be accompanied by enough information about the policy behind them. Over-familiarity with the subject-matter is often the cause of misunderstanding. It is easy to forget that the other man does not know all that you do. Ideally the information passed on should relate to the scope and responsibility of its recipient.

Announcements made to convey information to employees should contain statements of fact with sufficient explanation to enable the facts to be understood. The main point to keep in mind is that the writer is not showing off his own ability or status, but presenting information for others to absorb easily.

One is surprised at the number of executives who complain of "going to a lot of trouble to keep staff informed, but they simply don't read the information sent to them." When one sees some of the written information given to employees, one is no longer surprised; certainly nobody would *want* to read it. The writer should confine himself as far as possible to words that are in common use, and use the shortest word which expresses the meaning. Guiding rules are:

- Do not use a phrase to express a meaning which can be conveyed by a single preposition.
- Avoid the use of woolly abstract nouns whenever possible.
- Keep sentences as short as possible, preferably eight to eighteen words long, and limit them to one main thought.

Remember that always the reader will want to know:

"How does this affect me?"

In an official report on communications in industry, published under the title *People at Work*, a summary was made of the general attitudes to communications in the firms where surveys were carried out. The managers of nearly all the firms visited believed that good communications would give employees a better understanding of their work and of factors which might affect it, and would help employees to work intelligently and efficiently and to accept the need for change when it arose. Most of them also held that there was value in letting employees know what was going on in the firm generally, and that in the absence of facts, rumours, often unfounded, would take their place. Again managers were anxious to know what employees thought about the firm and the way it was run, so that they could take this into account in shaping their plans and policies. In all the firms, it was felt that the problems of establishing and maintaining good communications were considerable.

For their part, employees felt that they should have clear and definite information on matters necessary for carrying out their jobs. Employees also attached importance to arrangements for raising and discussing with the managers matters affecting their jobs and working conditions, and also the general running of the firm.

Discussing the background factors the report said that there were common features in the communications arrangements in all the firms visited. There were also significant differences—for example, in the range and amount of information communicated, the methods used and the extent to which exchange of views between managers and employees was encouraged and took place. In some measures these variations were due to background factors, such as the size and structure of the firm, the way in which the work was organised and the quality of the relationships which had been built up over the years.

In a large engineering works employing thousands of men on noisy production lines moving at a set pace, there were physical problems of communication which did not exist in a smaller firm with a few hundred employees working under one roof, each at his own speed, on relatively quiet operations.

A nationalised industry with widely dispersed units had consciously tackled its communications problems by developing an extensive network of committees and by making wide use of written material. On the other hand, a small compact firm was able to rely on frequent informal day-to-day contacts between managers, supervisors and men.

Shift working may be a source of difficulty, since workers on shifts may have little opportunity for contact with managers, supervisors and their own representatives. These difficulties existed but were not found to be acute at factories where the shifts rotated. They were serious in one firm where there was a permanent night shift.

Whether or not a firm has a history of steady demand for its products and of stable employment was also found to be an important factor. At one factory, where there had been a constantly high level of activity for years, and employees felt that their jobs were secure, critical situations in which the directors had to take urgent action to explain to the employees what was happening were unknown. At another factory, which was subject to substantial fluctuations in activity and employment, the directors had to be constantly prepared to deal with rumours of short-time working or redundancy.

In all the firms, three main methods of communication were used. On some matters, managers and supervisors talked with shop floor employees individually or collectively. For others, written material was used. On yet other matters, information was given to, and views were exchanged with, employee representatives, either at meetings of joint committees, or in the course of informal day-to-day contacts. The emphasis placed on each of these methods varied from firm to firm.

The first method—where managers and supervisors communicate with shop floor employees—is widely used, but where there are many intermediaries not only is the transmission of information slowed down but there is an increased risk of inaccuracies and misunderstandings creeping in. The personal factor often presents a difficulty, and there is frequently a reluctance to pass on information. Sometimes this arises because a man thinks that his status is enhanced by knowing more than his subordinates. Where written material is used this usually takes the form of handbooks, notices posted on works' notice boards, and work's magazines. Notice boards are, in fact, widely used, but all too often they are disregarded unless care is taken in siting and display, and in making sure that "dead" material is regularly removed. An increasing use is made of joint committees as a means of communication between managers and the main body of employees. Such committees serve as a channel of communication in both directions.

There is no doubt that accepted channels of communication reduce the scope for rumours and misunderstandings. It is difficult to eliminate altogether the "grapevine," but where there is a definite plan for communication with employees, the effect of the unofficial communications network is reduced to a minimum.

Suggestion Schemes

Employee information is not limited to information passing down the line from the top to the bottom. Much valuable information can pass upwards. Although upward communication is less frequent, a manager should tap the full resources of subordinates by encouraging creative thought and full expression of ideas, without making hasty judgment as to their worth.

Communications going downwards are highly directive and initiate actions by subordinates. Communications going upwards, however, report results or give information and make suggestions.

Some businesses run suggestion schemes to arouse the interest of the staff in the conduct of the business and to encourage them to co-operate by submitting practical suggestions. A suggestion scheme gives workers a sense of participation and initiative.

Achievement Factors in Corporate Communication

Disciplines like finance, personnel, company secretaryship and marketing have well-defined scope of operations together with modalities therefor. This is largely because of their intrinsic place in the organisational structure of any Corporation. In fact, the birth of any Corporation starts with the opening of wings for looking after these functions.

In this scheme of things corporate communication as a discipline is of recent origin. Corporate communication is viewed differently by different people. For some corporation communication is the same thing as organisational communication. Others think it as a mere "rehash" of public relations. Still there are those who equate it with management information systems, company publications, advertising, liaison and so on.

If corporated communication is not generally well understood, it is because of the fact that corporate communication is still evolving. The concept is an offshoot of the growing recognition, by top managements, of communication as a strategic resource in helping achieve corporate goals and objectives.

As the term implies, corporate communication encompasses all the communication activities undertaken within the corporate context, whether formal or informal, regardless of direction or flow information—top-down, bottom-up and horizontal.

Public relations is for shaping and projecting an image as a key element in the drive for success. Top achievers rightly consider a good image as a basic resource in the same way that they view finance or people. As the interaction between government, industry, environment, and public becomes extremely complex, public relations or PR becomes an inevitable component of corporate affairs.

Public relations is the corporation communicating with various publics with the objective of winning public understanding, acceptance and support. As Alejo Villanueva, President of Media Communicators, Inc. USA, said "PR is not just a question of form, of media mileage and of cosmetics. PR is a public recognition of a substantive performance. PR can very well mean Performance Recognition."

For any activity it is important to clearly know the target groups, information requirements for each target group, channels and sources of information. This needs a detailed and continuous exercise by a professional PR man. It is not a one-time activity but a continuous activity governed by changes in corporated goals, environment and modalities for achieving corporate goals through a well-thought out communication strategy. It will now be worthwhile drawing up an agenda for a PR or Corporate Communication Manager.

Managing PR Functions

The first and foremost item on the agenda of a PR manager is: help formulate corporate policies and strategies in the area of communication for internal and external publics. This is necessarily to be done in the back-drop of the corporate goals, the prevailing environment and the need for dissemination of information among various publics so as to help built a correct appreciation of the Corporation's working. This strategy has to spell out the PR goals, the target audience and the action plan for achieving those goals.

In big corporations like BHEL, ONGC and SAIL, detailed exercise is done for preparing a PR strategy for each year or for a couple of years. This document serves as a guideline to PR professionals both at the corporate and unit levels so that the overall projection conforms to a uniform pattern and approach. This does not, in any way, stifle the initiative. Rather, it helps working in a clear-cut direction.

Secondly, the PR manager has to scan the communication environment on a continuous basis for identifying and utilising the various communication tools for effective management. We have to understand one thing clearly that PR deals with human beings and not machines. That being so, human beings are susceptible to many currents, cross currents, vicissitudes and perceptions unlike the machines which operate as per set formulae. The communication manager has to make best possible use of various communication tools in keeping with the requirements of the top management.

The third item on the agenda is adaptation of organisational communication practices and processes to such policies. This means a close and continuous interaction between various functional groups in the organisation for evolving such practices and processes as will help create an understanding in public.

Fourthly, the communication manager has to oversee and regularly monitor the on-going communication activities in the organisation and identify the communication needs of members of the organisation or of units within the organisation.

Mainline Functions

An example will help better understanding of this aspect. During interviews for promotion from Manager to Senior Manager, the candidates were asked questions pertaining to areas other than those handled by them. In most of the cases, the candidates could not answer the questions even though they had already put in 10 to 15 years service in the organisation. They argued that right from morning till evening, they were busy in their own work area which did not leave them any time to collect information about other areas. But, then, the moot point is that a Manager has to make efforts to update his own knowledge and information about the more important aspects of the organisation and for this he has to evolve his own methodology to collect information and retrieve the same when required. It is surely expected from a Manager, aspiring to be a Senior Manager, that he knows about major activities of his organisation and not just about his own work-area.

Fifthly, the PR manager helps, in his own way, promote industrial peace, goodwill and efficiency within the organisation. The PR manager plays a complementary and supplementary role to the PR manager by projecting the achievements of the workers and building up their self-esteem as partners in the organisation's success and not as mere cogs in the wheel. A corollary to this function, the PR manager has also to help enrich the organisation relationship with the associated public outside the organisation, namely, government industries, clients and the public at large.

Last on the agenda of the communication manager is to conduct communication audit, recommend communication plans and execute them in the overall interest of the organisation. The main target groups for corporate communication strategy are internal publics which means all employees from the lowest to the highest and their families. Then there are customers, government functionaries, stock holders / investors, special interest groups and the mass media. For each one of the target groups, information requirements are varied because what is required by the company employee may not be of much interest to a government functionary.

The above agenda for a PR or Corporate Communication Manager is only illustrative and not exhaustive. The PR manager has thus a very important role to play in dissemination of information to various publics in a manager so that they develop a correct appreciation of the corporation's role and activities. It follows that he has to identify the target audience, work out information requirements for each target group and make use of various channels and tools of mass communication. Table 4.1 below spells out all the three aspects in an illustrated manner.

Table 4.1

Target Audience	*Information Requirements*	*Channels/Sources of Information*
1. Employees	Corporate goals and objectives	Regular staff meetings
	Update on corporate policies, rules and regulations	Management-Staff dialogue
	Company performance indicators	Company publications
	Career opportunities, social welfare (salary and wages, job security, working conditions, medical benefits)	Bulletin Boards Audiovisuals
		Informal channels (grapevine)
	Staff movements	Union publications
2. Top Management	Corporate philosophy and range	Technical reports
	Corporate Performance indicators (group rate, export, return on investment, profit, etc.)	Company publications and reports Audiovisuals
	Update on policies/strategies	Group management conferences
	Feedback from rank and file	*Ad hoc* bodies
	Government policies (particularly those related to trade and industry, finance)	Mass Media Government issuances (including laws, orders, circulars, etc.)
	Market information (prices, credit sources, interest rate suppliers, buyers)	
	Social-political trends (international and national/local scene)	

(Contd.)

Target Audience	*Information Requirements*	*Channels/Sources of Information*
3. Middle Management	Corporate philosophy	Group management conferences
	Performance/targets indicators	Technical reports
	Range of corporate activities	Company publications
	R&D efforts	Audiovisuals
	Feedback from employees	
4. Customers	Corporate philosophy	Mass Media (including trade/industry/publications)
	Range of corporate product services (including innovations)	Plant/office visits or tours
	Company contributions to the local/national community	Company publication
	Product/service attributes	
	Social and cultural community programme	
5. Government	Legal requirement (financial statements, articles of incorporation etc.)	Lobby groups
		Annual reports
	Adherence to legal statutes such as minimum wage, price control, environmental protection, etc.	Financial reports
		Trade and Industry Associations
	Industrial performance as it relates to employment, investment, research and development, exports and balance of payments, profits and taxes.	
6. Stockholders/Investors	Performance indicators	Annual stockholders meeting
	Quality of saving	Company publications
	Projection of future earnings	Mass media (including professional publications)
	Past earning records (financial track record)	Financial experts (portfolio advisers, security analyst, financial managers)
	Competitive position	Financial institutions (Bank)
	Management competition	
	Growth potential	

(Contd.)

Target Audience	*Information Requirements*	*Channels/Sources of Information*
7. The Mass Media	Corporate profile	Company PR/ Information Officers
	Socio-economic performance	Company Publications
	Future development plans and top management changes	Top management
	Company innovations in management techniques and social aspects	Industry leaders
	R&D activities	Trade Unions
	Industry trend data (particularly on employment, investment, pricing etc.)	News clippings/video files
	Top management views on major national issues.	
8. Special interest Group (consumers, environmentalists, etc.)	Product/service quality standards Result of government agency Product evaluation (e.g. Bureau of Food and Drugs, Bureau of Standards) specific corporate policies (pricing, technology transfer, wage and salaries, waste disposal)	Company publications Mass media Lobby groups

CHAPTER 5

Towards More Effective Corporate Communication: An Executive View

Introduction

A whole new approach is emerging in the role of corporate communication. Let us begin with an example from Indian Industry. Telecommunication equipment is supplied to the Indian P&T or the Indian Telecommunication Department by the three major central public undertakings, the Indian Telephone Industries, the Hindustan Teleprinters and the Hindustan Cables. Every fourth year was declared the "Year of Productivity," and as at least most of the government and public sector undertakings do, we have also given a report saying that we have exceeded the installed capacity. But the question was never asked whether it has been achieved in the most optimum way. We think that is not done.

We do not think we can get productivity by pushing our workers to work harder or anybody to work harder. It is something which we have got to provide them, either in terms of modern technology, tools, training or whatever it is, which can increase productivity. And here again we get caught in an objective, which has been enunciated in the technology policy. One of the objectives is to ensure the correct mix between mass production technologies and production by masses. In a light engineering industry like the telecommunication industry or electronics, it is our firm belief that we have to go in for mass production technologies, whether it is for keeping the quality or increase in the productivity or reducing the cost. From any account, mass production technologies will have to be incorporated in telecommunication industry at least in the upstream stage of component manufacture. Assembly and testing, perhaps to some extent, could be manual. But even here with new electronic equipment coming up, we have to go in for automated assembly because we cannot even handle the chips by hand, and we have got in for automated testing. So, in the telecom industry, automation, mechanisation, new technologies are perhaps the best means of activating productivity. A simple example will do. The ITI started production with pre-Second World War vintage equipment called Strowger equipment. They are employing 8,000 people today at Bangalore for producing 1.5 lakh lines of telephone exchange lines, the equivalent of one lakh unit. Sometime in the late 1960s we went in for a post-war electro-mechanical technology in the form of a cross bar exchange, for which we are employing now 3,000 for 2 lakh units. Recently we have concluded an agreement for the manufacture of electronic telephone exchanges where we will be employing only 2,000 people for a 5-lakh-unit production. So, in the telecommunication industry, in spite of talk about motivation, communication etc., appropriate technology and mass production technology alone can bring in the desired productivity.

Moving on to the telecom services, there has been some talk of yardsticks for measurement of productivity. We are not sure what yardsticks are to be used for productivity in a telecommunication service, a service which depends upon technology for the satisfaction of the customer. Should it be in terms of complaints by subscribers per month or per day; complaints or actual faults which we had rectified; is it the number of men employed per telephone, is it the revenue per telephone? We are not very sure how we define productivity or utility—the American term is utility—of a service unit. Here again, we do have yardsticks within the P&T Department in terms of the number of complaints, the maximum number of complaints beyond which special action has to be taken, the number of faults per subscriber per year, the number of effective calls put through out of the total number of calls booked by you and, by and large, in most of the metropolitan cities these yardsticks are generally being matched. The question again can be asked: How realistic are these yardsticks? When we say that 70 per cent should be the effective call, that means out of 10 calls booked only seven calls will mature, say within two hours. Is that a good yardstick when most of you who have been abroad, can get access there even through manual operator almost instantly? We agree it is not a good yardstick. But this is the yardstick which is possible with the type of network, with the type of investment, with the type of training, with the type of tools which we have provided to our people.

But if you are talking in terms of expenditure over the years, when you look at the trend in productivity, the expenditure per telephone has remained almost constant in spite of the additional DAs and additional pay revisions which have gone through. To that extent indirectly there has been certain productivity. And also we have got bonus payment to the P&T workers, to the telephone workers, on the basis of their achievement in 1976-77. And this also shows an upward trend from 96.4 in 1976-77 to 99.1 in 1981-82. But these are yardsticks which can be always questioned as to whether they are correct for a service organisation. How does one define it?

Our revenue has been by and large one-third of the gross block; which has also been accepted in the telecommunication industry all over the world—annual revenue being one-third of the gross from block is a fairly good return. And this also we have been achieving. Again, a question can be asked: whether it is due to the recent tariff hikes or is it really due to better service and better output. We must assure that it is partly due to better output and partly due to tariff hikes.

The staff expenditure as a ratio of the total expenditure can also be taken as a yardstick for productivity in an industry. All over the world it is about one-third, that is, the staff expenditure is one-third of the total expenditure because we have to have expenditure for the maintenance, maintenance of tools, materials etc.; and we have to give leave away, the pensionary benefits and so on and so forth. To look at the staff expenditure in terms of salaries, travel allowance etc., that is also about one-third of the total. Here also we seem to be in line with the productivity in other countries. But this may be again due to the low wages in our country. But the one thing for productivity which in the P&T Board we have been very actively looking at now is that we are having a unique and perhaps a dubious distinction of being the only country which is employing more than 100 people per thousand telephones. That is less than 10 telephones per employee, while the advanced countries like Japan, America, have got more than 100 telephones per employee, and even a developing country like Thailand has got 30 telephones per employee. So, that means they use one-third. So, this is one aspect which we are looking into, and we have taken a policy decision and are actively working towards reducing the work force by half or rather the work force per thousand population by half, that is from 100 to 50, by the end of the decade. There will be an approximately five-fold increase in telephones between 1980 and 1990, but the increase in staff, we are trying to keep at around 1.5 times. This is one trend of productivity. Probably this is not something which you have heard about in industry. But in a service organisation, especially in the context of telecommunication in India this is one trend in productivity.

It has been said in Parliament that during the ASIAD and during the NAM, we definitely gave better service. At least our statistics prove, however bad it may be, that there was better service. The number of complaints were down, the number of faults were down, the number of cable breakdowns were down. We have been asked as to why it is that we cannot continue what we have achieved during the ASIAD and NAM. We have no answer for that. We wonder if somebody can tell us how we rise to an occasion like the ASIAD or the NAM or the CHOGM. We do not know how people get motivated during these days and how we can continue to motivate the people throughout the year when there is no NAM or ASIAD. If somebody can tell us, we would be very happy to learn.

The third point which we will touch upon is regarding the telecom infrastructure as a means of productivity. We know how communication is extremely important for modern industry and commerce and how if the telecommunication infrastructure is not well developed, it hampers industry, even the export business.

However, there are certain hopes and certain restraints under which we have to work in expanding the telecommunication facilities and providing it with what subscribers should demand. It is not what you feel you should have but what you demand for the money that you are paying. At the beginning of the Sixth Plan we had about 20 lakhs telephones. We will be adding 14 lakh telephones during the Sixth Plan, 37.5 lakhs telephones during 1985-90 Plan and by the end of the decade we expect to have about 72 lakhs telephones. If we have 7.2 million lakhs lines by 1980, perhaps we will be able to give you a telephone within six weeks of your asking. Now this trend again is very deceptive because there are many theories in telecommunication about surplus demand and extrapolation of waiting list. Purely in terms of telephones, this itself will call for about 10,000 crores of rupees of investment. The order is about 25,000 rupees of investment per telephone. But there are some good signs and also bad signs in achieving this objective. Till about the 1980 the telecommunication was considered as a purely elitist service. There was a clamp on the investment growth rate. The Planning Commission permitted only about 6 to 8 per cent growth rate in telecommunication even though money was available. But in 1980 depending upon various studies done by outside agencies and also within the P&T, the Planning Commission permitted a growth rate of anything from 12 to 15 per cent. They have approved an expenditure of Rs. 10,000 crores during the decade—provided they can find the money. What has happened is well-known. In the last one year we were in a results crunch. And there has been a certain setback to the very ambitious plans which we had drawn up. But we are quite sure that with the lowering cost trends in equipment with electronics, even with the limited resources, we will be able to achieve the targets by the end of the decade.

Apart from telephones for industry and commerce, the country also requires STD and ISD. The hope is that almost all the district headquarters will be connected by STD in another four years, by about 1986-88, and STD will be made available within a district also by about 6 to 8 years. Of telex we hope to meet the demand of the present waiting list, at least by 1985-86. We are working towards giving a better international telex service, lack of which is hampering quite a lot of your export and import trade.

Concerning data communication, we have plans, and we have the telecommunication infrastructure on which data can be superimposed without much difficulty. We are now going in for videotex telex services. But here we come into another type of inter-related activity which has to grow hand in hand that is, computers. The days of very big computers in a central location with data process is over. Now it is distributed intelligence, data basis and home computers or home terminals. So, the computer policy and communication policy have to be inter-woven and taken together by some other administrations. We may have to have communication policy. There are efforts on the part of both the Department of Electronics and the Ministry of Industry to evolve a combined policy for computers and communication because that is an essential need for today's productivity.

CHAPTER 6

Successful Business Communication: A Manager's Roadmap

Introduction

In the modern age of information, the businessperson—manager, worker, consultant, director, owner or entrepreneur—is part of a larger order of things. The free flow of information between and among the various components of the corporate entity is of the utmost importance. You must keep your employees informed, get them involved, and motivate them with performance standards. Information is the key and information flow means having reliable systems.

Your business success depends on the use of resources: money, clients, physical assets, customers, professional advisers, and your time. The management process that you, as an entrepreneur, follow will include the development of ideas and strategies, the management of people and the administration of systems to ensure that your business flourishes. The development of ideas and strategies, as well as the involvement of people, requires facts and figures.

It is important that you understand how financial and non-financial information has to be collected, analysed, stored, and reported to you and other decision-makers who help the business to succeed. This chapter focuses on the types of information you need as an entrepreneur; on the various reports that you need on a day-by-day, week-by-week and month-by-month basis; and on the development of your systems to keep pace with your business growth.

Each year in many nations, business failures are analysed and the reasons for failure identified wherever possible. For example, in the United States the internationally known Dun and Bradstreet organisation regularly analyses failure in that country, and it finds that each year almost 80 per cent of failures appear to be due to managers of businesses being "trapped" in unfavourable positions. These situations would probably not have arisen if satisfactory information systems had been feeding management with relevant facts and figures. For example, many businesses were reported to have failed because their sales were too low. In such cases the business information system may not have reported the failure of sales to meet expectations. It is surprising how many owners do not know from day-to-day or from week-to-week the actual sales position of the business.

Other companies reported failure due to excessively high operating expenses. Could this be due to the fact that the information systems failed to accumulate expenses as they occurred, and failed to report actual expenses to management? Other businesses failed because of their poor collection policies. They made the sales, but couldn't collect the cash. Perhaps their information system failed to report credit sales, levels of debtors, ageing of debtors, and the flow of cash from debtors. Also, if cash was not being received from debtors, it might have to be obtained from another source. This would put a burden of additional interest on the company, and could contribute to eventual failure.

Sound and efficient information systems could have saved many of these failed businesses.

Many other businesses failed because too much capital had been tied up in stocks or physical assets. No business can afford to have too much cash in the form of excessive stocks or assets. It means that more cash might have to be borrowed at high interest rates, thus reducing the competitive position of the enterprise. The information system should monitor stock, as well as other physical asset investments and the return on these investments.

In brief, information is vital for business survival; but it is also vital for growth and development. Statistics from the United States emphasise that *lack of information* can lead to overspending or over-investment in assets. Entrepreneurs must have information on which to base their future strategies. The more complex the business, the more important is the information system. An unprofitable strategy (a poor investment strategy) may directly or indirectly lead to business failure. Thus, the information you are looking for includes:

- facts and figures for your business strategies that will enable you to make decisions on expansion, construction, additions to products or outlets, additions to factories or warehouses, and so on;
- information on your present financial position and obligations to external organisations, such as the amounts due to suppliers of goods and services, the amounts due to lenders of funds, the amounts invested by owners;
- information to help you, as the entrepreneur, to control the day-to-day operations of the business, such as cash receipts and payments, balances, sales, balances due to creditors, expenses, profits, actual results compared with prepared plans. You not only want the over-all picture; you also want the information system to provide you and your staff with an analysis by product/division/group/retail outlet, and so on; this is management information in the true sense of the term;
- information on the total investment in your business, and investment by division/asset/group, and so on. How much is invested in buildings? Vehicles? Stocks? Debtors? Cash? The system should highlight trends in investment as well as trends in profits;
- information on people, including the basic information required by law such as salaries and wages; information allowing you to identify the real costs of hiring and training key staff; information on people productivity and people investment.

Mention was made in a previous section of the importance of comparisons, both internal and external. Your information system should automatically provide you with internal comparisons, such as this month with last month, and probably with the same month last year. This might well be done weekly, monthly and quarterly. It should be possible to feed key industry statistics into your information system so that external comparisons can be made. As an entrepreneur, you should be vitally concerned with your information system; its quality; its ability to provide you and your staff with information in a form you want, when you need it; and its ability to develop and adjust to your needs as the business grows.

Focused Management Reports

A great deal has already been said or implied about the types of management reports that should flow from your information system. Certain types of reports should be available to you on a daily, monthly, quarterly and annual basis. Many entrepreneurs assume that the information needed for management can be obtained from the returns prepared for government and taxation authorities once a year. This is not so; and you, being entrepreneurial, will see the folly of relying on such annual reports.

Daily/Weekly Reports

The daily information you require is strictly operational. The facts and figures to meet your day-to-day requirements include: daily cash position; sales summaries (both cash and credit); cash payments; cash received from debtors; cash deposits in bank accounts; and closing cash balances. A simple form that could be used for this purpose is illustrated in Figure 6.1.

This form provides a simple system where cash balances are available at the beginning and the end of each day and can be reconciled with actual cash in the register. One form could be located with each cash register in your business, or all cash transactions could be centralised in one place in the business.

Don't be satisfied with *total* daily sales. Have sales analysed by product group *and* make an estimate of gross profit by product group, given estimated gross margins. The discussion on break-even analysis suggested that the daily cost of being in business could be related to daily gross profit estimates to indicate when (during each week) your business breaks even. Thus, your system should provide daily gross margin estimates and an estimate of the daily cost of being in business; this will allow you to see how you break even and produce profit on a day-by-day basis. The form reproduced as Figure 6.2 could be used to analyse day-by-day sales and margins with each member of the sales staff having a separate form.

Day	Date	Opening Balance Rs.	Cash Received			Cash Payments Rs.	Details Rs.	Bank Deposits Rs.	Closing Balance Rs.
			Cash Sales Rs.	Previous Credit Sales Rs.	Other Rs.				
Sunday									
Monday									
Tuesday									
Wednesday									
Thursday									
Friday									
Saturday									

Fig. 6.1: Daily/Weekly Cash Flow Summary

Day	Date	Product Group A			Product Group B			Product Group C			Total		
		Sales	G.M.%	G.M. Rs.	Sales	G.M.%	G.M. Rs.	Sales	G.M.%	G.M. Rs.	Sales	G.M.%	G.M. Rs.
Sunday													
Monday													
Tuesday													
Wednesday													
Thursday													
Friday													
Saturday													

G.M. = gross margin

Fig. 6.2: Sales and Profit Margin Analysis

From this information you can estimate daily profits or losses, and these can be accumulated day-by-day to indicate estimated weekly profits (losses). It can be expected that some trading days will produce losses while others will result in high trading profits. The main point is that you are "on top of" the trading facts, and can adjust your trading and cash flow strategy when necessary.

The progressive entrepreneur will also want daily details of inventory so that stock levels are controlled in relation to sales and cash flows. It has already been pointed out that many business failures are caused by poor inventory control. Standard inventory systems are available from consultants and equipment suppliers, and you should find a system that satisfies your business needs.

Monthly Reports

On a monthly basis your business should have available:

- a detailed profit-and-loss statement;
- an analysis of sales and inventory by product/service groups;
- an analysis of cash flow, debtors, creditors and financial commitments; and
- an internal ratio analysis revealing efficiency ratings and highlighting trends, with a comparison between your plans and your actual achievements.

This information would coincide with the meeting of your advisory board, the group that joins you in decision-making and strategy development.

Quarterly Reports

Naturally, the monthly reports would be available each quarter; but, in addition, the following information should be available for you and your Advisory Board:

- a detailed statement of your financial position;
- internal and external industry comparisons as measures of efficiency;

- trend analyses in more detail than would be prepared for each month; and
- information about your current business plant to allow you and your Advisory Board to review activities and project future plans.

Annual Reports

The major annual reports are the balance sheet, the profit-and-loss statement and the cash flow statement, which together with the composite quarterly reports provide the basis for strategic planning. You, the entrepreneur, must have a reliable information system because without a regular supply of facts and figures you are severely handicapped and are likely to make wrong decisions. The information systems in your business deserve your close attention.

Keeping Pace with Corporate Growth

Great strides have been made in recent years in developing sophisticated information systems for specific sectors of industry; and this rapid development of such a wide range of systems has created doubt and confusion in the minds of many entrepreneurs. If considering making a change, you should follow these guidelines:

- Seek initial advice from your advisory group, industry associates, government, small business agencies, professional accountant or consultant, and any other group that can give background information about information systems for your business, industry and location.
- Discuss your information requirements with equipment suppliers and systems specialists without making any commitments. Be specific—which requires that you do the initial homework. What do you want the system to do for you and your business team? Document your needs carefully.
- Inspect systems in operation in business similar to yours. Don't forget that it is important for you to see systems actually in operation. Talk to the owners of those

businesses. Are they satisfied with the system? What are the system's strengths? What are the weaknesses? How could it be improved? It is very important to be specific.

- Before committing your business to any system, seek further advice from specialists in the field and obtain guarantees from the intended supplier. These would relate to the introduction of the system, the training of staff, and so on.

The various decision options on processing data that are open to you are illustrated in Figure 6.3. You have to process data in some form and at some location. Your basic decision on processing is whether to process within your own business or in some other location. The other location could be an accountant's office or through a data-processing bureau. More and more small data-processing centres or bureaux are being set up to process data for small and medium-sized businesses. Some bureaux specialise in various industry groups and may be in a position to cover your weekly and monthly reports. For these reasons, it is essential that you seek advice from the groups mentioned above to allow you to make the right decisions.

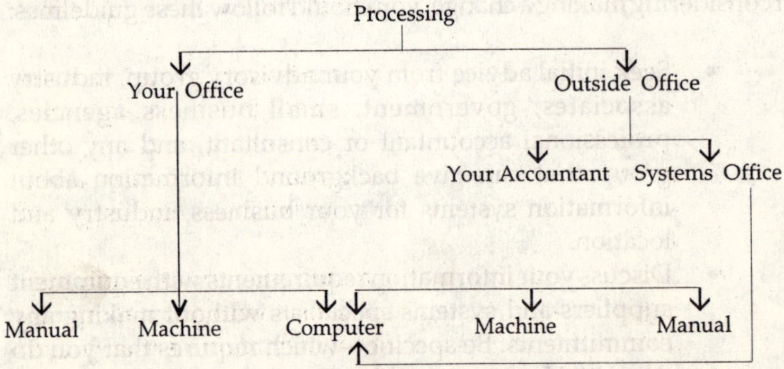

Fig. 6.3: Data-Processing Alternatives

The choice of location must be made with the *method* of processing in mind. There are three basic alternatives: the use of manual systems; the use of non-electric machines; and the use of computers of some kind. Related to those options are questions of capital investment in equipment (or the leasing of equipment); physical space required for equipment; hiring and training of staff; and the methods available to upgrade systems and staff.

Factors which might influence your final decision include:

- the size and complexity of the business;
- growth and development expectations;
- service facilities available for various system installations in your local region;
- the quality and quantity of staff available for various system types, and the training facilities available to staff so that systems can be upgraded;
- the volume of transactions to be processed; and
- financial factors.

Contrary to much that is written and said about systems, most entrepreneurs can obtain adequate and timely information for management decision-making from a manually operated system. On the other hand, it is a fact that mini-computers are becoming available in increasing numbers, and specific systems for industry sectors are available for you and your business. These so-called "management information packages" can often be purchased with the equipment, and may not require any or much modification to suit your specific needs. Another option open to you is to combine manual and computer systems, where internal manual systems give you day-to-day facts which are further processed and analysed by a computer for monthly and quarterly reports and analyses.

All this adds up to the importance of advice from specialists and experienced operators in your industry. Failure to obtain that advice initially might severely limit the ability of your system to expand with business development. It does not make sense for you to give careful attention to the planning, control and financial aspects of your business only to find that major problems arise because you and your colleagues lack the appropriate information to make decisions and control operations. Information should be the basis for all decisions. The more complex your business becomes, the greater is your need to develop a foolproof system for gathering information.

CHAPTER 7

Basics of Business Communication: The Power of Words

Oral Communication

Very often the spoken word works wonders for business. In any presentation you are making, if your listeners use more than one sense to receive your message, they have a better chance of remembering what you have said. Visual aids also assist the memory and give variety to a talk. A very brief subdivision of aids would be:

(*a*) symbolic or actual;
(*b*) two-dimensional or three-dimensional.

With all your visual aids the aims should be simplicity and clarity. Always prepare, so that you will know precisely how your illustrations will work out and the timing of their use.

We sometimes forget that visual aids have their disadvantages as well as their advantages. They cost money, take up a fair amount of time and thought and, for someone who makes very few presentations, they diminish flexibility. If they go wrong they invariably cause a certain amount of embarrassment and confusion. The number of times I have seen them go wrong is almost astronomical! My advice is to go prepared to deliver your talk if everything breaks down, and then you will at least avoid total disaster.

In any case you should always ask the question—can we manage just as well without them? Films, slides, epidiascopes and blackboards all have their place, but they should be kept firmly in it! They are *aids* not crutches. Besides this they should be visual and not visual verbals; they should not be just words written out on slides or charts, unless you are developing a complicated argument which may need headings or reminders of important points revealed one at a time. People often put words on slides and then proceed to read them off as though they were talking to children of young school age—don't do this. Your audience are quite capable of reading.

Proxy Idiom

When you use one object to represent another, you are using a symbolic visual aid. Surprisingly, this can often be more effective than the real thing. You can indicate size by using familiar objects such as pens, books, tables, or the room itself. Because your listeners frequently see such objects, they have a clear picture of what you are talking about; whereas they may seldom see the real object itself. You can use the objects in an average room to show size, shape and colour as well as texture. For example, you can show how the size of a component has decreased by comparing its original size with a book and its present size with a coin. Another general point arises here which is that we should always relate the unknown to the known even when we are not using visual aids. It is pointless to talk to a group of non-business people about millions of pounds, or cubic capacity, etc., without relating it to something with which they are in daily contact and can readily comprehend.

The other method is to show the object itself. If you talk about a transistor, then show one; if you are talking about some material, show a sample. If you can get your audience to hear and see what you are putting over or even to feel or smell it you will obviously make a much deeper impression. A picture is worth a thousand words.

Classroom Aids

These can be static or moving. Static aids include blackboards, flip-charts, flannel-boards, magnetic boards and projectors. Projectors can also provide moving visual aids.

Although blackboards are often considered old-fashioned, they still provide one of the best means of presenting two-dimensional visual aids. Their big disadvantage is that chalk (even the 'dust-free' variety) is usually very dusty and messy.

However, they are particularly useful for diagrams, keywords, or sketches. They have the following advantages:

1. you can rub out mistakes, or modify your picture, as you present your talk;
2. you can prepare your material beforehand or build it up as you go along.

An experienced speaker or lecturer plans his diagrams beforehand even if he is going to draw them as he goes along. A piece of quarto paper is roughly proportional to most blackboards, so this makes it useful for roughing out what you intend to put on the blackboard.

Keeping in Touch with Employees

It's a Spartan existence on America's last frontier, where the Alyeska Pipeline Service Company is laying the trans-Alaskan pipeline, the most expensive construction project in history. They work upto twelve hours a day, seven days a week, in which temperatures can fall to 55 below freezing! There are few women—no liquor. The only contact with the outside world is by radio telephone.

But the workers are kept sweet and hard working by big money—around $6,000 a month, and by (for construction workers) lush camp conditions such as carpeted, well-furnished rooms, well-stocked libraries and daily movies.

Cash is a crude but powerful method of communicating with the workers when the job is especially tough. One reason is the symbolic significance of money. During the national mineworkers' strike in the UK in 1972 one union leader said: 'Our men spend all day in dangerous, unhealthy jobs, yet their daughters, working as secretaries, earn as much as they do.' How much pay-turmoil is really about recognition and self-respect—both much harder to give than money.

Era of the Employee

Workers in many factories find it difficult to feel much self-respect: 'You'd treat a dog better than this, give it a longer leash,' a car worker complained. 'A man's work station is the length of the car body plus three feet either end and he has to stay in it.' In some plants a man can't even go to the lavatory until the spare man arrives to take his place on the track.

'When I'm here my mind's a blank. I make it go a blank.' It takes more than incentives to cut through cynicism as deep as this. Subtler communication techniques are needed.

I've heard of bakery workers who were so turned-off with their jobs that they simply walked out in mid-shift and didn't even come back for their wages.

Walter Reuther, the American union boss, in describing the plight of many industrial workers, evoked a Chaplinesque vision of men crushed in the cogs: 'The prospect of tightening bolts every ten minutes for eight hours a day for thirty years doesn't exactly lift the human spirit.'

The facts of industrial life can cause a tremendous build-up of frustration and resentment which vents itself in poor work, absenteeism, hostility to management—even outright violence. In *Working for Ford* Hugh Benyon reports bostic bombs being hurled by frustrated workers into rubbish dumps at one of Ford's UK plants.

"Mindless" Workers

How many bruising confrontations in industry stem from these pent-up frustrations? At a Liverpool factory in 1975 management and workers locked horns over the vital issue of where the wages should be handed out. The workers felt so 'bolshy' that they refused to allow management into the factory to distribute them there. Management retaliated by stopping workers going into the office block and collecting them there. A compromise was worked out. The wages were handed out through a side-window while workers queued in the rain.

How can you communicate with your work force in spite of the frustrations and aggressions that may exist? One hundred and thirty years ago, Disraeli wrote about 'two nations. . . as ignorant of each other's habits, thoughts and feelings as if they were dwellers in different zones or inhabitants of different planets.' Today a cleavage in social ethics still exists, and it separates the manager from his work force—unless he knows how to bridge the gap.

Close co-operation between the two sides of industry during the three-day week period in 1974 shows that genuine communication can take place. But too many managers still regard industrial relations as somebody else's business. Hugh Parker, head of McKinsey's consultancy operation in the UK points out that 'people who manage don't identify themselves with the interests of the managed. They stay aloof—at arm's length from the workers.' Here are some techniques for getting closer to your work force.

Getting Together

Many companies, such as the Japanese giant, Matsushita, find that the group session attended once a week, say, by the entire staff of a section or department or division is an effective communication method.

The meetings should be as informal as possible so that everyone is encouraged to talk. In a relaxed atmosphere management can explain its plans and policies and tell the employees what is happening to the goods they are producing—remind them of their important contribution.

Work can be freely discussed, improvements suggested, and the workers can buttonhole their bosses and air their grievances. Policies can be explained. The advantage of doing it this way is that once the whole group accepts the need for a change of plan or procedure, individuals who are hostile to management tend to adjust to the new conformity. Some men take pride in defying management but think twice before opposing their own work mates.

Employer-Employee Interaction

An engineering firm's management which in previous years had met union officials only at times of crisis decided to ask the union to meet them regularly, reason or no reason. So, once a week the two sides met—just sat and talked informally. For the first time each side found itself really listening and being interested in the other. Each side was able to explain its own point of view and, because of the informal atmosphere, really wanted to learn the other side's view.

Each meeting brought a quick exchange of pieces that brought both sides closer to their common objective—compromise, and, therefore, stability across the industrial board.

When the number of disputes in the factory dropped, management linked the trend with these informal meetings. Thus they soon paid for themselves many times over.

When people from the two sides of industry sit informally round the same table they begin to understand one another's viewpoint. When they sit round the table long enough and often enough they even begin to share the same values and talk the same language.

Of course the communication barriers will remain unless the unions feel that management are really listening during these meetings and will take action as a result of what they hear.

Understanding Union Leaders

Many unions are better at fighting management than at co-operating with it to achieve joint goals. One clue in dealing with awkward union branches comes from F.M. Thrasher's book *Gang* based on his work with delinquent teenage gangs. He found that the best way to influence these gangs was through their leaders. By concentrating attention on the leader and showing him ways of achieving status and security—the main motives for gang membership—by other means than the gang, Thrasher was able to change the attitude of the whole gang. The rest followed the leader's example.

Perhaps, after all, the best way to deal with the militant shop steward or wildcat leader is not to isolate him, not to seek less contact but to seek more contact with him. Bring him onto the works committees. Give him special responsibilities—and, therefore, status. Ask him to chair staff meetings or group sessions. In this way you will involve the man and his followers in management processes.

Or carry involvement a stage further. Ask the local union branch to advise management about discipline and conditions of work—the length and times of tea-breaks, holiday and overtime arrangements and so on. This kind of direct involvement in management creates a greater sense of responsibility in union members, a greater awareness of management problems.

Floor-Level Interaction

Supervisory interviews, held about twice a year, can raise morale and improve communication between employee and first-line management. Supervisors who are trained to conduct these interviews should be fully briefed about aims and techniques to ensure (a very difficult task) that employees will feel free to talk without inhibition.

During the interview, the employee is given an appraisal of his performance over the past half-year together with advice about how to improve. We need to remember that many workers lose heart because they genuinely don't know how they are measuring upto company expectations: nobody ever tells them.

Then it is the employee's turn to talk about his or her problems and grievances, or about anything else they want to get off their chests.

Western Electric has found that supervisors who are involved in these interviews become less dogmatic in their ideas, more willing to take account of the feelings of their subordinates. The first-line manager is brought into closer contact with his people, perhaps in spite of himself.

Success depends largely on the social skills of the interviewer, his ability to establish an easy relationship with the other person. Thus the provision of effective company training in this field is essential. Chances of success are improved when:

- *(a)* the supervisor holds the interview on neutral ground and not in his own office;
- *(b)* is careful not to show too much authority;
- *(c)* encourages the employee (by using appropriate counselling techniques) to speak his mind;
- *(d)* does not argue, disagree, express shock or disapproval.

Areas like these show clearly that communication is above all a technique when applied to industry.

The inevitable social and environmental stresses which crop up in the industrial organisation do not admit social contact between individual managers and employees in an entirely normal way. For the factory or the office is always an artificial environment in which individuals cannot choose each other's company.

The problem is compounded because of the frustrations and resentments that build up in the work force as a result to tedium and discipline. Such feelings are not dissolved by cash incentives, unless they are abnormally high.

In large organisations, formal patterns of communication will always predominate. But the trick is to promote better relations by encouraging informal communication between managers and employees.

This is not something that can happen overnight with some magic gesture. It will be the product only of a consistent management policy that sets out to win and deserve the confidence of the work force. To achieve that, management must not only accept the principle of good communication, but get down to the planning of a detailed campaign.

Such a campaign might be spearheaded by the techniques described above. But in any case, it will require the co-operation of the other side as a starting point.

Points for Discussion

Discuss 'the symbolic significance of money.'

Do you feel a cleavage exists today between the manager and his work force?

What is the principal value of group sessions?

What are the likely advantages to a manager in having more contact with trade union leaders?

Discuss the supervisory interview.

In-House Communication

Managers and workers have generally been to different schools. They live in different parts of town, go to different pubs, rarely mix socially. Neither learns the other's point of view. How many communication breakdowns in industry spring from this underlying experience gap? Perhaps nationwide comprehensive education would be a good long-term method of improving industrial relations in Britain!

No wonder that so many management announcements, filled with words like efficiency, productivity and profitability, fall on deaf ears: for managers are committed to these values whereas the workers' main aims at work are security and stable social relationships. Workers are group-minded whereas managers tend to be individualists striving for personal achievement and reward. To the manager, cash incentives seem the logical way to boost production. But the worker knows that striving for money might cut him off from his work-mates. How many bonus schemes have collapsed under the weight of this simple fact?

The manager needs to be aware of the cleavage in social ethics that separates him from his employees, and desist from making individualistic appeals to employees in trying to boost their production or improve their time-keeping.

Consider the problem of output restriction. To the worker this is a completely logical way of protecting himself against unreasonable demands or possible redundancies. Any attempt by management to convince individuals to the contrary will be fiercely resisted. Operatives will change their methods and raise their output only when the work group as a whole nods approval. To break through barriers of this kind, call the group together and explain why a change is necessary; offer new forms of security for old, *e.g.*, guarantee jobs and earnings; then leave them to *talk themselves* into a change of attitude. Only in this way can the emotional barriers be overcome. Of course, such an approach carries risks: the discussion may lead to a hardening of attitudes rather than a change of heart.

But sometimes the employees should be encouraged to make their own decisions. An experiment was carried out in a toy factory where girls had complained about the speed of a moving belt carrying components for assembly. After discussions a control dial was fitted to the work bench so that the girls themselves could control the speed of the belt. The girls were very pleased and morale soared. And the average speed at which the girls themselves ran the belt was higher than the speed they had complained about!

Through participation management can increase its control by seeming to relinquish it. Furthermore, employees happily implement changes which they have decided upon or agreed to. And that is a valuable effect, for change itself is the only constant in modern industry.

Egalitarian Approach

Henry Ford was touring a new automated engine factory with Walter Reuther, President of the Auto Workers' Union. When Ford remarked to Reuther, 'Walter, these machines never go on strike,' Reuther replied, 'True but they don't buy any automobiles either.' If you think about it Reuther's reply contains a sufficient reason for treating workers and their representatives with a special kind of courtesy and respect—the kind that would have seemed soft-headed a generation ago. One Managing Director at a motor components factory wouldn't agree with that proposition. When the union official called to talk about the case of a dismissed foreman the Managing Director sent a curt message saying he was too busy to see him. Next day the official made four 'phone calls only to be told each time that the MD was not available. So every foreman in the factory came out on strike in protest. Moral: avoid high-handedness—it doesn't pay.

Times have changed and workers have changed. Employees are better educated and more sophisticated than they were a few decades ago. The development of automation and electronics has caused a shift from craft skills to numerical control, with a consequent blurring of white and blue-collar distinctions. Employees are better equipped than they used to be to contribute to company plans and policies. Lord Feather, the former Secretary of the TUC, has said he'd like to see workers discussing such matters as manpower requirements, delivery dates, new machinery and other topics still widely considered to be the exclusive prerogative of management.

Many managers still jib at the thought of introducing wide-ranging consultative processes, fearing that to do so would be to relinquish some of their powers. Perhaps they are right. Perhaps each extra piece of participation machinery represents a real transfer of authority. But perhaps too the most formidable communication barriers in British industry can only be overcome by this kind of radical transformation.

A powerful braking-force on the trend towards decision-sharing is the undemocratic nature of most companies in Britain. The votes that control them go to money not people; the running is done by a small and powerful group of directors; power rests at the apex. No doubt within the next few years company law will be reformed to bring the voice of the work force in greater measure into the boardrooms. Such a reform is long overdue, for there are many areas where the experience of the man on the job can do much to improve methods and efficiency. As Mary Parker Follett pointed out half a century ago, the man who works with the machine is as expert about it in his way as the man who designs or the man who buys it. This is the assumption at Parish Instruments of Richmond, Surrey, where informal meetings were held on the factory floor during protracted tea breaks: company plans and problems are openly discussed with the Managing Director joining in.

At Rowan Engineering of Glasgow the staff decide most matters in the company, right down to electing managers and fixing their salaries. Matters of policy are decided by all employees. This approach has relieved the company of many financial problems. At Scott Bader job applicants are interviewed by some of the people they will be working over. While in the Computer Management group all levels have identical desks, the same carpet and the same amount of space. The Managing Director, in the middle of a large open-spaced office, may be freely approached at any time by anybody. As a result of this free communication many problem areas have been revealed and ironed out. One of the company's founders said 'We are like an army with only officers—the computer is our only private soldier.'

Labour Leadership: The Liberal Equation

Through his union the worker has more direct influence over the conditions of his everyday life than he exercises by his vote at a General Election. But many managers see only the negative side of union activity, although the positive side is far more important. Think of how joint consultation in the coal mines enabled the smooth introduction of full mechanisation and the planned closure of five hundred pits during Lord Robens' time. Sir William Swallow has attributed his success in avoiding serious strikes at Vauxhall while he was at its head to the habit of constant discussions with the unions, so that grievances could be spotted as soon as they arose and acted on 'in minutes or hours.'

Talk to the workers' representatives and take them into your confidence: for they are a valuable communication channel for conveying information and feelings upwards and downwards, and for explaining management's plans and policies to the work force. The modern union boss talks about wages and prices in terms indistinguishable from those used by the CBI. Management and the unions are partners in industry if only they would acknowledge the fact.

Professor Tom Lupton of the Manchester Business School has shown that even the disruptive side of union activity may serve a positive purpose. The entire trade union machinery of strikes, ballot, go-slows, etc., acts as a kind of battering ram, smashing down barriers, forcing management to listen and to make necessary changes, clearing the ground for realistic policies.

Ensuring Upward Communication

Good upward communication gives management the information it needs for sound decision-making. It brings employees' on-line experience to bear on company problems, and acts as a kind of early warning system about shop-floor problems and grievances. Yet in many firms upward communication works in low gear. Often the cause is a lack of listening ability in managers combined with over-reliance on formal channels for feeding information upwards. The inability to listen at top levels strangles the desire to tell at lower levels. According to M.H. Knowles, an industrial psychologist, many managers are constitutionally incapable of listening to subordinates. According to Knowles, it is the neurotic, authoritarian personality who tends to get himself promoted into a managerial position. Such people are incapable of expressing their own feelings or of listening properly to others.

But sometimes employees themselves are to blame for poor upward communication. Most of us tell the boss only what we think will please him, feeling we can't afford to expose our failures and weaknesses. In a study of fifty-two managers, Read found that men on the way up tend to restrict information about their problems because they want to please the boss and preserve comfortable work routines. The inevitable results of this kind of self-imposed censorship is that bugs in the system multiply. The 'ever open door' might as well be slammed shut if the men on either side of it won't talk frankly to each other.

There is much that the individual executive can do to stimulate upward communication with his own department or unit. For instance, he can seek personal contact with employees and attempt to learn their point of view, their goals and values. Other possible actions include:

(a) holding regular meeting with employees to discuss their problems and grievances;

(b) finding out which communication methods are preferred by employees and using them, *e.g.*, the shop steward may be preferred by employees as a channel of upward communication;

(c) regularly checking that foremen are passing upwards information, ideas, grievances received from the shop floor.

This kind of systematic communication eats up time. But far more time can be spent ironing out the misunderstandings and grievances that arise when upward communication is neglected.

Why not use some of the following administrative techniques for stimulating upward communication in your own organisation?

Set up a special section to collect information about employee attitudes and grievances. The information could be collected by anonymous questionnaires or by confidential interviews which are then sent to top management for use in policy-making.

Confidential exit interviews would help you to discover workers' real reason for leaving and perhaps several serious shortcomings in the company will be revealed.

Using an employee counsellor can have the double effect of boosting morale on the shop floor and revealing grievances before they become storm centres.

Informal get-togethers over coffee can greatly stimulate upward communication within the management team.

Polaroid Corporation employees can telephone a special number and state their grievances or question. Answers are sent direct to the employee and then printed in the company newspaper. Other companies fix certain times when top executives are available for phone calls from employees on any topic.

Workers' Views and Suggestions

Most employees have their own special work methods. They find short cuts. They develop quicker and easier ways of doing their jobs, like the machinist who raised his output by making a short rod for guiding a cutting tool. By tapping this kind of know-how, suggestion schemes not only reduce operating and production costs but also increase employee participation in company affairs.

Suggestion schemes act as a powerful stimulant to upward communication. That is why the Industrial Welfare Society has been supporting them since 1918. Today they operate in thousands of companies—sometimes with great success. One manager reports that a new company suggestion scheme paid for itself in the first week, because valuable ideas for cutting waste and rationalising the work-flow were among the first to be contributed. Westinghouse Corporation reckons that in one year it saved more than a million and a half dollars through implementing suggestions. Yet it paid only a fifth of that amount back in awards.

Generous cash awards for accepted suggestions are an essential component of any scheme. As some companies have discovered, a tight-fisted policy by the suggestion committee can kill interest in the scheme and damage morale. Cash keeps the ideas flowing. Hundreds of money-making ideas for boosting productivity were dropped in the BLMC suggestion boxes after the company offered a new Mini car every month for the best suggestion. Many firms even pay for good rejected ideas as an acknowledgement of time and effort spent and as an encouragement to employees to keep trying. Some firms reward the section or department as well as the individual for an accepted suggestion and claim that this is a good way of raising morale throughout the plant.

In most companies suggestion schemes are used exclusively for ideas about technical improvements. But why not widen the scope of a company's suggestion scheme by inviting suggestions about company plans, policy and managerial methods then relying all these suggestions direct to the Board.

ORAL INTERACTION: MULTIPURPOSE APPROACH

Meetings

No business or industrial organisation can get along without a large number of meetings (unfortunately!). Meetings, when properly run, are probably the most valuable of a company's means of communication. They are certainly necessary if we are to promote:

(a) Understanding and willing acceptance of the company's policies and procedures;
(b) A correct understanding and tolerance of people's needs and desires; 'two-way' exchange of constructive suggestions and ideas; intelligent co-operation;
(c) Savings of time, of repetition and paperwork.

But meetings cost money. We have to calculate the salaries of those present, the cost of time taken by those who helped prepare for the meeting and produced the necessary documentation and the cost of lighting, heating, ventilating and perhaps even renting the meeting room. It is imperative, therefore, that we use the time spent in meetings profitably, and that the leader and participants achieve the objectives of every meetings arranged.

Meetings vary between these two extremes:

1. Highly formal, complete with chairman, secretary, agenda, usual minutes and formal rules of procedure;
2. Very informal—*ad hoc* meetings about current business often attended by close colleagues on first-name terms.

In the day-to-day working of an organisation the first type of meeting is fairly rare. Besides this, there are many good books on formal meetings, whether they be for companies, local government or voluntary organisations. And as this book is about communicating anyway, we will content ourselves with looking at the conduct of an informal meeting.

Agenda

We have attended (and conducted on occasion!) meetings that have ended more from sheer exhaustion than for any other reason. I have attended (and still do!) meetings which I regard as a waste of time. The reason often starts with, as indeed in most forms of bad communication, an unclear and inadequate preparation. When you are thinking of calling a meeting the following rules will be helpful:

1. Establish a valid purpose for calling the meeting. A meeting may be called:

(*a*) to give information;
(*b*) to get information;
(*c*) to solve a problem; or
(*d*) to secure certain positive attitudes.

The leader and participants must know at any point in the conduct of the meeting which of these four objectives is applicable.

2. Consider carefully whether the purpose could not better be achieved by some other means, such as a memorandum or a series of telephone calls.
3. Consider when the meeting should be held. Make sure all the relevant people are available, the facts or documents are to hand and that the meeting is not being held *after* the decision to be taken thereat should have been taken.
4. Establish who should attend. If a decision has to be reached you need people to be present who have the power to make that decision. Sometimes full participation will not be expected, as will be the case when you are calling a meeting to hear a statement of policy, a definition of responsibilities or to receive instructions.

If at all possible you will avoid inviting the 'difficult' member. He is one who talks too much or at length, constantly talks off the subject and is generally quite illogical. He is also impatient and wants a decision without a thorough investigation. He's always unwilling to consider alternatives or compromise, and makes dogmatic unsupported statements; he gives no reasons, and the points he makes always need clarification or illustration. He does not pay attention but always whispers and interrupts. And he always comes to the meeting *you* are conducting! He needs firm leadership, and the use of questions addressed to him will usually go a long way to disciplining him.

Unsuccessful Meetings

Before we go on to the conduct of meetings let's look briefly at the problems which occur all too often. First of all, meetings are often held for the wrong reasons, *e.g.*, the organisational structure may not have kept pace with changing needs. *Ad hoc* committees set up to deal with a particular problem sometimes become fixed. Some groups may even be meeting purely out of habit—there may be a regular Thursday morning meeting at 10.00 a.m. with nobody examining whether or not the meeting should still be taking place. There may be inadequate advance information, or faulty composition of the group. The leader may be vague about the subject or purpose. There may be no provisional plan, there may be bad handling of the time factor or physical conditions may be inadequate. Meetings may be held simply because managers feel inadequate. They do not have the courage to make the decisions necessary so they call a meeting; or indeed they may even use the meeting to delay making the required decision.

Meetings may also be unsuccessful because some items had apparently been decided beforehand. Or there may be too much emotion present, while lack of control may allow too many people to talk at the same time. There's always a serious problem if the chairman or leader is biased. Key issues may not be defined nor main issues clarified, so that there will be several red herrings present throughout. Some people may never open their mouths throughout, while others may have no idea at the end of the meeting of what has been decided. Diffident members may even be discouraged or snubbed.

Then at the end the progress may not be summarised, minority views ignored and inaccurate quotation of contributions. Unsettled points may be left 'in the air,' and finally the required action may not be formulated.

Effective Meetings

First of all see that none of the above problems occur! Then let's think first about physical conditions. Make sure the temperature of the room is conducive to work—not too cold nor too hot. Ventilation is very important and fresh air keeps participants alert. Noise can be very distracting. There should be a bright atmosphere about the room, with comfortable furnishings—these have a definite psychological effect. Refreshments can revive people, particularly at a long meeting, but do make sure that they are not brought in during a closely-argued discussion. Arrange the seating so that all members can see each other easily—an oval shaped table for larger groups can be suitable and a horseshoe or 'U' table for groups of fourteen or over. If possible, a company should have a few properly equipped conference rooms available on the premises of different sizes and suitably sound-proofed. Of course, meetings do not always have to take place in a room—a few colleagues talking in a corridor may be all that's necessary, and if the right decision is reached in those (or any) circumstances you can be assured the meeting has been successful.

There are really three stages to any meeting—before, during and after.

You have to decide what you want to achieve through the group of people who will be present. Are you out to sell them some idea, a new company policy, to solve a problem or to secure certain positive attitudes? Do you want them to take a decision that you know they will be committed to without any pressure from you.

Then you have to know the subject being discussed inside out. Do plenty of homework; collect, sort, and arrange all the relevant information. Prepare a workable timetable for your own use, apportioning relative times to major and minor issues. Be well armed in relation to possible questions and/or objections.

Prepare an agenda, which is merely a list of items to be discussed; it covers all relevant points in the right order. The early items should not be controversial and important items should not be left until the very last, at which time some may have had to leave (to attend another meeting possibly!), while those remaining will naturally be tired. It assists pertinent discussion of items on the agenda if they are all divided into sub-sections if appropriate, and all items should be specific and concrete. Often for small meetings held on a regular basis agendas may be dispensed with, but even so, the leader of the meeting should always have one for his own use. Try to have the agenda sent out in good time (obviously statutory meetings have set amounts of notice which must be given), so that all members can themselves be fully informed on the issues to be discussed. If you do send a note with the agenda make sure it tells those attending what the subject is all about and that you are inviting their participation.

Adequate preparation, as in any form of communicating, will greatly help the effectiveness of the meeting, bearing in mind that all of us have opinions, prejudices and attitudes to everything under the sun, and don't forget to have any visual aids or reports ready in plenty of time.

Conducting the Meeting

Start on time. Repeat—start on time! Welcome members, especially newcomers. Emphasise the work to be done. State the topic, problem or difficulty with which the meeting is to deal. You may wish to outline the situation giving rise to the topic, and outline what is appropriate for discussion and what it not. Outline the procedure to be followed in the case of groups not meeting on a regular basis.

Define technical terms being used, and remember the subject for discussion must be simply and clearly expressed and all ambiguous words must be clarified. The vague statement of a subject is probably the cause of most futile discussion. It is often a good idea to put the subject before the meeting in the form of an impartial question; one advantage of this is that a question at least provides the framework for the answer.

People called to a meeting tend to bring their immediate problems with them. They may even have decided views on the matters they know are going to be discussed. So you must put them at ease and focus their minds on the purpose of the meeting. An informal call to order is usually all that is necessary to get their attention, and then you begin your brief introduction. After this you may ask a direct question or a question of the group as a whole. The leader must draw out all relevant information, viewpoints and experiences. He or she must make sure that all available information is before the meeting and get further information from members as is necessary. He must stimulate thinking and get the meeting to examine the experience and judgement of all. The member who insists on talking must be interrupted—you can thank him for his seven points and tell him before he continues with the other seven you would like to discuss the ones just made. Everyone—both sides—at a meeting can and should be heard—but not indefinitely. Encourage those who tend to be quiet. Link the speakers together and provide the channel through which they speak. But talk yourself only when you must. Cajole the members into brevity, but try not to choke off discussion until it comes to an end. Wait until you get from the feeling of the meeting that time has come for the particular debate or argument to be wound up. You, as a chairman or leader, are running the meeting, but don't make it too obvious. The top leaders keep the show going and ensure that everyone stays contented and awake, and the finest chairmen are those who use good humour, quiet tact and gentle persuasion.

Summarise the developments of the discussion from time to time and refer to any changes of opinion. State points of agreement and disagreement, state intermediate conclusions as they are reached and make sure of members' understanding and acceptance of summaries. A particularly good time to give a summary is when you notice that uniform thinking has been reached on one phase of the subject and no really new contribution is coming forward. There should, of course, be a summary when each intermediate conclusion is reached. Summaries are also useful to bring discussion back to the point and purpose of the meeting when the subject has been extended beyond profitable limits.

Establish the final conclusion reached, state the main points contributed at the meeting, mention any minor disagreements, make sure your summary is fair and that all the members understand it. It should make clear to people just what they have achieved and what further action they have committed themselves or the organisation to taking.

Try to finish the meeting on time. If this looks like being impossible then ask the members if they wish to extend the meeting for another half-hour or so.

At the very end thank the members for their contribution to the group achievement.

The majority of informal meetings are supposed to lead to changes in the work situation. You may wish to send a brief summary in writing to all those present, outlining the decisions reached and the action to be taken as a result. In any event there should be a permanent record of what took place. If your summary at the meeting itself has been clear you won't have people saying 'Oh I didn't think we agreed to that.' People do not contest what they have created. Formal minutes and informal notes also serve as a starting point in any further meetings on similar subjects.

Working Through Committees

A committee is a person or group of persons to whom something is 'committed.' It is, therefore, possible for one person to form a committee—probably the most effective committee of all! It is usually a small body of people appointed by a parent body to meet to discuss particular matters which are defined in its terms of reference. Recommendations are expected to be made to the parent body, where the committee is an advisory one. But decisions are expected from a policy committee. Committees may be homogeneous where all the members are of similar interests and status, they may be mixed, or joint. Many companies have joint consultative committees (also called works councils), comprising representatives of both workers and management and meeting at weekly or monthly intervals. Normally these joint consultative committees do not negotiate conditions of work; they discuss matters of common interest to management and labour such as methods of improving efficiency, safety and welfare. The balance of management and worker participation varies, but it is usual to have equal representation or a slight bias in favour of the workers. These committees are of special value in improving communications within a company.

Most professional institutions, learned societies and voluntary organisations make extensive use of committees. The council would be the main body. There would also be a small executive committee through which most of the business is conducted, and reports thereof would be periodically presented to the council for approval.

There are several advantages of the committee system of management.

1. Committee work can be said to be a highly significant feature of modern industrial life and a sign of democratic control in that it is constituted by the free votes of an elected assembly;
2. the specialised knowledge of diverse people is pooled for the common good;
3. the continuity of the committee is assured regardless of changes in its personnel.

In addition to the joint committee mentioned above there are also standing committees, *ad hoc* or special committees, and the old favourite, sub-committees.

Standing committees are those formed for specified purposes only. These are used mostly by local government and for Parliamentary affairs. County councils, for example, often have a finance committee, a planning committee, a general purposes committee, etc.

Ad hoc or special committees are those formed for special investigations and are usually dissolved when their reports are submitted. The inauguration of a pension scheme or the installation of a computer are items that would be dealt with by an *ad hoc* committee whose members would have special knowledge and experience in these fields. The formation of these committees leaves the parent body free to concern itself with the major business of the institution and with policy.

Sub-committees are occasionally formed to relieve a larger committee of detailed work and their activities are limited to that particular work. Examples are a transfer committee of a board of directors or a finance committee of a governing council.

As well as a good means of communication there are intricate psychological and social motives underlying committee work. Executive control by individual to individual is sometimes fraught with complicated emotions and some inhibitions. But sitting down with others round a table in committee provides an opportunity to shed those inhibitions. People are there to voice opinions, exchange ideas and contribute to the decision and there is, therefore, a kind of anonymity which pervades committee work.

Committees generally tend to be reasonably formal, with their own rules as to quorums, proposals, resolutions, minutes and all matters of election and procedures. They make a very large and valuable contribution to industrial, local governmental and professional life of the United Kingdom and embody a proud tradition of service.

Brainstorming Sessions

In our society more and more of the daily operations of business, education and government are being directed by groups of people—committees, boards, councils, and conferences. Certainly any business or professional man spends much of his time participating in discussions; in fact, his effectiveness in his job may be very largely determined by his skill in discussion. Although discussion varies in method from group to group, the following should serve as a good working definition: discussion is a co-operative process by which a group of persons exchange and evaluate ideas and information about a mutual problem in order to understand or solve that problem.

There are generally two purposes of a discussion group which may be independent or inter-related:

(*a*) to exchange ideas or opinions; and
(*b*) to reach an agreement or make a decision.

The least any discussion can do is to inform each participant of the other members' knowledge and opinions about the subject under consideration. Sometimes this is the only purpose of the discussion but often the exchange of ideas is merely a preliminary to making a decision. In either case the pooling of information and the expression of the divergent opinion are very valuable methods of getting a broad understanding of the problem and of providing a sound basis for making a decision. If it is desired to reach an agreement there is no doubt that through the give-and-take of discussion individual beliefs are often modified and a consensus reached. If a consensus should prove impossible at least the range of disagreement may be sufficiently narrowed so that a clear understanding of the remaining basic differences are arrived at.

The various types of discussion group with which you and I may be expected to be involved are: Study groups, Committee Meetings, Panel discussions, or Symposium discussions.

A study group is normally quite an informal affair. A speech or lecture is given, after which there is a mutual exchange of information. The ideas and information exchanged means that those present learn something from each other as in the case of conventions or seminars where men and women in the same business profession tell each other of experiences they have had or detail the results of their research or methods of dealing with common problems.

We have already dealt with Committee Meetings.

Panel and Groups

Where a group is too large to engage in effective discussion or many of its members are too uninformed for such a discussion to be mutually profitable, a small group—usually about three to six individuals—often discusses the problem on a platform before a larger group. The individuals in the panel are chosen because they are well informed on the particular topic and can supply the facts needed for intelligent discussion or because all of them are known to represent points of view held by a considerable part of the audience and can act as spokesmen to express these viewpoints.

Seminars and Conferences

Very common in America. They arise where a small group of people usually four or five give a series of short six or seven-minute speeches each presenting a different viewpoint or aspect of the particular subject being discussed. They are common at large conventions were experts are asked to talk on varying subjects or several aspects of the same topic and they are also used to report the findings of various groups attending a conference.

Both the symposium and panel discussion are often followed by an open forum, where the participants answer questions put by those in the audience. The general principle of the symposium and panel discussion is that one small group do most of the talking while the larger group listens and asks questions.

When leading a discussion, state the topic, problem or difficulty with which the meeting is to deal, outline the situation giving rise to the topic problem or difficulty. State the purpose of the meeting so that everyone present knows what is appropriate for discussion and what is inappropriate. The vague statement of the subject is probably the cause of most futile discussions. The subject must be simply and clearly expressed and all ambiguous words must be defined. Some subjects at meetings are put so broadly that it is extremely difficult to know just what the field of enquiry is.

Then throughout the discussion there must be order. This does not necessarily imply great formality; in fact in small discussion groups formality would be entirely out of place. Order does require, though, that only one person talks at a time and that each member be consistently courteous. Some definite procedure must be followed as I have already indicated, otherwise the discussion wanders too far afield. Every member must co-operate. If each person insists on having his or her own way the discussion will get nowhere. Members of the group must have a willingness to discuss points of view other than their own and there must be some agreement to compromise. There are no doubt occasions when compromise is neither desirable nor possible but reasonable compromise should always be the objective. The more each member knows about the other members the more they will be able to judge the value of their remarks and the better they will be able to secure the approval of their own.

As a leader of any discussion you should always:

(a) prepare a time-table;
(b) outline a clear introduction;
(c) know the final objective;
(d) know the intermediate objectives;
(e) frame appropriate questions; and
(f) quote any relevant case examples.

For the ordinary member of a discussion group you must learn that, while if you keep quiet, you will learn a good deal, you will not thereby help solve the problem. Develop, therefore, the ability to present your ideas clearly and tactfully and learn to bring them in at the most strategic time. Don't delight in scoring points off your colleagues—a committee meeting or discussion group is not a game. And always do your homework first.

Briefing Sessions

Briefing sessions are a systematic and checkable method of downward communication involving managers and supervisors at all levels. All of those who are intimately concerned with time spent in the Services know what 'de-briefing' groups are and the principle holds good in an industrial situation. They bring people together in small groups under their immediate boss in order that any situation can be explained to them face to face. Consequently they, in their turn, are able to ask questions and so understand not only what is happening but why. They help keep everyone in the picture and are ideal in a scattered organisation.

The key person in explaining management's point of view is the immediate supervisor, and while it takes supervisors' time, it is necessary for it to pay dividends. By using supervisors to explain management policies the supervisor is made a more effective boss, because he who communicates is he who leads. At a time when more and more supervisors are joining trade unions it is essential to bring home to them, whether or not a union represents them to negotiate conditions of employment, that this in no way affects their vital role as the first line of management.

The items for briefing are those which affect a man's will to work effectively. They will, therefore, be items about the job-quality, safety, changes, progress, performance of the group; and those things which affect all workers personally—promotion, employment policies, security, and so on.

Normally a form is given to each supervisor with the items to be briefed printed clearly thereon with a space left after each item for a note of any points which the briefer must especially emphasise. Briefing should not only be checkable but be checked which is best done by managers sitting in now and then on a briefing session. Briefing sessions should take place with no fewer than six nor more than twenty persons present. This greatly facilitates the number of questions and answers which can be handled during the session.

More and more large companies are using briefing sessions to inform their workers of matters affecting their work and are very complimentary of the results being obtained.

Points for Discussion

To what points would you give attention before calling a meeting of supervisors to discuss increased measures for safety in your particular factory?

What rules do you consider to be important in running a meeting?

Do you consider it essential that all members speak at a committee meeting?

What is the value of sub-committees?

What various types of situation can you think of where the application of a discussion group would be helpful?

Customer Care

Ask yourself: Who's the most important person in any company? If you believe the managing director is the most important person in the company you're obviously going to go a long way. But, take it from me, you'll never be a salesman. For the most important person in any commercial organisation in the world is the customer or consumer, the ultimate purchaser of the product or service. Without him, you're dead, no matter how sophisticated the accounting procedures or management techniques.

Yet all too often the consumer is the most neglected person in the world. Instead of seeing him as the foundation of the business, he is seen as a necessary irritant to be suffered in the cause of profit, like the businessman who wrote to the managing director of a large chain of hotels complaining about the condition of the bed clothes in his hotel room. By mistake, back came his original letter with the managing director's instruction to his secretary: 'Send this nut the bed-bug letter!'

Of all relationships a commercial organisation has to develop and cultivate, nothing—but nothing—is more important than its relations with its customers. This applies whether you are selling industrial plant on a multi-million pound scale or washing-up liquid.

The starting point, therefore, is a company's reason for being in business.

Says Professor Theodore Levitt in his book *Innovation in Marketing*,

> . . . the object of a company's efforts ought to be to offer a cluster of value satisfactions such that people will want to deal with it rather than its competitors.'

The next point we have to consider, in that case, is what the customer wants. Professor Levitt gives an example,

> 'Thus if you sell pianos it is obviously critical to find out among other things what people buy pianos, who they buy them for and what all the problems are in connection with using a piano.'

The answers he discovers are that

> . . . Adults buy pianos but mostly for their children. The piano is not just a noise making instrument or a pleasure giving tension-relaxing contrivance; perhaps for many buyers it is most important as a symbol of cultural elevation. They want their reluctant children to play an instrument whose presence in the house brings credit to the parents.'

But, of course, there are plenty of reasons why piano sales are nowhere near as high as the manufacturers would like '. . . the resistance of children, the tediousness of learning to play, the competition of hi-fi and so forth. Hence to design a better piano, a more compact piano, a more beautiful piano, a cheaper piano, or to expand the number of retail outlets for them may be much less effective than developing a faster and more congenial way of enabling people to learn to play more easily,' says the professor.

Given this reasoning, which is applicable to every product under the sun, we have the rational basis for a customer relations programme.

Right Product

The basic product, we assume, is acceptable to the consumer. If not, the whole selling operation is a fraud. I am not saying that every product must be so attractive and so valuable that consumers cannot resist buying it. That would be absurd. Instead, I believe, every product should have a basic consumer appeal otherwise sales would be minimal and the need for a customer relations programme non-existent.

Next, the product must be pitched at the right price. Like the politician, you can convince some of the people some of the time. But a successful product must be pitched at the correct market price otherwise, again, there is no sale and no customer relations operation. Finally, the product—and this is the first stage of any promotion programme—must be presented in the most attractive form for the consumer. The degree of presentation or packaging, of course, depends on what is being sold and varies from product to product. Try selling perfume in a plain brown envelope and you'll soon see why the packaging is so expensive.

Sales Staff

This is the extension of the attractive receptionist syndrome. Basically there are two kinds of salesmen; salesmen who sell and salesmen who handle enquiries from potential customers. Clearly, it is much better to have salesmen who actually go out of their way to sell. This might sound a truism. But go into any store any day of the week and you can spot the good salesman a mile away. It is in a company's interests, therefore, to select the right sales staff and train them to their own specific requirement.

New staff should be given a formal guide to any company, its philosophy, its products or services and its market. How often have customers been told by a member of a company, 'I don't know if they sell that; I'll have to check.' Apart from the obvious benefits of a more informed staff, it can help promote the sales attitude throughout the organisation. Sales staff proper should be trained—not only in the use of the product they are selling but in salesmanship as well. This doesn't mean everybody should be a huckstering door-to-door salesman. It means that staff should be doing their job to the best of their ability. Think of the investment a company makes in a single salesman. It is foolish not to try to realise that investment.

Sales training is also a valuable safety factor, for it ensures that any sales force, by and large, follows the established selling methods. I say by and large because obviously nobody can monitor every sales opportunity encountered by every salesman. But it helps to cut down any extreme approaches.

Some companies go as far as writing out every possible sales approach and counter-approach imaginable. The sales force have to master these before they are allowed on the road. It might be mildly bureaucratic but it safeguards the company from extreme abuses and guarantees a fair response to the ultimate customer.

Sales Promotion

This is the land of advertising and public relations. There are many definitions of different sales promotion activities. In the end, however, they are all aimed at presenting the product to the selected market in order to persuade people to purchase. The actual purchasing decision, however, has to be clinched by the salesman. Advertising delivers the customer to the doorstep. The salesman completes the sell.

Lesson number one is to present a consistent image to your market place. It is difficult enough trying to recall familiar names or signs. The company with a diffused image has little chance in establishing and maintaining any consumer loyalty. Having launched a consistent image, the next stage is to create the 'come hither' appeal for a product. This is either termed the 'value satisfactions' of the product if you're a follower of Professor Levitt, or the unique selling proposition, if you're a student of American marketing techniques. Either way, it means the sales promotion material must present the best possible argument for buying the product in the most attractive way. A good salesman does this automatically when he is talking to his customer. It is a little more difficult attempting the same thing on paper to a wide audience. It is largely because of this basic problem that so much advertising is accused of talking down to people. Unfortunately, it is a fact of life that those who complain, don't like plastic daffodils; those who don't complain do like plastic daffodils.

Overall sales promotion can stretch as far as sponsoring round-the-world yacht races or simply arranging taste-ins at local supermarkets.

Point of Sale

Point of sale is virtually sales promotion on the shop counter. It is difficult enough, runs the theory, to get the potential purchaser inside the store. Then once inside, he is still faced with a bewildering choice. Point of sale material is supposed to swing him over that final hurdle.

The nearer we get to the actual purchasing decision the more careful must be the actual sales approach. The different provisions of the trade descriptions legislation control the sales information. The new credit legislation governs hire purchase terms and the true interest charges being made. Both are key figures in any customer relations programme. The more enlightened companies have anticipated these provisions in their sales promotion activities.

The Sale

Now the sale proper. Everything so far has been designed to bring the consumer to the actual point of purchase. Now that we have brought him so far the problems are still not over. Not only the interests of fair trading but customer relations demand he is still protected from abuse.

First, the product must measure up in every way to the descriptions he has been given. Not only is this natural justice but it is also commercial commonsense since an angry customer is going to cause more time and trouble than the margin allows. An angry customer is also likely to damage the company's reputation as well.

Second, any accompanying guarantee must be spelt out in full. Schreiber Furniture Centres, for example, do this admirably. Everybody buying furniture from any Schreiber Furniture Centre receives a written pledge from the chairman, Ch. S. Schreiber:

> 'I pledge the Schreiber Company to provide well-made furniture at fair prices; to honour delivery dates; and to refund or replace without delay if any piece of furniture is ever seen to be less than we claim.'

Which is, of course, the ultimate in customer relations. Whether other businesses follow suit or not this should certainly be their aim.

Third, any accompanying financial enquiries must be conducted with the consumer in mind. Most hire purchase or credit sales demand a credit enquiry on the purchaser. Because of the dangers of accusations about the invasion of privacy, the provision of inaccurate information and so on, it is becoming more and more prudent to inform the consumer that such a check is being made and to give them the opportunity to comment on any information provided.

Delivery

Schreiber has already made the point about deliveries. Probably nothing causes so much ill-will as delivery dates. Invariably, it is difficult to be quoted a delivery date; if a date is quoted it is rarely honoured. The customer continually complains. The salesman exhausts the goodwill he established in the course of the sale. By the time the delivery is actually made the credit supply is at an end.

Far better to follow Schreiber's approach. Quote reasonable delivery dates—and keep to them. Nothing is more likely to win consumer goodwill. The situation is even worse in the industrial area. As a country we are recognised for our failure to keep delivery dates. As a result customer's turn to overseas suppliers again and again. Not only is it in the consumer's interests that we solve this problem it's in the country's interests as well.

Installation

Once a product is delivered, the battle actually begins—especially if the product has to be plugged in and switched on or operated in even the simplest way. For I often believe this country leads the world in preparing instruction books that don't instruct, thus bungling up a major area of communication.

We've all experienced the situation. There is your brand new shining product. You've probably saved up for it. It is three weeks late on delivery. And there's the instruction book and you cannot understand a word. Or you get half-way through it and get struck. There is a technical term you don't understand and so on. Nothing is more infuriating or likely to put you off a company for life. It seems so obvious. The first thing any company should do is make the customer appreciate its products. Yet nothing is so difficult. I've even come across British companies circulating instruction booklets in French and German to consumers buying their product in this country!

Putting out an instruction booklet that anybody can understand might not seem important in the total business context but it is invaluable in the eyes of the consumer.

After Sales Service

Stories about the poor quality of after sales service are legion. Communication again often breaks down on the part of the company. Many stories are also based on the after sales engineer turning to the broken-hearted consumer with the gallant enquiry, 'What did you buy this for then. . . ?' But the frightening thing is that they are probably right!

For some reason or other few companies believe in the value of a first-class after sales services. Which seems amazing. For, in my book, after sales service consolidates the first sale and prepares the way for the next.

We all know the fantastic success achieved by Volkswagen in their overseas sales territories. Within months of breaking in they seem to scoop up the sales. And the reason? They always consolidate their after sales service operation before they attempt to sell a single car. If a Volkswagen customer needs a spare part it's on the spot.

Many other manufacturers concentrate on sales from the beginning. As a result they are rarely able to keep pace with the speed and efficiency of the Volkswagen service.

Complaints

Straightaway, let me admit there are two kinds of people who complain: the professionals and the people who genuinely feel they have cause for a grievance. Unfortunately, however, both kinds can bring a company into disrepute. It is in a company's interests, therefore, as well as being natural justice to service any complaints as quickly as possible. A number of companies establish complaints departments to deal with customers. In some cases such a department operates under a fictitious name in an attempt to personalise the service and make the aggrieved customer feel he is dealing with a person rather than a machine.

Again, different companies prefer standard letters to deal with complaints while others operate a complaints questionnaire. Overall, there are only two rules when it comes to this critical area of customer relations: acknowledge all complaints promptly and act on all complaints promptly. Give every complainant the benefit of the doubt and you're unlikely to come unstuck. At the same time one should monitor the level and subject of all complaints. For the complaints department have often been able to show up the inadequacies of any quality control procedures not to mention any basic product deficiencies.

Customer as Shareholder

The advent of consumerism coupled with the increasing democratisation of share ownership has brought this area of consumer relations to the attention of more and more companies in recent years. And it works both ways. Companies are becoming more eager to turn investors into consumers and consumers into investors. For in the days of bids and counter-bids it increases company loyalty. New shareholders in consumer companies often receive a personal letter from the chairman as soon as their name appears on the register. Others include a booklet outlining the consumer products of the company concerned and the places they can be purchased. A few companies have gone a stage further and arranged factory tours and office visits for their shareholders. One brewery kills two birds with one stone by holding their annual general meeting at their head office which is then followed by a tour of the brewery. Some hotel groups have begun to consider cut-price shareholder weekends during the off-seasons of the year. Shareholders feel they are more involved with the company than simply filling in a proxy card at the time of each AGM. The company, of course, benefits by filling the hotels but, in the end, both sides are happy.

I have listed ten key areas for any company to examine their customer relations. The sooner they start the better.

Points for Discussion

Comment on this statement: Of all relationships a commercial organisation has to develop and cultivate, nothing, but nothing, is more important than its relations with its customers.

What do we mean by sales promotion'?

Why is the point of sale so important?

CHAPTER 8

Information Quality Control and Evaluation

Management Initiatives in Ensuring Information Quality

The responsibility of top management in information system quality control is to establish the overall organisation structure, select the information system executive, approve the information system plan and budget, and evaluate performance. Some examples of top management duties are:

- Establish domain of responsibility and authority of information systems function.
- Select information systems executive.
- Approve the information systems charter, the information system long-range plan, and the yearly budget.
- Approve major hardware and software systems.
- Approve major applications.
- Review results against plan and evaluate information system performance.
- Review and approve information system procedures for quality assurance and control.

The top management responsibilities listed above may be exercised by individual top management personnel, or a committee structure may be used to do much of the work prior to final decision-making by top management. In the committee approach, an information system steering committee composed of top management of the organisational functions performs evaluations and makes recommendations for action.

Information Systems Management Control and Quality Assurance Duties

The information systems executive has the responsibility for organising and supervising the various control and quality assurance activities in information systems. Examples of duties are:

- Establish and supervise quality assurance procedures for applications developed in-house or obtained as packages.
- Establish and supervise various information system control functions.
- Establish and monitor procedures to measure and report evidence of quality: error downtime, reruns, application repair maintenance, etc.

Information System Control and Quality Assurance Functions

There are certain control and quality assurance functions that need to be performed in information system operations. In large installations, performance of these functions may require a special staff; in small installation, they may be part-time duties for an individual performing other activities. The major functions are:

1. *Librarian*: This function maintains custody of programmes, files, and documentation. These resources are issued based on an authorised of uses or special authorisation. The custodial activities include record keeping.
2. *Processing control*: This includes logging in and checking input, checking progress of jobs, reconciling control information for applications, checking output and distributing it to authorised recipients, maintaining error logs, and following up on error correction.
3. *Access control*: This function is responsible for control of physical access to the installation and control of access through terminals. Duties include follow up on violations of systems access rules.
4. *Database administration*: This include control over access to and use of database, enforcement of data integrity rules, and establishment and enforcement of standards.

5. *Back and recovery:* This function is reasonable for preparing backup copies of programmes, files and database, etc.
6. *Application development quality assurance*: This function includes review of controls planned for an application and review of adequacy of testing during development.

End-User Control and Quality Assurance

Users have quality assurance duties as participants in application and database development and maintenance. There are also special control and quality assurance considerations when users develop their own systems, to be discussed later.

Users quality assurance duties require knowledge of context of data, user participation in both input and output, and the organisational control principles of separation of functions. Knowledge of context means that users are able to identify individual data because it does not fit or is not reasonable. This ability represents situation-dependent data validation because the validation criteria may not be formulated until the user is faced with the specific invalid instance. For example, the user may recognise a personnel record showing that a person was born in 1961 and graduated from a university in 1975 as probably being in error. A validation test for this relationship could have been designed, but it is likely to have been overlooked. The user should be responsible for reporting such probable invalid data; procedures should exist to facilitate reporting to such instances and provide feedback that they have been corrected.

When a user prepares input for a batch system and also receive the output, this is one bases for quality control duties. For instance, the user may develop a control total of input data provided to data processing and check control totals on output against the input control total. The user may check output with other data such as checking the total on listing of accounts receivable with the accounting ledger total for accounts receivable.

The organisational control principle of separating functions that a person should not be responsible for incompatible functions in terms of ability to make errors or commit fraud. The same person should not have custody of assets and do all accounting for the assets. The initiation of transactions should be separated from the data processing of the transactions to produce financial records.

The separation of functions increases the probability than an error by one person will be detected by another. Also separation of function reduces the likelihood of fraud because it would require collusion. In the case of information processing, the division of functions is manifest in:

Requirements that a transaction in error be returned to the initiation area rather than being corrected by data processing.

Policy that data processing may not initiate transactions or master file changes.

User controls and user control duties in applications.

Quality Assurance for Application

A large proportion of the procedures related to an information system application related to quality assurance. These include handling of exceptions, detection of errors, error correction, and various exception error, and control reports. In a typical application, from 25 to 50 per cent of activities and programme code are for quality assurance. The same factors apply to database. Quality assurance is, therefore, a significant issue in application design, operation, and maintenance.

Conditions for Quality Assurance

There are three conditions that underline quality control in application: organisational commitment to quality, information processing discipline with respect to operations, and redundancy to achieve error control in the application design. Specific quality assurance procedures rely upon these three conditions.

The organisational commitment to quality in the results of information processing is not merely a statement of support; quality assurance requires extra effort and extra expense both in development and in operation. However there are significant differences in quality requirements among applications. There are different quality requirements by different organisations and different functions within the same organisation. This means the commitment to quality may differ among organisations and applications but the commitment should be appropriate to the conditions.

Information processing discipline is an element in overall organisational discipline. The term "discipline" is used in the sense of diligently following established procedures. It implies an acceptance of the need for careful attention to quality. Information processing discipline is institutionalised in the use of forms, screen design and procedures for input, output, and error handling. It is transmitted to new employees by training, supervision and example. For example, and older employee tells about the time she stayed until midnight locating an error caused by a sloppy transaction document. This transmits a message about the seriousness of errors and the diligence expected of employees in locating and fixing them. As a new employee gains experience, acceptance of data processing quality assurance procedures is strengthened. The success of many quality assurance procedures depends on the existence of such information processing discipline in the organisation.

Redundancy was explained in connection with information concepts. Redundancy in information processing consists of an extra element, process, or procedure that would not be required if there were complete assurance that the data and procedures were without error. Some examples of redundancy in computer data processing are:

Parity bid to detect errors in electronic circuitry or data communication lines.
Longitudinal parity bit on magnetic tape blocks to detect and correct errors.
Check digit added to identification codes.
Control totals on batches of data.
Run-to-run control totals.
Echo of input at VDT entry.
Verification of input data by rekeying and comparing.

Redundant data or redundant processing procedures provide the basis for very effective quality assurance procedures. However, there are three costs associated with the redundant elements; the cost of obtaining the redundant data or doing the redundant processing, the cost of error detection and error correction for the redundant elements, and the cost of the assurance procedures themselves. For examples a control total comparison used to detect loss or non-processing of data in a batch of data items requires the control total to be computed, the control total to be recomputed if there is a difference between the control total and the processing total, and either manual or programmed comparison of the two totals.

Quality Assurance in Application Development

The development cycle is designed to support quality assurance in terms of developing a system that meets requirements. Some quality assurance processes are:

- Information requirements determination processes to ensure complete and correct requirements.
- Sign-offs at each phase of development to assure adequate review and agreement on the system to that point.
- Programme development procedures for quality control. These include structured design, structured programming, independent review of programme logic, and programme testing.
- Conventional installation testing.

Development quality assurance procedures can be operated in a co-operative mode, an adversary mode, or a combination. In the co-operative mode, quality assurance is considered a responsibility of the entire development group. Finding errors is viewed as an aid to assist members of the group to achieve a better result. An example of the co-operative approach is a structured walkthrough for programmers. A member of the project team "walks through" programme logic and procedures with the rest of the group the objective is to improve the programme not to evaluate the programmer or analyst.

In the adversary mode, a separate quality assurance or testing function is established. The persons doing the quality assurance and testing receive organisational rewards for finding weaknesses and errors and identifying the source of the errors. The staff of the quality assurance function monitors application development projects and evaluates them in terms of processes being applied to achieve quality and in terms of the quality of the result. The separate function provides an independent evaluation of both project management relative to quality assurance and the application that is produced. The quality management relative to quality assurance and the application that is produced. The review consists of an independent evaluation of project risk and project plans in the light of the risk. Project reviews are conducted on a periodic basis during the development to assess progress. Special reviews may be made to deal with problems that arise.

The advantages of the separate quality assurance function are independence of the function, demonstration of organisational time and resource commitment, and specialisation in quality assurance. The disadvantages are primarily that quality assurance is then divorced from application development and resistance to separate quality assurance personnel may reduce their effectiveness.

Specifications for Application Design

Applications designed with high regard for quality assurance in operation tend to have low error rates. Some example of features that aid in assuring quality and low error rates are the following:

- Design of input documents and screens to elicit input natural sequence with labels, boxes, and menus that clearly identify what is to be input.
- Expanded echo of input data to provide data provide opportunity for visual verification. For example, code 3175 is input; the echo of the input is "Code 3175: engine mounting."
- Presentation of sufficient information on output for recipient to verify processing. "70 dozen widgets at $0.72 per dozen = $50.40."
- Control totals on output to allow checking against other control totals.
- Audit trail references to allow tracing of end result back to constituent parts or tracing a part upto the result.

The cost of data increases with the quality requirements. A tendency to request higher quality of data than is required can be costly. Accounting data on cash, customer billing, etc., needs to be very exact; data on sales by product by area can be less exact and yet be completely satisfactory. Additional accuracy and completeness are achieved at the cost of redundant data and controls at a variety of points in the processing cycle.

Maintenance of Application Quality

According to system theory, a system will run down and become disorganised unless matter and energy are applied to overcome the natural tendency to entropy. For information system applications, the negative entropy is application maintenance; this refers to either repairs of errors or enhancements. If repairs are not made, users lose confidence in the system and fail to use it or to provide inputs. If enhancements are not made, users may switch to alternative source of information.

The process of maintenance follows a cycle of identification, analysis, performing changes, and testing. The identification to errors and proposed enhancements in crucial to the maintenance of system quality. Procedures need to be established for feedback from users on need for changes and from maintenance personnel to users. If the application is "owned" by one function, this function can assign responsibility for working with maintenance personnel. If there are many users, there may need to be a user group responsible for resolving conflicts.

Maintenance of Data Quality

The principle of entropy also applies to stored data. The maintenance of data quality requires continuous inputs of resources. In assessing the establishment of databases, an important factor to be considered is the probability that the integrity of the data can be maintained. The assessment should also consider the risk from a degradation of data quality. The ability of an organisation to maintain data quality depends on both organisational factors and data factors.

1. *Length of error-effect cycle*: If errors have an immediate effect, organisational resources will be applied more readily than if the effect of error is longer term. Errors in the billing file are, therefore, more likely to receive attention than error in the employee information file.

2. *Regularity of measurement*: Data collection that is scheduled that is scheduled at frequent, regular intervals is more likely to be regularised through institutional procedures. Occasional, *ad hoc* data collection is likely to be forgotten or done poorly. A regular, weekly report of competitor intelligence from sales as part of expense reports is more likely to have high integrity than an occasional intelligence report.
3. *User-provider link*: It is more difficult to maintain high quality when the function providing the data has no organisational link with its users. If the data is received from an external source, the organisation cannot impose its own quality control stands.
4. *Provider data discipline*: The extent of data discipline in a function is a result of the background, training, and culture of the function. For example, the accounting function tends to have greater data discipline then marketing.
5. *Ease of verification*: Some data items can be easily checked by comparison with other stored data or by comparison with physical evidence. The credits to accounts receivable are easily verified by the debits to cash.

Given these factors affecting data quality and the difficulty of maintaining data quality over time, organisational procedures can be applied to increase the probability of maintaining suitable quality. There can be regular comparison with physical evidence, such as inventory counts. The objects of data collection may be requested to review their records for correctness and completeness. Records may be reviewed on a cycle basis by persons who can recognise errors. For example, the purchasing department may review two per cent of the vendor files each week. Training and supervision may be utilised to instill and appropriate level of data discipline.

Quality Assurance with User-Developed Systems

User-developed applications are an approach to overcoming problems of backlog of new applications, system that do not meet user needs, and implementation failure. Users are provided with application development tools and given training and assistance; they take over the responsibility for requirements determination, development, implementation, and maintenance. There are unique quality assurance problems associated with user-developed systems, primarily because of the elimination of the analyst role in the design of controls for the application.

Development tools can be used which automatically include control procedures or prompt users to include them. Some also provide appropriate documentation as a by-product of user development.

The policy approach is to establish policy for adequacy of testing and documentation. For example, a policy may establish different testing and documentation guidelines depending on the importance of the problem, the duration of the system, and the task interdependencies involved. Four levels of testing might be:

No testing or non-developer review
Minimal testing and peer review
Medium testing and external review
High level of testing and formal external review

The quality assurance procedures summarised above reflect a balance between letting users have complete responsibility for developing their own systems without organisational controls and having a formal quality assurance process that must be applied to all user-developed systems. The same level of formal process for all cases would stifle creativity and experimentation, but the lack of any organisational controls subjects the organisation to an unacceptable level of risk.

Post-Audit Evaluation of Information System Applications

The last phase of the system development life cycle is a post-audit. This is reviewed by a task group. The audit group reviews the objectives and cost-benefit representations made on behalf of the project and compares them with actual performance and actual costs. If also review the operational characteristics of the system to determine if they are satisfactory. Documentation is reviewed for backup and maintainability considerations. Control and security provisions are examined. The results of the post-audit are intended to assist in improved cost justification and management of future projects, improvement in the application under review, or cancellation of the application of it is no longer justified.

Applications may be evaluated in terms of measures of system value. They may also be compared with the reports of technical, operational, and economic feasibility by which they originally justified.

Evaluation of System Value

One of the most severe problems with the post-audit evaluation is the difficulty of determining system value. The ideal measure, as of any investment of organisational resources, is a determination of the impact of the system on organisational effectiveness. Since few changes can be isolated so that their effects on overall organisational functioning can be measured, substitute indicators must be used. The most logical place to look for such measures of system value is the immediate environment where the system is being used. Methods can be determined for measuring the *effectiveness* of the user as a result of having received the output or service from the system. Some methods of indirectly measuring system value are:

Significant task relevance	Results of system use are directly observable. For instance, an office support system results in improved turnaround of documents. For a decision support system, task relevance is *improved decision quality* which is often difficult to observe but sometimes possible to approximate through users' subjective estimates.
Willing to pay	Users may be asked to specify how much they are willing to pay for a specific report or system capability. This type of estimate will be very imprecise unless it is linked to an actual transfer price.
System usage	System logs may permit measures of system use, or users may be asked to estimate their user of the system. This is only appropriate for systems whose usage is voluntary.
User information satisfaction	Users are asked to rate their satisfaction with such aspects of the system as response time, turnaround time, vendor support, accuracy, timeliness, format of outputs, and confidence in the system.

Measures developed according to any of the above methods are probably most effective if given both before and after a new system or system enhancement is introduced. This provides a comparative indicator of improvements. System value assessments should not be made shortly after a system is implemented; an excess of programme errors, difficulties in learning and adjusting to new procedures, and general resistance to change may bias significantly both user satisfaction and system usage. With many voluntary-usage systems, initial use may be very high and will gradually taper off to a steady level once the novelty of the system has worn off. Another caution is that some applications cause subtle changes in the structure and behaviour of organisations in ways that were not anticipated, and these changes may be difficult to uncover through the simple measures described above.

An information system faculty member who did significant amounts of writing plus some administrative duties acquired two microcomputers. One was provided to his secretary. The other one was placed in his study at home where he did much of his writing. Communication was established for transfer between the two machines. After a year and a half of experience, some roles and duties had changed.

> The faculty member now composes at the keyboard where previously all keying was done by the secretary.
> Faculty member frequently keys in all text and data for document and secretary puts in final form, including page breaks, checking for misspelled or mistyped words using software, and printing on letter-quality printer. Previously, he read for errors and format.
> Faculty members sometimes dictates to secretary who keys text. To do further work, he either takes diskette or receives text over communications line. He makes corrections directly at his microcomputer and sends corrected text back to secretary. Previously, he always marked changes in pen which secretary keyed.
> Secretary writes programmes, using microcomputer application development system to do complex reports.
> Secretary builds files on the microcomputer for administrative lists, mailing, etc.

- Secretary has learned to send files to a large computer for special printing and to prepare graphical output. Previously, faculty member was responsible for all computer technology.

Technical Evaluation

The questions asked during a technical evaluation are similar to those used to determine whether the application was technically feasible. Some examples are:

- Is the data transmission rate fast enough to handle the data?
- Is there sufficient secondary storage to keep the necessary data?
- Does the CPU respond to all requests within the specified time period ?

When applications are installed, subsequent evaluation may disclose that they operate ineffectively because the technical capabilities of the hardware or software cannot support them properly. An online real-time operation may be very slow because the computer involved has insufficient capacity to handle the workload. A communications network may adequately handle the workload but the more costly than had been anticipated. Another common problem is that transaction volumes were underestimated, so that secondary storage for online processing has inadequate capacity.

Operational Considerations

Operational considerations relate to whether the input data is properly provided and the output is usable and used appropriately. Evaluation of application should examine how well they operate with special reference to input, error rates, timeliness off output, and utilisation. Some research on utilisation of output suggests the need for periodic evaluation of applications. In a study by Gee, 64 line managers at the middle management level of manufacturing companies were interviewed and asked to evaluate control information items they received as being used substantially or as being irrelevant or background information. Of 579 items, 46 per cent were considered to be irrelevant or useful only for background. In a further investigation, 49 middle managers were asked to classify items of control information as vital important, or background.

There is a tendency not to terminate a report once it is started. Even though it may not be used, there often is a feeling that it might have utility in the future. Various methods can be used to identify unused reports:

- Termination of the report to see if anyone asks for it when it does not arrive
- Periodic review of all reports by a task force
- Transfer pricing for reports to provide incentives for managers to eliminate those that are unnecessary.

Economic Evaluation

The original proposal for an application included an economic evaluation. In the post-audit economic evaluation, the actual costs are compared with actual benefits. The costs can be estimated with reasonable accuracy at post-audit, but many benefits may still be difficult to measure. After making these estimates, an economic evaluation may be computed. For example, a revised return on investment may be calculated.

The economic evaluation may be useful beyond the specific application examined. For management purposes, the evaluation may aid future decision-making to identify the costs of applications for which an economic return was not expected or could not be estimated. For example, the reasons for the application may have been:

- Mandated by law or changes in external systems
- Required in order to meet competition
- To establish or maintain a competitive advantage or innovation
- Improvements in organisational performance that are expected are difficult to measure.

If economic evaluation shows that the return-on-investment objective will not be achieved or other benefits. In other words, the costs of development already incurred are no longer relevant; they are sunk costs and cannot be altered by the decision. Frequently, therefore, an application that has less benefit than anticipated may still have sufficient future benefit to pay for operating costs and future maintenance costs.

Evaluation of Current Hardware and Software

The purpose of evaluation of existing hardware and software is to determine if all resources are needed, if some resources should be replaced with improved hardware or software, if a rearrangement of resources will improve effectiveness, or if additional resources will increase the effectiveness of the system. Some examples of actions resulting from performance evaluation of the existing hardware-software system are:

- Addition of a new data channel or dropping a data channel not being used.
- Replacement of a low-speed data channel with a high-speed channel.
- Addition to main memory capacity.
- Change in disk storage units.
- Change in disk organisation.
- Change in database management software.
- Change in communication network.
- Replacement of order entry application package.

The methods and tools for evaluation of the hardware-software system are hardware and software monitors, system logs and observations, and simulation.

Evaluation by Use of Performance Monitors

Hardware monitors are sensing devices attached to selected signal lines in the computer hardware to measure the presence or absence of electrical impulses. For example, a sensor might be attached to measure the time that the CPU is in wait state. Another sensor might measure channel activity. The monitoring device does not affect the operation of the computer hardware. It requires no primary storage and the CPU cycle times. The data from the sensor probes is routed to counters. Periodically the data in the counters, together with the time determined by an internal clock, is written onto magnetic tape or other output medium in computer-readable format. It is periodically summarised by use of a computer programme and reported in an analytical format.

Monitors can collect data on both CPU and peripheral device activity such as disk storage. The major shortcoming of hardware monitors is that they cannot identify the programme which is being measured unless monitors is that they can not identify the programme which is being measured unless the location of the programme in memory is known. Most computers of reasonable size use relocatable programmes and have more than one programme in memory at a time; this reduces the effectiveness of hardware monitors for measuring specific programme efficiency. The operating system normally resides in a fixed partition in memory, so its activity can be measured.

Software monitors are computer programmes. They reside in main memory and require execution time; they interrupt the programme being executed to record data about the execution. They, therefore, slow down the execution of the programmes they are monitoring. One approach to reduce the amount of interruption is to sample the activities being executed rather than to measure them continuously. Software monitors can identify particular programmes or programme modules within the operating system environment. Peripheral device activity is not measured directly but can be estimated from the CPU commands.

Hardware and software monitors can be used to detect idle resources, bottlenecks, and load imbalance. Inefficient use of resource owing to excessive wait time can be measured. This wait time may be caused by insufficient channel capacity, excessive seek time by disk storage devices, inefficient overlapping input-output and processing, etc. The monitors assist in identifying the causes of inefficiency.

Some remedies to be applied following performance monitoring and analysis of the results include:

- Changes in equipment
- Recording of programme segments
- Redesign of disk storage files
- Restructuring of access to disk storage records

The results from "tuning" of hardware-software systems have been significant. A 25 per cent reduction in execution time for the few jobs which normally take most of the processing capability is not unusual.

Evaluation by Use of System Logs and Observation

The system log may provide data useful for evaluation. This is especially true of small installation which maintain simple logs of jobs, job times, etc. An analysis of the system log may indicate problems with reruns, variations in job running times or excessive machine failure. The log may also be used to develop a distribution of jobs by time required. Such a list generally reveals the impact of, for example, few large jobs or a stream of small jobs.

Observation of computer operations is useful in detecting inefficient scheduling of resource use and inefficient applications. Some of inefficient scheduling or poor operating procedures are:

- Processing delays for operator to locate files, mount tapes or disks, load forms, or perform similar functions
- Excessive requirements for operator response at console
- Delays caused by lack of training in proper restart procedures when processing is interrupted

Simulation

Simulation is used primarily to chose a new system can also be used to study the effects of proposed changes or addition to existing installations. In this approach, the analysts defines mathematical models of representative computer runs and descriptions of existing or proposal computer configuration and operating system. These are input to a software package which produce a series of reports representing how, the workload will be processed. Simulation is useful, once a problem has been identified, in analysing various alternative solutions. Its drawbacks are that it is expensive to set up and run.

Evaluation of Proposed Hardware and Software

A frequent decision in information systems is the acquisition of new or replacement hardware or software. These are often major purchases with significant organisational implications. The process of evaluation for a new or major replacement hardware-software system will vary depending on the level or experience by the organisation using computers, the urgency of replacement, and other factors. A general approach consists of steps such as the following:

- Requirements study
- Preparation of specifications
- Obtaining vendor proposals
- Evaluation of proposals

The basis for this approach is that the organisation should undertake sufficient analysis to specify its requirements and request proposals from vendors based on the specific requirements. The vendor proposals are systematically evaluated relative to the requirements, and a decision is made. This approach is in contrast to a common method of asking a single vendor to propose hardware and software without any organisational study and specification.

The Study Group

If the hardware or software acquisition is major, a high-level study group or committee should be formed. Some smaller acquisitions may benefit from an advisory group of users. The high-level study group will be described as the model for both groups. A high-level committee should usually consist of middle-management personnel who represent the principal functions of the business, plus an executive from the systems function.

The study group should be provided with technical staff support. For an organisation that already has a computer installation and is studying the value of a new or expanded system, this support can come from the data processing systems staff. For an organisation without prior experience, the use of outside consultant for support is frequently advisable.

Requirements Study

The purpose of requirements study is to investigate the present hardware or software system, evaluated the need for a new or replacement system outline the characteristics of a tentative system, evaluative the cost and effectiveness of the tentative system, and evaluate the impact of the tentative system on the organisation.

From the information obtained in the requirements study, the group formulates the characteristics of the one or more tentative hardware and software systems, then makes rough estimates of cost and ability of each alternative to meet performance objectives. From these tentative systems, one of which should usually be a modified version of the system in use, a tentative system having the specified characteristics is selected as the preferred solution and is then analysed further in terms of personnel impact, cost-benefit, and suitability to the firm's needs. The system solution is by necessity very general, since it is not tied to a particular hardware or software vendor.

The cost-benefit study summarises the benefits to be expected from the system, the expected cost, and expected savings, if any. A reasonable life estimate for medium- to large-scale equipment is five years; for microcomputers, the life before obsolescence is considered about three years.

The results of the hardware-software requirements study together with the recommendations of the study group are summarised and presented for top management approval. If the project is approved, the next step is to prepare a manual of specifications for use in procurement.

Preparation of Specifications and Obtaining Proposals

The manual of specifications defines specifically what is to be accomplished by the proposed hardware-software system. It is a fairly detailed document based on data collected in the requirements study. The document serves both as a summary of the proposed system for internal purposes and as a statement for use in inviting proposals from vendors of hardware and software.

Evaluation of Proposals

Evaluation may be simple if only one vendor can satisfy the specifications, but in general several vendors will respond with proposal worthy of consideration. Since there are a number of considerations, both quantitative and subjective, one evaluation method is to rank each supplier by a point system. For each criterion for evaluation, a number of points is assigned as a potential total, and then each vendor is rated by being award part or all of the potential points.

- Operating system evaluation
- Very high level language evaluation
- Procedural language evaluation
- Database management system evaluation
- Software package availability evaluation
- Other software evaluation

The major questions that need to be addressed are whether the proposed hardware or software will perform the job in the time allowed, its relative cost, and its flexibility to expand as more applications are needed. Most computer systems can provide for growth by the addition of equipment options. For example, a stripped-down minimum-memory computer may have its power increased by addition of faster input-output, more storage, or special software packages. A compatible "family" of computers allows the organisation to move from one computer in the family to a larger size without reprogramming. The evaluation should include not only the existing software but also the probability of promised software being available on schedule.

In evaluations of hardware and software it is usually desirable to run test programmes. The vendor will usually provide time for testing.

When equipment is being evaluated, the alternative of a mixed system should be considered. Several firms offer "plug compatible" peripherals which have higher performance at a lower cost than the computer vendor's units. The main disadvantage of these independent peripherals is in the added management problems of dealing with more than one vendor and coping with responsibility for equipment-caused failures.

For a new computer system or major software package, the study group should conduct an independent analysis of system performance. The real criterion for measuring system performance is throughput; if actual jobs cannot be run and timed, then substitute measures must be used. There are several substitute comparison methods, but the most common is standard benchmark analysis in which standard problems of a type normally performed are code and time to perform the standard task is estimated or measured by running it. For example, a standard problem might be to read 10,000 records sequentially from disk storage and print them. Standard benchmark problems usually reflect typical jobs are not a sample of the complete processing system as it will operate.

Auditing or Information Systems

Organisations use auditors as independent evaluators. There are basically two types of auditors: independent auditors and internal auditors. Auditors who specialise in auditing activities related to information systems are generally termed EDP auditors. The roles of independent and internal auditors are different, although they perform many activities that are similar. Auditors can have a significant effect on quality and control of computer processing.

Independent Auditors

A major role of independent auditors is to attest to the fairness of financial statements. This professional judgement is based on evidence obtained and evaluated by the auditor during an examination.

Accounting Procedure and Information System

When accountants are designing some changes in the current information system, they should recognise that some employees might resent the suggested changes even if these modifications contribute positively to the company's goals. A systems change ordinarily will require certain individuals to perform their jobs differently from the past. A change from the normal routine can be frustrating. To reduce this frustration and thereby foster positive employee attitudes toward a systems change, the accountants should encourage the employees to *participate* in the systems study. This participation includes not only keeping the employees well informed regarding the reasons for change but also encouraging them to make suggestions in areas where they feel changes are needed. The employees should be motivated to accept a new system if they contributed to its development.

Since the job of accountants is to communicate relevant information to people, they must have an understanding of how people perceive information and then reach decisions from it. Basically perception is the specific meaning that an individual attaches to a communicated message. Identical information may be perceived differently by two people partly because of their dissimilar backgrounds. Thus accountants should be familiar with the basic psychological characteristics of the decision makers to whom they will communicate, so that their messages can be designed and communicated so as to allow the best possible organisational decisions.

A production supervisor, for example, typically thinks in terms of physical manufactured units rather than dollar production costs. Thus, if the Alan Company's basketballs exceed the standard quantity during a specific week, the accountant should communicate this unfavourable variance to the supervisor in terms of the excess raw materials used rather than merely report the excess dollar cost of the raw materials entering production. Because of the supervisor's background, he or she should have a better understanding of the production inefficiency of physical units rather than dollars are emphasised. As a result, the supervisor will likely be motivated to correct the production inefficiency.

Quantitative Approach

The *operations research* field includes various quantitative techniques to aid management decision-making. Some of these techniques are statistical analysis, linear programming, PERT analysis, waiting-line theory, simulation, and regression analysis.

Modern accountants use quantitative tools to increase the effectiveness of the information they provide to management. For example, due to increased sales of sporting goods equipment and the resultant need for additional productive capacity to meet these sales, the Alan Company's accountants could be asked to help management to decide whether to build a new production plant across town or expand the current plant. The accountants would attempt to project the future costs and benefits associated with both alternatives and then make a recommendation. Because costs and benefits associated with both alternatives and then make a recommendation. Because the future involves *uncertainty* and the accountants are trying to forecast the future operating results from two alternative actions, their analysis might be made more meaningful by using statistical probability theory.

As another example of accountants' use of quantitative techniques, assume that Alan Company's management is attempting to determine the optimal sales mix of its sporting goods products to maximise the company's total contribution to maximise the company's total contribution margin. The company's accountants can aid management's decision by preparing a linear programming analysis of the various sales mix combinations.

Let us assume that the analysis and design steps of a systems study have just been completed for the Alan Company and the recommended changes are ready for implementation. To aid this process, the accountant who participated in the systems, study can develop a quantitative PERT network diagram of the specific activities required for implementing the new system.

A few of the quantitative techniques that accountants can employ to perform their organisational functions more effectively have been briefly described here. The examples illustrate the accountant's use of quantitative techniques in business situation involving decisions that affect the future.

Computer Mainframe

Electronic data processing has significantly changed accountants' functions in an organisation. Prior to computerised business information systems, accountants often spent a large amount of their workday manually processing data. In many firms, the computer has taken over the build of these data-processing tasks and thereby allowed accountants to become more involved in decision-making in their organisations. The computer's making in their organisations. The computer's ability to handle an organisation's routine book-keeping has been a major cause for the growth of managerial accounting. Accountants are now concentrating on the design of systems, the development of budgets, and the recommendation of future managerial actions in a wide variety of operational areas.

The accounting subsystem must continually interact with the EDP subsystem. A large quantity of the input data to the computer must be provided by accounting. Accountants should understand the capabilities as well as the limitations of a computer so that they can perform their jobs effectively. In fact, the computer's ability to execute complex mathematical calculation in a short time period has been an important stimulus for accountants increased use of operations research quantitative techniques when providing information to management.

Overview Remaining Text Materials

Many of the contemporary studies assume that the student has prior knowledge of the hardware and software concepts associated with electronic data processing. The supplement includes the student with an understanding of computer fundamentals, terminology, and so on. Because modern business systems often have computerised processing of accounting data, accounting employees must be familiar with the capabilities and limitations of computers and be able to communicate with EDP employees. The materials on computers presented in other sections will expose the students to essential computer concepts that should enable them to function effectively within an EDP environment.

The current chapter has examined the role of accounting information systems in today's business world. For accountants to contribute to the development of efficient and effective business systems, they must have a good understanding of management concepts and how these concepts affect the design and operation of accounting information systems. Continuing Part One of our text, will, therefore, emphasise those management concepts of importance to accountants working within an accounting information system. Budgets are quite useful to management as planning and controlling tools. Because most students have been exposed to the computational aspects of preparing budgets, on budgetary accounting information systems, will stress the important contributions of budget systems to managerial planning and controlling activities. Various ways in which a computer can be utilised in a company's budgetary information system will also be examined in this chapter.

A vital role of an accounting information system within an efficient and effective organisational system is to aid the collecting, recording, and storing of financial data as well as converting these data into useful managerial decision-making information. Thus, Part Two will examine several data-processing approaches used by companies to enable relevant information to be provided to their managements. The emphasis throughout these three chapters will be on data collecting, recording, and storing within a computerised accounting information systems environment. The major subject is the use of *data bases* within accounting information systems. To complete Part Two of the text will provide a detailed illustration of both a manual and a computerised accounting information system for processing an organisation's accounts receivable business transactions.

To reduce the risk of errors and irregularities in an accounting information system's functions of collecting, recording, and storing business data, a system of *internal controls* is essential. Part Three will analyse in depth the topic of internal control within both manual and computerised data-processing systems. As a means of both preventing and detecting fraud within companies' computerised data processing systems, the performance of good *audit* procedures is extremely important. Therefore, to complete Part Three.

Accountants often participate in systems studies to help a company solve its problems associated with a lack of good information flow for managerial decision-making. Part Four will examine the activities that are essential when performing a study of a company's information systems problems, emphasising accountants' functions in systems study work. A large part of the discussion in these four chapters will involve accountants employed by consulting firms and participating in systems studies of operating problems. The major emphasis throughout Part Four will be on a systems study to convert an organisation's manual accounting information system to a computerised system.

Case Analysis: An Analogy

Once upon a time the president of a large chain of short-order restaurants attended a lecture on "Human Relations in Business and Industry." He attended the lecture in the hope he would learn something useful. His years of experience had led him to believe that if human relations problems ever plagued any business, then they certainly plagued the restaurant business.

The speaker discussed the many pressures which create human relations problems. He spoke of psychological pressures, sociological pressures, conflicts in values, conflicts in power structure, and so on. The president did not understand all that was said, but he did go home with one idea. If there were so many different sources of pressure, may be it was expecting too much of his managers to think they would see them all, let alone cope with them all. The thought occurred to him that may be he should bring in a team of consultants from several different academic disciplines and have each contribute his part to the solution of the human relations problems.

And so it came to pass that the president of the restaurant chain and his top management staff met one morning with a sociologist, a psychologist, and an anthropologist. The president outlined the problem to the men of science and spoke of his hope that they might come up with an interdisciplinary answer to the human relations problems. The personnel manager presented exit-interview findings which he interpreted as indicating that most people quite their restaurant jobs because of too much sense of pressure caused by the inefficiencies and ill-tempers of co-workers.

This was the mission which the scientists were assigned: find out why the waitresses break down in tears; find out why the cooks walk off the job; find out why the managers get so upset that they summarily fire employees on the spot. Find out the cause of the problems, and find out what to do about them.

Later, in one of the plush conference rooms, the scientists sat down to plan their attack. It soon became clear that they might just as well be three blind men, and the problem might as well be the proverbial elephant. Their training and experience had taught them to look at events in different ways. They decided that inasmuch as they couldn't speak each other's languages, they might as well pursue their tasks separately. Each went to a different city and began his observations in his own way.

First to return was the sociologist. In his report to top management he said:

> "I think I have discovered something that is pretty fundamental. In one sense it is so obvious that it has probably been completely overlooked before. It is during the rush hours that your human relations problems arise. That is when the waitresses break out in tears. That is when the cooks grow temperamental and walk off the job. That is

when your managers lose their tempers and dismiss employees summarily."

After elaborating on this theme and showing several charts with sloping lines and bar graphs to back up his assertions, he came to his diagnosis of the situation. "In brief, gentlemen," he stated, "you have a sociological problem on your hands. He walked to the blackboard and began to write. As he wrote, he spoke:

"You have a stress pattern during the rush hours. There is stress between the customer and the waitress..."
"There is stress between the waitress and the cook..."
"And up here is the manager. There is stress between the waitress and the manager..."
"And between the manager and the cook..."
"And the manager is buffeted by complaints from the customer."
"We can see one thing which, sociologically speaking, doesn't seem right. The manager has the highest status in the restaurant. The cook has the next highest status. The waitresses, however, are always 'local hire' and have the lowest status. Of course, they have higher status than bus boys and dish washers but certainly lower status than the cook and yet they give orders to the cook."
"It doesn't seem right for a lower status person to give orders to a higher status person. We've got to find a way to break up the face-to-face relationship between the waitresses and the cook. We've got to fix it so that they don't have to talk with one another. Now my idea is to put a 'spindle' on the order counter. The 'spindle' as you choose to call it, is a wheel on a shaft. The wheel has clips on it so the girls can simply put their orders on the wheel rathar than calling out orders to the cook."

When the sociologist left the meeting, the president and his staff talked of what had been said. It made some sense. However, they decided to wait to hear from the other scientists before taking any action.

Next to return from his studies was the psychologist. He reported to top management.

> "I think I have discovered something that is pretty fundamental. In one sense it is so obvious that it has probably been completely overlooked before. It is during the rush hours that your human relations problems arise. That is when the waitresses break out in tears. That is when the cooks grow temperamental and walk off the job. That is when your manager lose their tempers and dismiss employees summarily."

Then the psychologist sketched on the blackboard the identical pattern of stress between customer, waitress, cook, and management. But his interpretation was somewhat different:

> "Psychologically speaking," he said, "we can see that manager is the father figure, the cook is the son, and the waitress is the daughter. Now we know that in our culture you can't have daughters giving orders to the sons. It louses up their ego structure.
>
> "What we've got to do is to find a way to break up the face-to-face relationship between them. Now one idea I've thought up is to put what I call a ' spindle' on the order counter. It's kind of a wheel on a shaft with little clips on it so that the waitresses can put their orders on it rather than calling out orders to the cook."

What the psychologist said made sense, too, in a way. Some of the staff favoured the status-conflict interpretation while others thought the sex-conflict interpretation to be the right one, the president kept his own counsel.

The next scientist to report was the anthropologist. He reported:

> "I think I have discovered something that is pretty fundamental. In one sense it is so obvious that it has probably been completely overlooked before. It is during the rush hours that your human relations problems arise. That is when the waitresses break out in tears. That is when the cooks grow temperamental and walk off the job. That is when the managers lose their tempers and dismiss employees summarily."

After elaborating for a few moments he came to his diagnosis of the situation. "In brief, gentlemen," he stated, "you have an anthropological problem on your hands." He walked to the blackboard and began to sketch. Once again there appeared the stress pattern between customer, waitress, cook, and management.

> "We anthropologists know that man behaves according to his value systems. Now, the manager holds as a central value the continued growth and development of the restaurant organisation. The cooks tend to share this central value system, for as the organisation prospers, so do they. But the waitresses are a different story. The only reason most of them are working is to help supplement the family income. They couldn't care less whether the organisation thrives or not as long as it's a decent to work. Now, you can't have a non-central value system giving orders to a central value system.
>
> "What we've got to do is to fins some way of breaking up the face-to-face contact between the waitresses and the cook. One way that has occurred to me is to place on the order counter an adaptation of the old-fashioned spindle. By having a wheel at the top of the shaft and putting clips every few inches apart, the waitresses can put their orders on the wheel and not have to call out orders to the cook. Here is a model of what I mean."

When the anthropologist has left, there was much discussion of which scientist was right. The president finally spoke,

> "Gentlemen, it's clear that these men don't agree on the reason for conflict, but all have come up with the same basic idea about the spindle. Let's take a chance and try it out."

And it came to pass that the spindle was introduced throughout the chain or restaurants. It did more to reduce the human relations problems in the restaurant industry than any other innovation of which the restaurant people knew. Soon it was copied. Like wildfire the spindle spread from coast to coast and from border to border.

Range of End-Uses

Standard Building Service Company of St. Louis is a 15-year-old company that provides janitorial services for office buildings and industrial plants. Standard was purchased five years ago by Leslie Waller, and at the time of the purchase, annual sales were approximately $ 500,000. In three years he was able to double the sales volume to the present level $ 1,000,000; but for the past two years, sales volume has remained relatively constant. Waller attributes the lack of growth of the past two years to his being unable to call on new accounts because the business has grown to such an extent that his full energies and time are required in solving the myriad of problems that arise each day. He recognises that the few new accounts he does obtain do no more than offset the normal turnover of accounts lost each month.

Janitorial services are usually performed after the tenants have left the building for the day; consequently, very few of Standard's employees start work before 6 P.M. Waller has found from experience that in order to keep employees, he must offer them at least 20 hours of work a week. On the other hand, very few people seem willing to work more than 25 hours a week. As a result, the work force of approximately 275 men and women are part-time employees. Waller also found that by hiring persons presently employed he is assured of stable, motivated employees. However, since his employees are working full-time elsewhere, there is considerable resistance when supervisors expect an above-average amount of work from them.

A recent analysis of the 121 accounts serviced by the company shows that 40 customers require the services of only 1 person working a maximum of 25 hours a week. Thirty-five accounts require 2 people with total man-hours ranging from 35 to 50 hours a week. Fifteen accounts require an average of 100 man-hours a week, thus utilising the services of upto 4 employees. There is one large industrial plant that requires 500 hours of service each week and approximately 20 workers. The remaining 30 accounts range between 100 and 400 man-hours each week, and require between 4 and 16 employees.

Waller is not sure which size job yields the most profit. Jobs are priced on a rule-of-thumb basis and depend upon the type of floor surfaces, the amount of building traffic, number and types of offices, and other similar factors. Waller and one of his two full-time supervisors estimate the manpower requirements for each new job. An analysis of company records shows that for the past five years, variable costs—direct labour and materials average about 80 to 85 per cent of total revenue.

The full-time organisation consists of Waller, two supervisors, a secretary, an accountant, and a supply man who also maintains some of the larger pieces of cleaning equipment such as the floor polishers. In addition, there are five part-time supervisors, each of whom supervises 40 to 50 workers in a given geographic area of the city. Most of their time and energy is spent in delivering supplies and materials to the various buildings within a given geographic area of the city. They also reassign personnel as the need arises and collect the weekly time cards. The two full time supervisors have no specific duties assigned to them nor is either one responsible for the work of any particular part-time supervisor.

At the present time Waller has only two sources of information to guide him in the operation of his business. One of these is customer complaints, which serve as a check on the quality of the work. The other source is the weekly payroll, which is prepared by a local bank. Each week time cards are submitted to the bank and from these records payroll checks are prepared. The bank also maintains the necessary social security and income tax records. In addition, a summary is prepared showing the total man-hours per week for each job. At present, no consistent use is made of this information. However, on the occasions when he has examined these weekly reports, Waller has found that the total hours per week run as much as 400 hours in excess of the number of hours used in computing the price of services. There is no record of the use of supplies for each job.

Identifying Transaction Source

An accounting "business transaction" results from any monetary event that causes a change in an asset, liability, owner's equity, revenue, or expense account. Remember, separate accounts are maintained in an organisation for every monetary item so that information is available regarding the dollar balances of these individual financial items—the dollar balance of *cash*, the dollar balance of *accounts receivable*, the dollar balance of *notes payable*, and so on. Transactions can occur from business activities between a company and either some external party or an internal party. For a business transaction to enter an organisation's accounting information system. It must be quantitative and also be measurable in monetary terms.

Business transactions result in the creation of *source documents*. To illustrate, assume that a customer of the Alan Company purchases several footballs. This sale will trigger the preparation of sales invoice by an Alan Company sales clerk. The sales invoice represents a transaction *source document*, which is the basis for entering the football sales transaction into the Alan Company's accounting information system.

Source documents represent visual evidence regarding the occurrence of business transactions. In many companies today a financial transaction is not subject to entry into their accounting information systems until proper source documents are prepared and approved. The types of source documents used by businesses will vary depending on each firm's special operating characteristics. A few of the more common source documents used by business organisations, in addition to the previously discussed *sales invoice*, are as follows:

1. *Purchase invoices* reflect the bills received from another company for the quantity and cost of inventory items or other assets purchased from the company.
2. *Receiving reports* reflect the actual quantity of inventory items or other assets delivered to a company from another company.
3. *Bills of lading* reflect the freight charges on physical goods shipped to a company.
4. *Employee time cards* reflect the number of hours worked by a company's employees during a specific pay period.
5. *Voucher checks* reflect the payees and amounts paid for various goods and services.

By utilising source documents, a company can collect its transaction data for subsequent entry into the accounting information system. Furthermore the transaction source documents represent the starting point in a company's *audit trail* through its information system's accounting cycle. The efficient collection of accounting data in a format in which they can be properly reflected within an accounting information system.

Daily Transaction Document

After accounting data are collected on a source document, they are recorded in a company's journal. A journal is kept within an accounting information system to provide an organisation with a chronological record of the economic activities that occur throughout its life. If, for example, a managerial executive needs information regarding specific economic activities that look place on June 12, 1998, the executive can turn to the page of the company's journal used on that data. It should be noted that if a company processes accounting data with a computer, the journal might be maintained on a storage medium such as magnetic tape. In this case, a computer printout of that day's journal entries would have to be prepared.

In many organisations a league volume of monetary transactions occur during accounting periods, but normally these transactions can be classified within a few broad categories. The classification of transactions by categories permits the firms' accounting information systems to process efficiently the hundreds or thousands of monetary events that take place. Furthermore, the enormous volume of transactions is one of the major factors causing many organisations to replace their manual accounting information systems with computerised accounting information systems. Some of the more common categories of business transactions are:

1. the purchase of economic resources (*i.e.*, assets),
2. the incurrence of operating expenses,
3. the sale of products and services, and
4. the receipt and payment of cash.

A very important category of business transactions commonly found in a manufacturing firm relates to the accumulation of production costs associated with the firm's "work in process inventory" and "finished goods inventory" accounts. To review the processing of business transactions and to emphasise the relevant information that is generated from business transaction processing, we will discuss each one of the four broad categories of transactions just described.

1. *Purchase of Economic Resources*: In a merchandising firm, two major types of asset resources acquired are:
   - *(i)* inventory (a current asset) and
   - *(ii)* equipment such as cash registers and display racks (long-term assets).

The basic journal entries to reflect the acquisitions of these types of asset resources are as follows:

(1)	Acquisition of Inventory	
	Merchandise inventory	X
	Accounts payable	X
(2)	Acquisition of Equipment	
	Equipment	X
	Due to equipment Suppliers	X

If cash is paid immediately for the acquisition of inventory or equipment, the transaction would be classified under category the receipt and payment of cash. Examining journal entry (1), the "merchandise inventory" account is a general ledger asset account that accumulates the total costs of all inventory items acquired for eventual sale to customers. In those companies that sell several products, a subsidiary inventory ledger would likely be maintained. This subsidiary ledger would contain a separate account for each inventory item. The use of individual inventory accounts within the subsidiary ledger enables a company's managers to know the quantity and cost balance of every inventory item. This information, which is not provided by the general ledger inventory account, is essential to management in planning the acquisitions of additional inventory product items and in analysing slow-moving inventory items. If a company has a large number of suppliers from whom it purchases inventory on credit, detailed managerial information regarding the dollar amounts owed to each creditor is essential so that future cash disbursements can be planned. In addition, for those creditors offering cash discount terms such as 2/10, n/30, the company needs information about the specific cash discount terms of each creditor so that the various creditors can be paid within the allowed discount periods.

The accounting information system can provide management with data concerning accounts payable liabilities through the utilisation of an accounts payable subsidiary ledger. Within this subsidiary ledger, a separate account is maintained for each creditor, indicating such things as the dollar balance due and cash discount terms available.

In journal entry (2), the general ledger "equipment" account is debited for long-term asset acquisitions. To provide management with detailed information about each piece of equipment an equipment subsidiary ledger containing a separate account for each equipment item can be used.

2. *Incurrence of operating expenses:* The basic journal entry to recognise a company's operating expenses is shown below:

Operating expenses	
Wages expense	X
Payroll taxes expense	X
Rent expense	X
Advertising expense	X
Utilities expense	X
Wages payable	X
Taxes payable on wages	X
Rent payable	X
Advertising payable	X
Utilities payable	X

To determine the operating expenses for "wages expense" and "payroll taxes expense" as well as well as the liabilities for "wages payable" and " taxes payable on wages," detailed payroll data would have to be maintained within a company's accounting information system. A payroll subsidiary ledger containing a separate account for each employee would likely be used. The accounting information system must accumulate within this subsidiary ledger specific payroll data about every employee for both tax and financial statement reporting purposes. In a manufacturing firm, the accounting information system must be designed to distinguish between production wages and non-production wages. Regarding production wages, a further distinction is necessary between the wages of direct labourers and indirect labourers. The wages earned by non-production employees, on the other hand, are recognised as operating expenses of the period in which they are incurred. Because of the large volume of computations often required in payroll, computerised payroll processing is a tremendous time saver.

The expenses recorded for rent, advertising and utilities are reflective of typical operating efforts in carrying out a company's business activities. The month-end dollar balance of the advertising expense account, for example, would likely be of interest to a company's marketing manager. By relating the balance of this account to the company's month-end sales account balance, the marketing manager has a basis for evaluating the effectiveness of various advertising endeavours.

3. *Sale of product and services*: A merchandising firm (such as a hardware or clothing store) sells a *tangible* product to its customers, whereas a service organisation (such as a law firm or medical clinic) sells an *intangible* product. Presented here are the basic journal entries to reflect the revenue-earning functions of (1) a merchandising firm and (2) a service organisation (in our example, a law firm)

(1)	Merchandising firm	
	accounts receivable	X
	Product sales revenue	X
	Cost of merchandise sold	
	Merchandise inventory	X
(2)	Service Organisation	
	Accounts receivable	X
	Legal services revenue	X

If cash is received immediately at the time merchandising firms or service organisations perform their revenue-earning functions, the revenue recognition transactions would be classified under the receipt and payment of cash. Several detailed records supporting a merchandising firm's journal entries that reflect its product sales are maintained within the firm's accounting information system. To provide credit and collection department manages with information regarding the dollar balance owned to the firm by each credit customer, an accounts receivable subsidiary ledger could be used. The total of individual customer account balances within the subsidiary ledger should equal the total of the general ledger accounts receivable account. Many companies that have a large volume of credit-sales transactions use computers to maintain their accounts receivable subsidiary ledgers. Once a week, for example, credit-sales transactions of a company together with customer payments can be recorded by the EDP subsystem's computer to update the accounts receivable subsidiary ledger. In addition, the computer can be programmed to prepare a weekly accounts receivable against analysis and customer's monthly billing statements. The merchandising firm can also maintain a product sales subsidiary ledger to support the various *credits* to its general ledger product sales revenue account. This subsidiary ledger might include such detailed information as sales by product lines, sales by individual salespersons, and sales by regions of the country. These types of sales information would be extremely vital to the firm's marketing managers in evaluating prior periods' sales activities and in forecasting future sales.

The second journal entry illustrated for the merchandising firm assumes the use of a *perpetual* inventory system, whereby the cost of merchandise sold expense account and the merchandise inventory asset account are updated at the time of each sales transaction. Separate detailed subsidiary ledgers can be maintained within the accounting information system to support the cost of merchandise sold and the merchandise inventory general ledger accounts. The cost of merchandise sold subsidiary ledger would include detailed cost information about each product item sold. This information, as well as information from the product sales subsidiary ledger, enables accounting employees to analyse the profit margins of the firm's various product lines. With the foregoing information available, the firm's marketing managers can better plan their company's future sales mix of specific products by emphasising those product lines having the largest profit margins.

As discussed previously, a subsidiary inventory ledger provides important information for planning the acquisitions of additional inventory product items and for analysing slow moving inventory product items.

Since a law firm does not sell a tangible product, its journal entry to reflect earned revenue would include only a *debit* to the accounts receivable account and a *credit* to the legal services revenue account. For those service organisations that bill customers for work performed, the use of accounts receivable subsidiary ledgers would provide them with important information regarding the dollar balance owed by each customer. In a service organisation that provides a variety of services, a subsidiary ledger to support the organisation's general ledger revenue account can provide useful information for managers. For example, the law firm's subsidiary ledger relating to its legal services revenue general ledger account would contain specific information about the firm's earned revenues from each of its many legal services. By examining this subsidiary ledger, the partners of the law firm are able to analyse the types of legal services that are earning the greatest revenues.

4. *Receipt and payment of cash:* Many business have cash receipts from two major types of transactions:
   (1) cash sales and
   (2) collections of accounts receivable from previous credit sales.

The basic journal entry to reflect cash receipts from these two types of business transactions is as follows:

(i) Cash Receipts

Cash
Product sales revenue
Accounts receivable

As discussed previously, subsidiary ledgers can be maintained for each of the general ledger accounts (*i.e.*, product sales revenue and accounts receivable) *credited* in the preceding journal entry.

It is quite common for most companies to make cash payments based on previously incurred liabilities. Therefore, the following journal entry is representative of an organisation's cash payment activities.

(ii) Cash Payments

Accounts payable	X	
Due to equipment suppliers	X	
Taxes payable on wages (separate account would be used for FICA taxes paid, withholding taxes paid, etc.)	X	
Rent payable	X	
Advertising payable	X	
Utilities payable	X	
Cash		X

Each of the *debits* is to a liability account, indicating a reduction in the liability as a result of making a cash payment. For any of the liability accounts in which there is a large volume of transactions, a subsidiary ledger providing detailed information about the individual transactions affecting the account can be maintained.

Current information regarding a company's cash account balance is very important to management. In those organisations having a finance subsystem separate from accounting, the finance managers are responsible for their company's cash planning. Cash planning involves a projection of the future *sources* of cash and the future *uses* of cash. Following a company's cash planning activities, the cash account should be monitored quite closely by the finance managers. This monitoring of cash enables the finance managers to ascertain whether the actual cash activities are in line with the original cash planning projections.

If, for example, the cash account balance is becoming too large, the finance managers should examine possible investment opportunities for this excessive cash. Because the build up of cash within an organisation's checking account does not contribute to a positive rate of return on assets, the finance managers may want to consider investing excessive cash in more productive assets such as marketable securities. On the other hand, should the cash account balance become too small, a company may find it difficult to meet some of its liabilities that are coming due. Consequently, the finance managers will have to investigate possible sources of cash to avoid being delinquent in paying many liabilities. If an unanticipated capital acquisition becomes necessary, a heavy drain on a company's cash balance can result. To obtain the needed cash for the purchase of an expensive piece of equipment or other long-term asset, the finance managers may want to consider issuing bonds or selling additional stock.

Step 3: Posting business transactions from the journal to the general ledger and determining individual account balances.

Within an accounting system, a *general ledger* is a "book" containing detailed monetary information about an organisation's various assets, liabilities, owners' equity, revenues, and expenses. A separate account is established for each type of monetary item in a business firm. Without information available to both external and internal parties regarding the dollar balances of the firm's many assets, liabilities, and so on, successful business performance would be difficult because effective organisational decisions by external parties as well as internal parties are often based on specific account balance information. If the Alan Company's personnel manager, for example, wants accounting information concerning the total wages paid to employees after the first quarter of the year, he or she can refer to the page in the general ledger where the T account for wages expenses is located.

Step 2 of our accounting cycle involved the recording of business transactions in a journal. As was emphasised during the step 2 discussion, the journal provides a chronological record of all monetary events occurring in a company and indicates the accounts and amounts of the *debits* and *credits* for every business transaction. However, this journal fails to provide information regarding the individual dollar balance of the various financial items in a company. For example, if an organisation's managers wished to know the monetary balance of their company's accounts receivable asset, they would find this information in the specific T account maintained for accounts receivable in the general ledger. The journal, on the other hand, would not provide information regarding the actual dollar balance of accounts receivable. Rather, it would include only the various *debits* and *credits* that were recorded to the accounts receivable account during a specific time period. Therefore, to provide specific debits and credits recorded in the journal for accounts receivable must be transferred to the T account for accounts receivable in the general ledger through a process called *posting*. After the posting process is completed, the dollar balance of each general ledger account is determined.

For a company to have effective accounting information system, both a journal and a general ledger are necessary. The major benefit of a journal is that it provides a complete chronological listing of an organisation's monetary transactions. The journal tells the "complete story" of each business transaction, because the debit and credit parts of the transaction are shown together with a short explanation. However, without a general ledger, it would be rather difficult to determine the monetary balance of the individual accounts. The general ledger takes over where the journal leaves off by providing information regarding the dollar balances of an organisation's accounts. On the other hand, the general ledger does not disclose in one location the complete picture of an economic transaction. For example, the *debit* part of a transaction may be recorded in account number 200 of the general ledger, whereas the *credit* part of this same transaction may be recorded in account number 380. Functioning together in a company's accounting system, the journal and the general ledger provide relevant information about the monetary transactions that have occurred. The posting process provides a cross-reference between the two.

Preparing a Trial Balance

The time period over which companies prepare financial statements is determined by individual company policy. Because income taxes, both federal and state, must be paid to the government each year, a firm must prepare financial statements at least once a year as a basis for computing its tax liability.

When a company wants to prepare an income statement and a balance sheet all of the posting work must be finished so that the dollar balance of the various general ledger accounts, which are used in preparing the financial statements, can be determined. Assume that the Alan Company prepares monthly financial statements. Therefore, by the end of every month, all of the company's posting from its journal to the specific general ledger accounts should be completed. Upon completion of this posting work, each general ledger account balance is determined so that the company will know the dollar amounts of its individual accounts.

After these account balances are computed, a financial schedule called a trial balance is prepared. A trial balance lists all the general ledger accounts together with their end-of-period dollar balances. The trial balance facilitates:

1. the determination of whether the *total debit* and *total credit* account balances are *equal* and
2. the preparation of a company's financial statements.

The trial balance is just what its name implies, a "trial run" to ascertain the monetary equality of an organisation's accounts with *debit* and *credit* balances before the organisation's financial statements are formally prepared.

Other Document Uses

After finishing of the accounting cycle, a company's general ledger accounts have dollar balances within them which represent the account balances at the end of a specific time period. Before preparing the company's financial statements, however, certain adjustments may be necessary in the accounts. The need for adjusting journal entries within an accounting information system is based on two accounting principles:

1. the periodicity principle and
2. the matching principle.

The *periodicity* principles is derived from the word *periodic,* which means "occurring at regular intervals." In accounting, we assume that after a specific time period a company can accurately determine the dollar balances of its general ledger accounts and then prepare its financial statements. This process is commonly called adjusting and closing the books. At the end of a month, for example, when a business firm wants to prepare its income statement and balance sheet, the *periodically* principle assumes that the firm is at a specific "cut-off point" in its operating activities and can, therefore, provide relevant financial information to interested parties such as potential investors, creditors, and management.

These parties do not want to wait until the end of a firm's life to acquire financial information. They want it at specific times throughout the organisation's operating life. The periodicity principle enables a company to provide financial statements at specific time intervals prior to the company's termination. Furthermore, an organisation *should* attempt periodically to present to its financial statement users the most accurate income statement and balance sheet possible. This will give them reliable information for financial decision making regarding the organisation.

The objectives of the *matching* principles is the accurate computation of a company's net income as well as the accurate determination of dollar amounts for balance sheet accounts each time the company's financial statements are prepared. An organisation should recognise "revenues" when they have been *earned*, either by selling products or providing services to customers and "expenses" should be recognised upon receiving a *service* from someone or something. The matching principle attempts to relate accurately a company's *revenues earned to the expenses incurred* in earning those revenues prior to the preparation of the financial statements.

Basically, there are four major types of adjusting entries possible at the end of a company's accounting period, as described in the following list:

1. Adjusting entries for *accrued liabilities.*
   Example:

Wages expense	X
Accrued wages payable	X

2. Adjusting entries for *accrued assets.*
3. Adjusting entries for *prepaid assets.*
   Example:

Insurance expense	X
Prepaid insurance	X

4. Adjusting entries for *advanced payments by customers.*
   Example:

Advanced payment for services	X
Services revenue	X

These four examples of adjusting entries do not represent all the types of adjustments necessary or a business firm at the end of its accounting period. However, they do illustrate the adjusting-entry concept. At the end of an accounting period, when a company wants to prepare financial statements, it should strive for accuracy within the financial data. To achieve this accuracy, all the monetary activities during the accounting period should be examined and a determination made if anything has happened that is not presently recognised in the accounting records. If unrecorded economic events exist, adjusting entries are required. After all adjusting entries are recorded, an organisation's financial data have been updated. The resulting financial statements reflect a more accurate picture of the organisation's business activities for the accounting period, thereby providing better information for decision-making to the statements' users.

After a firm's adjusting entries are recorded in the journal, the debits and credits of these entries are *posted* to the correct general ledger accounts in the same manner as the regular business transactions recorded during the accounting period. Upon completion of the posting work, the updated monetary balances of those accounts affected by the adjusting journal entries are determined. Once this is done, a company's financial data are current for the preparation of its financial statements. Preceding the preparation of the income statement and balance sheet, however, is an *adjusted trial balance*. Because a trial balance is prepared after all business transactions during an accounting period are recorded and posted and each general ledger account balance is determined, the equality of total debits and total credits within the accounts is ascertained before the adjusting journal entries are recorded and posted. The purpose of preparing this second trial balance (called the adjusted trial balance) is to determine if the quality of debit and credit account balances still exists following the adjusting entry process.

Preparing Financial Statements from Adjusted Trial Balance

When the adjusted trial balance is finished and thus reflects the updated financial data, the financial statements can be prepared. The adjusted trial balance contains all the information needed for the preparation of the financial statements.

An organisation's revenue and expense accounts are *subdivisions* of the owners' equity accounts. The major reason for utilising separate revenue and expense accounts is to provide better information about a company's operating activities to management and other interested parties. Remember, however, that a business firm's net income or less belongs to its owner. Therefore, at the end of an accounting period, a company records and posts *closing entries* to eliminate its individual revenue and expense account balances and transfer the net income into the owner's equity account. Because revenue and expense accounts are subdivisions of the owner's equity accounts, whose balances are closed at the end of an accounting period, revenue and expense accounts are often called *temporary accounts.* On the other hand, balance sheet accounts are not subdivisions of any other business accounts whose balances are closed at period-end, and are thus often called *permanent accounts* or *real accounts.*

CHAPTER 9

Company Image and Art of Effective Presentation

Scenarios and Schemes

Every company employee presents a particular image of that company. Let us assume that you are describing a movie you have recently watched to a friend or you are telling your parents about a new watch that you want to buy. You may be making a presentation in class, facing a job interview or describing the benefits of your product to a customer. In all these situations, what is common is that you are attempting to present something—an idea, your own self or your product. "But isn't that effective communication" you may well ask. Quite right the basic concepts are the same, after all presentations are all about communicating, however, in the business environment of today they need to be understood in depth.

Let us accompany O.P. Sharma from an advertising agency who is going to make a presentation to his client.

We asked O.P. what was the objective of the presentation and how was he going to go about it.

"Well, I have taken over this account a week ago from my ex-colleague and I have to present the new advertising campaign designed by us for them. I have prepared a few transparencies, but most of my presentation will be without any aids. I am quite comfortable taking spontaneously," he replied.

We were most impressed with O.P.'s confidence, so we followed him to witness this presentation in action and at the same time learn something in the process.

On reaching the client's office we met Balu, the Brand Manager who took us to a large conference room, well equipped with an Overhead Projector, Slide Projector, Screen, boards, TV, VCR and cassette player.

When O.P. asked Balu, "Aren't we having it in your cabin?" he was informed that the Vice President Sales, Marketing Manager and both the Zonal General Managers were also to be present for the presentation.

"But!" exclaimed O.P., "you didn't tell me about this. Anyway I will manage."

Soon the audience, looking formidable, took their seats and the presentation began.

O.P. greeted everyone and introduced himself to the managers and then told them he was going to talk to them about the new campaign.

"Just a minute," said the Vice President Sales, "could you first tell us about the earlier campaigns. I am new to this company but I do remember a campaign of two years ago which was very popular with the consumers and when it was changed, the sales had dropped. Why was that changed?"

O.P. looked visibly shocked at this question and responded by explaining that he too was new to this assignment and hence was not familiar with the earlier campaigns. However, Balu intervened and answered the query.

O.P. continued and to display his first transparency switched on the OHP. Well, nothing happened. The OHP did not work even though O.P. tried all knobs and switches. Finally, Balu got up to call their maintenance person and then there was a long pause with the managers grimacing and looking at their watches.

Finally the General Manager asked O.P., "Have you done any specific research to come up with the campaign theme?"

O.P. vigorously nodded his head and told them that a study was conducted before finalising on the theme and positioning of the product.

They asked O.P. to share the study findings with them. O.P. looked through his papers and had to tell them that he was not carrying the study findings but would surely send it across to them later.

After some wait, the OHP was repaired and the presentation started. O.P. went through the first transparency and then had to look through all the others for the second one. He then rushed through his presentation throughout which he continued to address only Balu. Soon, the Marketing Manager and the Vice President Sales got involved in their own separate discussion. One of the GMs looked at his watch and drummed his fingers on the table impatiently while the other was shuffling through his papers.

Finally, as the presentation drew to a close and O.P. asked everyone to comment on the new campaign. The General Managers said that they were not too excited about the campaign and had no idea why such a theme had been suggested.

However, they all felt that the agency should give it some more thought and come back for another meeting.

Once these managers left, Balu asked O.P., "How come you are not carrying the report on the study conducted? The person who used to come before you always carried a copy of documented background information which could be circulated to all present. I wish you had seen the presentation yesterday by Mediatrackers. It was so smooth and captivating. In fact, we had slotted twenty minutes for it but spent close to forty-five. Anyway there is nothing that can be done now. Maybe for the next presentation it would be a good idea for you to also bring along your boss."

What is your opinion of the manner in which O.P. went about his presentation, and what do you feel went wrong?

Let us examine this from the beginning.

O.P. went for the presentation without knowing the profile of his audience.

He could not build on the presentation objectives or give the required background material.

He had not even checked the equipment as a result of which, he had to waste a lot of time.

He had not even arranged his transparencies in order. Then to top it all our friend was only interested in making the presentation to Balu and ignored the other senior managers which naturally resulted in them losing total interest.

Imagine the repercussions of this presentation and its impact on future business between the client and O.P.'s agency.

Preparing for an Effective Presentation

So let us draw out the elements that make a presentation interesting, informative and effective in terms of gaining the desired response.

(i) Identifying the target audience.
(ii) Understanding and framing the objective of the presentation.

(iii) Researching the subject by consulting books, meeting experts or others.

(iv) Preparing the structure of the presentation, *i.e.*, the opening, the main points and the close or conclusion.

(v) Rehearsing the presentation prior to the final one to check for

- content
- structure
- time taken
- any issue that may require special attention

(vi) Checking the location of the presentation so as to

- understand the seating arrangements
- ensure all electrical connections are working
- arrange all media aids that you may need like a slide projector, over head projector, mikes, TV and VCR and ensure that they are in order and they are functioning.

(vii) Reconfirming the presentation venue and time with all concerned.

(viii) Reconfirming the size of the audience and their profile as well as roles in decision-making.

(ix) Plan and arrange all material you may require for the presentation

- your slides or transparencies or flip charts
- material to be given to the audience
- any aids like brochures, photographs or video films

(x) Budget for the presentation in terms of

- Material
- Manpower, *i.e.*, any other people required, any specialists
- Venue
- Transport

We asked Rajan Bhansalkar, a senior manager in an organisation selling office automation products, how he goes about making presentations to his clients.

"You see, for an effective presentation, preparation is critical. In this preparation, I try to answer questions like:

— who is the presentation to be made to
— what is the purpose and objective of the presentation
— where is the presentation to be made
— what is the duration
— what material or media aids are required

Once I have planned all this, I then need to concentrate on the delivery of the presentation to the audience or 'how to do it.' To begin with I try to make the opening very interesting and memorable because this is the time to win or lose the audience. In fact, the endeavour should be to keep the audience interest alive throughout the presentation. This speaks of the skills of the presenter." he added.

"But Rajan, just being a good presenter is not sufficient. What about your contents? Suppose your presentation was very complex or had a lot of numbers, how do you present it then?" we asked Rajan.

"That is the next important step in presentation delivery— the content. The matter of the presentation should be such that it answers all pertinent questions, given the pre-defined objective. One must make sure that the presentation helps the audience in either taking a decision or being informative for future decisions. Any figures or claims in the presentation should be given along with the source of information so that it is credible to the audience."

"And, to make even the boring contents interesting, one can make use of a lot of examples. Or else, statistics and numbers can be presented graphically to retain audience interest. Cartoon characters are also often used to enhance interest levels and ensure information retention in particularly dry presentations."

Well, we get your point Rajan. So if one was to inform an audience that an 'X' number of blood vessels are there in a human body, this same information can be presented more interestingly by saying that if you were to join all the blood vessels in the human body, end-to-end, it can be wrapped eight and a half times around the globe.

A business presentation, therefore, can easily be evaluated on its effectiveness and interest generating ability on the three main parameters:

(a) Presentation Contents

One needs to evaluate certain aspects of the contents or the matter that is to be presented, keeping in mind the audience profile and the objective of the presentation:

- — Will the presentation answer all the questions in your mind?
- — Are the facts presented sufficient and are supported by sources?
- — Does the presentation help you to take decisions or establish a future course of action?
- — How is the presentation structured? Is it too long and repetitive that it becomes boring or is it too short?
- — Are the contents of the presentation well structured to allow it to flow smoothly?
- — Is the opening of the presentation made interesting with an example, a visual, an interesting fact, humour?
- — Is the close of the presentation interesting enough to be remembered?

We were attending a presentation being made on Media Planning to Advertising professionals. As the speaker took his position he said, "I first want you to answer few pertinent questions that you should know as media planners." He then proceeded to ask about ten questions which made the audience sit up and wait very eagerly for answers to them which he tied in with the rest of his presentation. The result was that for the next hour and a half the attention of all was riveted to the speaker.

When we talk of making the opening and close of the presentation interesting, it is so because research shows that audiences generally remember what is said in the beginning and the end more. When stated graphically, the following picture emerged.

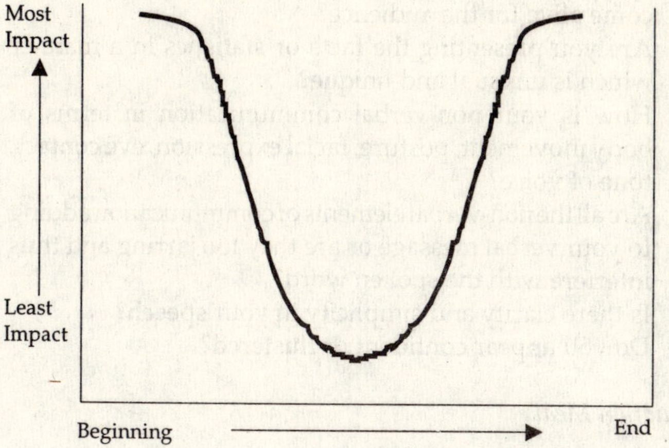

Audience Memory Curve

Therefore, an opening should be effective and brief. The close should have a conclusion or a summary of the presentation rather than the use of phrases like, "That's all I have to say" or "that's about it."

(b) Presentation Skills

Presentation skills are critical because a person can through his style make the presentation interesting or boring. There are quite a few speakers who make us want to listen to them carefully. They create such a high level of interest in the subject, that the audience sit up and look forward to listening to them.

Can you think of some speakers like that? A political leader? A faculty? A colleague or superior?

Observe them carefully next time and try to understand what specific presentation skills do they possess.

Typically you must keep in mind the following factors while making a presentation:

— Is every member of the audience involved?
— Is the audience comfortable with the flow and pace of the presentation?
— Are you presenting the points crisply or is the presentation too rushed or too slow?

— Are your examples illustrative? Can they make the issue come alive for the audience?
— Are you presenting the facts or statistics in a manner which is unusual and unique?
— How is your non-verbal communication in terms of body movement, posture, facial expression, eye contact, tone of voice?
— Are all the non-verbal elements of communication adding to your verbal message or are they too jarring and thus interfere with the spoken word?
— Is there clarity and simplicity in your speech?
— Do you appear confident or flustered?

(c) Presentation Media

People in an audience have a limited attention span. Even if they are interested in what you are saying, a part of their consciousness is thinking of something else and if they are bored, this tendency increases.

So what is it that you can do to hold their attention?

The answer lies in the use of audiovisual aids during the presentation.

The commonly used visual aids for business presentations and the imperatives for each are:

Over Head Projectors

— To use this media, the presenter should keep in mind that he does not obstruct the view on the screen by his own position.
— The OHP can be used for on line additions or changes during the presentation.
— The size of the letters on the transparencies should be readable.
— Coloured pens can be used to enhance the impact.
— The transparencies should not have too much matter on them that they appear cluttered or too little that they are too bare.
— To add impact and keep the attention of viewers focussed on the point of discussion, a presenter may mask other points on the transparencies.

Slide Projectors

- These can add to a presentation's visual appeal by high quality reproduction of photographs of let's say products, markets.
- To use this aid the presenter needs to switch off all lights in the room for better picture quality.
- The slides should preferably be multi-coloured, which makes them visually more appealing.
- While preparing the slides for presentation, one must be very thorough about the contents because no on line changes can be made in these.

TV/Video

- The presenter needs to check and adjust the sound and picture quality.
- The story on video should be cued at the starting point before the presentation so that one does not waste time looking for what is to be shown, and in the process loosing audience interest.
- To maximise audience attention and to enhance visual impact all lights should be dimmed.
- The presenter must, introduce and sum up the story so as to give it a context.

Flip Charts/Posters

- Mostly prepared by hand, these serve the purpose if the audience is small.
- Posters are mostly pre-prepared and can be used creatively, depending on the theme.
- Flip charts allow the flexibility of on line use.

Raju Krishnan, from the Corporate Planning division of an organisation tells us that, "in the use of the audiovisual media one must make sure that all these aids assist a presenter. Therefore, the timing to display these has to be very appropriate. Also, the choice of which aid to use must be based clearly on the content, objective, time duration of the presentation and the audience profile."

We asked him to explain this with some example and Raju narrated the following incident. "As part of our Corporate image building exercise, we had adopted a few villages in Haryana. The development of these were our responsibility. To educate people about issues such as sanitation, education for all etc., we decided to hold talks for them. The villagers were asked to gather at a central place in the village for these talks. However, the attendance was poor and many left while the address was still on. Seeing this, we did some rethinking and hit upon the idea of making a film on these issues. When this approach was used, the response received was much better and far more positive because the villagers were much keener on watching a film."

"Even in the film we used some popular faces from the Hindi screen and the theme used a lot of humour. This ensured total involvement and the message hit home strongly."

There is a lesson in the experience Raju has shared. Understanding your audience psyche, their background and likes / dislikes is critical to successful presentations.

Let us summarise the learning from this chapter.

- Presentations are an important communication in the new business environment.
- To make a presentation, the presenter should be well prepared about what is to be said, to whom, why, when, where and how.
- Presentations can be evaluated on the basis of:

  — Presentation Content
  — Presentation Skills
  — Presentation Media

- Presentation contents need to focus on the objectives and have to account for audience profile.
- Key skills for effective presentations include: ability to involve audience, use of examples and confidence.
- Commonly used visual aids, which enhance impact of presentations include:

  — Overhead projectors
  — Slide projectors
  — TV/Video
  — Flip charts/Posters

Art of Written Communication

How often has it happened that when you begin to write a letter, you just keep staring at the blank page in front of you, wondering what to write?

Or you are supposed to submit a report on your activities to your boss, and you think, "How should I phrase it? Should I write about the sales trends, competition or dealer activities?"

These are situations which each one of us has probably faced when trying to put words, thoughts or information on paper, be it in personal or professional life. But what does written communication involve in a business environment and what is its importance? Does business writing require any skills?

In this chapter we will attempt to answers these questions.

Can we start by posing a problem to you? Understand the following situation and try to frame a reply to it.

Your organisation has set up a new office in Bombay, after a successful run in Madras and Bangalore. You deal in office maintenance services, which cover providing manpower and material for day to day maintenance of offices. You save your clients this headache for a small premium. Please frame a short letter of introduction which will get the reader interested in your service and make him call you for more details and a round of discussions.

Now review your letter on the following parameters.

— the layout and format
— the use of language
— does it serve the purpose
— how soon does it get to the point
— does it create interest/motivate the reader to respond
— is it professional and organised

Did you really think of these issues, while framing your letter? Perhaps not! And if you really work at the purpose this letter is supposed to serve, you will understand that the language, layout and proposition can actually bring down the effectiveness, thus costing business. But let us discuss these specific issues in the chapters that follow.

Importance of Written Communication

We spoke to Aditya Rajramani, a Sales Manager of an organisation manufacturing fast moving consumer goods. He said, "when I had joined the company as a Sales Representative, fifteen years ago, I was a very high achiever. My territory was doing well. Then all of a sudden the sales dropped. It was because the competition had become active in my area. In spite of repeatedly telling my Marketing department to give us some support, nothing happened and we lost major business to competition. I was extremely disheartened and raised this issue in our conference. I was asked by the Sales Manager for copy of those requests. I had to tell him that all the requests had been on the phone or personally. He looked shocked and told me that since nothing was on record, no action could be taken. It was he who then sat with me and explained that unless every such inter-department communication is documented, there would be a lack of information for my superiors, resulting in their inability to take any follow-up action. Also, a written note is more difficult to overlook or ignore. From that day on, I have made sure that all interactions, within the company or with customers or dealers are comprehensively documented by myself or my subordinates."

Gayatri, Guest Relations Manager at a Hotel had more to add. "Written communication is an important tool to keep in touch with your customers in order to be able to give them a personalised service. In fact, in the recent past, one of our clients had booked our conference facilities and had asked for some additional equipment which our Salesperson had agreed to arrange for. However, our salesperson had to go on an unplanned leave and we had no idea that something had been committed to the client. On the day of the conference, when the client did not find the additional equipment he was livid and that was the last business interaction we had with them. Therefore, in order to avoid such situations, we now insist on confirming in writing to our clients all that was discussed verbally and also keep a copy of all the correspondence for our own record."

Hence we can now put down the reasons for the importance assigned to business writing as:

— What is in writing is on record and cannot be ignored.

— The written document can help provide information and confirmation of all verbal discussions held.
— It helps in generating prospective customers through introductory letters or mailers.
— Written communication in the form of a letter, fax, telex, etc., helps in saving travel time and costs.
— To a customer, a written note helps in taking a decision. For example, a proposal submitted will carry all information on the offer being made and the terms and conditions and thus facilitating in the decision-making process.
— Corresponding regularly with customers helps in maintaining them and creating a positive image about you and your organisation. For example, large hotels, boutiques or stores, credit card companies and magazines send regular information, greeting cards and discount coupons to their customers.

Elements of Business Writing

Let us for our purpose consider Business writing as having two essential elements

- Letters
- Reports

And we shall also cover "Resume Writing" for our benefit.

Business Letters

Consider the letter below:

> Gp. Capt. Tawakley (Retd.)
> 111, Aurobindo Apartments
> Alipur Avenue
> Alipur Road
> Calcutta
>
> Sub. : Complaint of Refrigerator
> Ref. : Your letter of 10.8.94
>
> Dear Sir,
>
> We have received your letter of 10.8.94, complaining about the refrigerator that you had purchased from our company branch office in Calcutta about a month back. We have checked with them and were informed that they have not been notified by you regarding the complaint till date, even though you have stated in your above referred letter that you had called them up regarding the matter last month.
>
> You may now please contact them for this complaint in our Calcutta office only.
>
> Yours Sincerely,
>
> For Superkool Refrigeration Systems

If you were the customer receiving this response to your complaint from a company, how would you have felt? Does it build the reputation or image of the company in your mind?

Does it give you any help or reassurance? Has it given the customer an indication of a course of action or given the name of the contact person and phone number in Calcutta office? Is it indicative of personalised service? Does it even appear to have been written correctly?

On carefully examining this, we find that the letter could be reworded in the following manner:

Superkool Refrigeration System
1010, Himalaya Bhawan,
Tolstoy Marg
New Delhi
13th August 1994

Gp. Capt. (Retd.) R.N. Tawakley
111, Aurobindo Apartments
Alipur Avenue, Alipur Road
Calcutta

Dear Sir,

Sub. : Complaint of Refrigerator Model 2001
Ref. : Your letter dated 10-8-94

We are in receipt of your letter of 10-8-94 regarding the cooling problem in our refrigerator model No. 2001. We appreciate your bringing this to our notice as also the delay in service from our Calcutta office.

In order to process the same efficiently and quickly we have initiated the following from our end:

(a) Your complaint letter along with action recommended has been sent to Mr. Jajwade, Service Manager in our Calcutta office (copy enclosed).

(b) As per information received by us on telex, the Service Engineer, Amit Biswas will visit you on 16th August, 1994 to rectify the problem.

(c) In case you need to speak to either Mr. Jajwade or Mr. Biswas, they are available from 9.00 am to 10.30 am at the following address:

Superkool Refrigeration Systems
Ashoka Building
Park Street, Calcutta
Phone No. 245389/245390

(Contd.)

Mr. Biswas will call you up to confirm your availability on 16th August '94.
We regret the inconvenience caused due to the delay in service from our end. In case of any future needs, please feel free to write to us.

Thanking you,

Yours Sincerely
For Superkool Refrigeration Systems

Anil Sreedharan
Manager Customer Service

CC : Mr. Jajwade/Amit Biswas
Encl. Copy of note sent to Calcutta office

Compare the two letters and examine what are the changes that have been made in the second one.

When writing a business letter the following issues must be kept in mind:

1. The language used in the letter
   — Are the words used simple and clear
   — Is the style and tone pompous or courteous and formal
   — Is the message structured logically
   — Are the sentences too long and confusing or crisp and clear
2. The contents of the letter
   — Is the opening paragraph relevant and makes the reader go through the complete letter
   — Is the letter addressing the relevant issues precisely and clearly
   — Is the conclusion suggesting that next course of action and is it formal and non-pleading
   — Is the close appropriate

3. The structure of the letter
   — Is the date mentioned
   — Is the name and address of the receiver spelt correctly
   — Does the letter have an introductory paragraph followed by main body and then a concluding paragraph
   — Does the letter close with the name/designation of the signatory

Therefore the elements of any business letter are:

(a) Address
Avoid lengthy geographical details. Spell the name and designation of receiver correctly. Type close to the left margin.

(b) Salutation
In situations when you know the receiver personally or well, use of informal salutations like, 'Dear Ajay' is acceptable. In a business like situation a more formal 'Dear Mr. Wahi' or 'Dear Sir' is more appropriate.

(c) Subject (optional)
A specific topic of the letter, not too broad or lengthy, should be given to give a context to the letter.

(d) Opening
(Get to the point and state the objective). The opening paragraph should give the reader a reason to read further.

(e) Body
Address the relevant issue by stating the problem and also the solution. For example, in a letter of offer state why your product is the ideal solution for a customer's problems through a feature, advantage, benefit analysis, a cost benefit statement and a competitive analysis.

(f) Conclusion
It must suggest the next action recommended or being taken when requesting for an appointment in an introductory letter or a direct mailer. Do not leave the

action inconclusive like "Kindly confirm the time and date of meeting whenever convenient.' More appropriate would be "Kindly confirm if a meeting on Tuesday the 14th morning or Wednesday the 15th afternoon at our office is convenient to you.'

(g) *Close*

As per the situation use a formal close like 'Yours Sincerely For XYZ Ltd.' or an informal close such as, 'Cordially,'. Enclosures should be mentioned as also the people to whom a copy of the letter is being given.

We were speaking to Sumati Desai, a Public Relations professional and she said "in business writing or even personal writing, we all face a writer's block, which results in questions like 'what do I write?' or 'how should I put it?' or 'where do I start?' To avoid this, it is advisable that one makes a point-wise structure of the matter to be written."

"What kind of a structure should it be Sumati?," we asked.

"In a structure, clearly state the objective of the communication, be it a report or a letter. You must know what do you want to achieve by writing this—inform, persuade, clarify, suggest, apologise etc. You must be clear about what information can be sent as an enclosure with your written communication—brochures, list of references, client list, etc."

"Is there anything else that is imperative?"

"Well, when I am to send a proposal or a letter to a customer, I like to know the receivers background. If he is a technical person then the communication needs to be technical in nature in order to appeal to him, but in case of a layman a simpler and more easily understandable message needs to be framed."

Business Reports

Yes, it is critical to be clear about the 'why', 'how' and 'who' for business writing but what happens in case of a report? Reports, as we know, are essentially a management tool. Even the most capable managers must often rely on other people to observe and collect information for them. This could be in the form of letters or memos and even pre-printed formats. Research reports of course are known to run into volumes, also.

Although much can be said, there are essentially three key components, common to all types of reports:

— accuracy of information
— format, style and organisation (must respond to the reader's needs)
— conclusions/recommendations (need to be drawn for course of action)

Let us first discuss the factors which effect format, style and organisation of a report.

Factor	*Possibilities*	*Implications for format, and organisation*
WHO originates it?	Voluntary reports prepared at writer's own initiative	Require plenty of introductory information to explain purpose of report
	Authorised reports prepared at the request of another person	Require less introductory material than voluntary reports; should be organised to respond to the reader's request
WHAT subject does it cover?	Sales reports, compensation policies, affirmative action plans, engineering proposals, research studies, progress reports	Presentation dictated by characteristics of subject (for example, detailed statistical information summarised in tabular format)
WHEN is it prepared?	Routine, recurring reports prepared on daily, weekly, monthly, quarterly, or annual basis and transitional	Require standard format that facilitates comparisons from one period to next; need relatively little background information
	Special, nonrecurring reports prepared in response to unique situations	Do not need standardisation, require plenty of background and transitional information
WHERE is it sent?	Internal reports prepared for use within the organisation	Can be relatively informal; written in memo or manuscript format
	External reports sent to people outside the organisation	Should be relatively formal in tone; written in letter or manuscript format

(Contd.)

Factor	*Possibilities*	*Implications for format, and organisation*
WHY is it prepared?	Informational reports providing facts	Organised around sub-topics
	Analytical reports providing analysis, interpretation, conclusions, and often arguments	Organised around conclusions/ recommendations or logical recommendations
HOW will it be received?	Receptive readers Skeptical or hostile readers	Arranged in direct order Arranged in indirect order

"Is there an appropriate way to make a report?" we wondered. To find an answer, we joined Romy and Mohit, Senior Marketing Professionals in a snack food company.

They were planning targets for the second half of the year. They explained to us that for this planning exercise they need reports from each Sales Representative on their market working, sales trends of different products covering pack sizes in each market, information on competition, impact of any promotional activity, dealer performance and outstanding reports.

Let us relate to you their conversation.

Romy: Mohit, just look at this report that your Nasik Sales Rep has sent. It is so thick and lengthy. I have no time to read the complete thing. Do you know briefly what this is all about?

Mohit: (Looking through the report): This fellow has sent so many figures, sales comparison of each pack size with competitor products and pack size, movement of stocks from each dealer and market and a comparison with last year period also. This is detailed but does not help us right now.

R: Has he atleast given any conclusions somewhere briefly or stated what was the response to the schemes given on Soya Chips? Other places gave us a good response on this scheme.

M: He hasn't mentioned what was the response to the scheme but is still talking about the scheme that he had suggested to us earlier. He says that would have been a better scheme to introduce in the market.

R: Well, does he have anything to say about competitor's activity?

M: (Looking upset) : All he has to say is that there are problems with a new competitor on prices and margin. No mention of this new competitor or his product, price and margins.

R: What is the use of this thick report when it is not helping us take the decision we need to. This person has wasted a lot of time and effort in writing a useless report and our time is wasted in trying to make head or tail of it. I think we should define the structure of a report for all our Sales staff to avoid this situation.

M: I think that's right. Otherwise we either get such detailed reports without any conclusion and analysis or very sketchy reports with important facts missing. I think the first thing that each report should have is an Executive Summary so that we get a snapshot of the complete report at a glance.

R: Yes, and each report should be in points and each point should be brief. Any data should not be given in a paragraph form, it is difficult to grasp it or analyse it, don't you think?

M: It would be better to put all data in a tabular form like that Search research agency does. The complete data is so easy to decipher and interpret that way. They even highlight the main points or key issues with a highlighter or print it boldly. That is really helpful in focussing on main points.

R: Their reports are undoubtedly good. I think we should also make it necessary for each report to have neat headings like Sales Trend, Market Working, Competition activity and so on and also at the end their recommendations, suggestions for support required. In fact, each representative should also make his action plan for the forthcoming month.

M: Yes, now a proper structure has emerged. I will send this immediately to all concerned so that it can be implemented right away.

On the basis of this conversation we can list out some important elements of effective report writing:

(a) Begin with an Executive Summary and provide a snapshot of the report.
(b) Make the report point-wise and brief.
(c) Tabulate all data, give an analysis and rationale for it.
(d) Highlight key issues.
(e) Make recommendations and suggestions for further support required from any other department.
(f) Make an action plan or suggest the future course of action.
(g) The report should be conclusive and comprehensive enough to help in decision-making.

It is not the quantity of the paper used to make the report, but the quality of the report and its ability to assist in taking a decision for future planning and action.

To achieve this it is important that the report is stated factually without any personal biases colouring it.

Resumé

What is a Resumé and why is it an important document for professionals?

A Resumé is a 'snapshot' of an individual giving information about his family, educational and professional background, his interests and achievements. The document can also cover career objectives, past track record and work towards establishing suitability for the position under consideration.

When asked why is a Resumé so important, Rajat, an upcoming professional says, "Afterall, the employer gets to know you only through your resumé. Based on this he decides whether he should meet you personally or not. The very purpose of the resumé is to gain an interview or an audience with the employer. Therefore, it is an important document which helps in creating that first impression about a person. Imagine if you send a hand-written, disorganised and untidy bio-data to an employer, what is the impression you are creating?"

Truly, the bio-data is the first hurdle in the selection process and can be the deciding factor in getting an audience with the employer.

So the question that comes to our mind is how do we find out what employers really look for in a resumé?

We spoke to specialists—*i.e.,* Placement consultants and Human Resource/Personnel Managers—people who go through thousands of resumés every year. They complained of the following problems:

- Too long—the resumé is not concise, relevant, and to the point.
- Too short or sketchy—the resumé does not give enough information for a proper evaluation of the applicant.
- Wordy—descriptions are verbose, with numerous words used for what could be said more simply.
- Too slick—the resumé appears to have been written by someone other than the applicant which raises the question of whether the qualifications are exaggerated.
- Amateurish—the applicant appears to have little understanding of the business world or of the particular industry, a lack revealed by including the wrong information or presenting it awkwardly.
- Poorly reproduced—the print is faint and difficult to read.
- Misspelt and ungrammatical throughout—the applicant lacks verbal skills important for the job and shows poor judgement in failing to have another person proof-read the resumé.
- Lacking a career objective—the resumé fails to identify the applicant's job preferences and career goals.
- Boastful—the overconfident tone makes the reader wonder whether the applicant's self-evaluation is realistic.

- Dishonest—the applicant claims to have expertise that he or she does not possess.
- Gimmicky—the words, structure, decoration or material used in the resumé depart so far from the usual so as to make it ineffective.

Let us now examine the bio-data given below:

NAME	:	SUSHIL KUMAR
DATE OF BIRTH	:	26-06-71
MARITAL STATUS	:	UNMARRIED
FATHER'S NAME	:	R. KUMAR
CONTACT ADDRESS	:	A-24, 1ST Floor Sarojini Naidu Marg, Delhi
CONTACT TEL. NO.	:	2278519

Educational Qualifications

Examination	*Institution*	*Year*	*Division*
Course in Sales & Marketing Management	NIS	1992-93	Result Awaited
Senior Secondary	CBSE	1989-90	II
Graduation	Delhi Univ.	1990-93	II

Extra Curricular Activities

Captain of school team in cricket and football

Experience

1½ years—Panex India Ltd., New Delhi, Sale of Electronic Typewriters

Sushil Kumar

Well, if you were an employer, looking for a Sales Professional with result-orientation, ambition and good communication skills how would you react to this bio-data?

- Does it give you sufficient information about the person's educational qualifications—which subjects has he studied in graduation or which university has he studied in?
  - For example—a background in commerce/economics may be more relevant than History for a sales job.
- His professional qualification, *i.e.*, the Programme in Sales & Marketing is for what duration; is it a diploma or a certificate or a degree?
  - Are all these qualifications well structured, *i.e.*, is the information given in chronological/reverse chronological order?
- What about the work experience? Should it not have been mentioned before extra curricular activities?
  - Does it tell you much about the nature of work or responsibilities handled by this person in Panex? When did he work for this company?
- How about the overall structure of the bio-data? Some matter is in capital letters while some is in smaller case, thus no continuity is maintained throughout.

From all this, what impression do you form of this individual? Certainly, not a positive one. And chances are that he may not get that interview call he was looking for.

A Resumé should have the following key elements:

(i) Personal Details:

— Name, Age and Address

— Family background

To be given in a manner that it adds value to you as a person. For example, belonging to a family of achievers/professionals adds to your credibility.

— Interests/Hobbies
Job related interests must be highlighted. For example, participating in debates, public speaking or dramatics could be a plus for many jobs.

— Membership of clubs/professional bodies
These could indicate professional or personal interests and lifestyle.

(ii) Educational Background:

— Schooling
The name of the school and scores/marks in boards should be mentioned. A lot of companies respond well to public school backgrounds.

— College
Name of College/University along with course and aggregate scores should be stated.

— Special achievements in school and college
Any prizes won, any specific participation in an event or leadership roles handled. For example, a school project that is taken up requires some organisational ability.

(iii) Work Experience:

— Cover all jobs. There should not be any unexplained time gaps

— Current job should be highlighted and description of nature of work, position, responsibilities should be given.

— Any accomplishments, growth, special achievements and contributions should be talked about.

— All this information should be stated in reverse chronological order, *i.e.*, start from current job and end with first job.

(iv) Career Objectives (optional)

— Should be specific and should cover both long-term and short-term plans.

— Should be tied in with the job being applied for.

(v) *Other Details:*

— References

— The people being referred to should know you professionally and not be personal friends.

— Languages known

It is a positive for a Sales & Marketing job.

— Additional skills that will aid you in the job applied for, *e.g.*, Knowledge of computers.

The key characteristics of a good resumé include:

— Neatness
— Simplicity
— Accuracy
— Honesty

Take a look at the chart below, which details some facts and fallacies about the resumé.

Fallacy :	The purpose of a resumé is to list all your skills and abilities.
Fact :	The purpose of a resumé is to kindle employer interest and generate an interview.
Fallacy :	A good resumé will get you the job you want.
Fact :	Hundreds of thousands of good resumés cross employers desks every working day.
Fallacy :	Your resumé will be read carefully and thoroughly by an interested employer.
Fact :	Your resumé probably has less than ten seconds to make an impression.
Fallacy :	The more good information you present about yourself in your resumé, the better.
Fact :	By including too much information, a resumé may actually kill the reader's appetite to know more.

Let us summarise the learning from this chapter

- Written Communication in a business environment is critical for purposes of maintaining a record and confirmation of verbal discussions.

- Most common forms of written communication in business are Letters, Proposals and Reports.
- When writing a business letter, the language used, the content, the structure and the background of the receiver should be considered.
- Elements of a business letter are the address, salutation, opening, main body, conclusion and the close.
- A business report should be written in a manner that it helps in decision-making or future planning.
- When preparing a business report, begin with an executive summary, present the information in brief points, tabulate and analyse data, give recommendations or suggest a course of action.
- A resumé is not meant to get you a job, but an interview.
- A resumé should have all relevant information like personal details, educational and professional qualifications, additional knowledge, achievements.

CHAPTER 10

Communication and Documentation: Export Management Procedures

I. Obtaining Documents Connected with Transport of Goods

Airway Bill (A W 13)/Air Consignment Note (ACN)

The receipt issued by an airline or its agent for the carriage of goods is called airway bill or air consignment note. It is issued in terms and conditions of the contract of carriage of goods. It is not a document of title and it is not issued in a negotiable form. It is the most important cargo document issued by a carrier or its authorised Cargo Agents. It combines several purposes.

Since the goods are delivered to the consignee (receiver) mentioned in the AWB after identifying himself as the party named in the airway bill as consignee/receiver and against payment of charges, if any (depending upon the terms of carriage, if the consignor (exporter) wants to retain control over the good until payment/commitment for payment is made for the goods, he should consign the goods in the name of a third party like foreign correspondent bank. This will serve dual purpose. Firstly the importer will not be in a position to take delivery of the goods unless he obtains the delivery order/documents from the foreign correspondent bank thus safeguarding the payment for the goods and secondly in case of difficulties/frustration of contract of sale, the exporter/banks handling the export documents have got better control over the goods.

- Documentary evidence of the conclusion of the contract of carriage;
- Proof of receipt of the goods for shipment;
- Freight bill

— Certificate of insurance (if carriers' insurance is requested by Shipper);
— Customs declaration;
— Guide to carriers staff in handling, despatching and delivering the consignment.

Since the goods reach the destination within the shortest time, usually on the same day or the next day, it becomes the duty of the seller to inform the buyer of the despatch of the goods by the use of telecommunication system to avoid unnecessary additional charges to the buyer.

Types of Airway Bill

An AWB shall be either an AWB referred to as an "Airline Air Waybill" with pre-printed issuing carrier identification or an AWB referred to as a "Neutral Air Waybill" without pre-printed identification of the carrier in any form.

Description and Distribution

The AWB is a non-negotiable document. It consists of three originals and six to eleven copies in case of an "Airline AWB" or of three originals and nine copies in case of a "Neutral AWB". Each part of an AWB set bears in the two top corners and in the lower right corner an AWB number composed of the three-digit carrier code number followed by a serial number of eight digits including a check digit placed in the extreme right hand position of the serial number. A sheet of identification labels with pre-printed AWB number—to be fixed on the pieces of cargo—may be attached.

The three AWB originals (Part 1, 2 and 3) bear on the reverse the conditions of contract and all have the same validity. The various parts of the AWB are disposed of as follows:

Original 3: Blue: (for shipper to be given to the shipper and to serve as:

(*a*) proof of receipt of the goods for shipment;
(*b*) documentary evidence of carrier's and shipper's signature to the contract of carriage.

Original 1: Green: (for issuing carrier) is retained by the carrier issuing the AWB for accounting purposes and to serve as documentary evidence of carrier's and shipper's signature to the contract of carriage.

Original 2: Pink: (for consignee) to accompany consignment to final destination and to be tendered to the consignee on delivery.

The other parts are copies of the originals, each to be used as indicated at the bottom. Not more than the following parts are removed from the AWB-set by the cargo agent:

(1) Original 3 (for shipper) (2) Originals 1 (for issuing carrier) where required by the airline whose Airway bill is issued (3) Copy 9 (for agent)

Validity and Duration of the Contract of Carriage

The validity of the carrier's contract of carriage starts when the AWB is executed, which is said to be when

The AWB is signed by the shipper, or on his behalf, and

It is signed by the carrier, or on its behalf by a cargo agent approved by the issuing carrier.

The validity of the carrier's contract of carriage expires when the consignment is delivered to the consignee stated on the AWB.

Responsibility of Completion

In accordance with the Warsaw Convention, the Hague Protocol and the carrier's conditions of carriage the shipper shall prepare the AWB. The shipper is responsible for the correctness of the particulars and statements relating to the goods which he inserts in the AWB or which are inserted on his behalf. The shipper will be liable for all damage suffered by the carrier or any other person by reason of the irregularity incorrectness or incompleteness of the said particulars and statements, regardless of whether the AWB is completed by himself, or on his behalf by the carrier or its authorised agent. With his signature, the shipper simultaneously confirms that he agrees to the Conditions of Contract as set forth on the reverse side of the AWB and to the Conditions of Carriage.

Completion of Air Waybill

The various boxes in the specimen AWB have been numbered to correspond with the numbers of the paragraphs below.

The purpose of these numbers is to illustrate the correct use of each box. They will not be found on the AWB. The issuing carrier referred to below is the airline whose AWB form is used.

The boxes shaded and with title are for carrier's use only.

The boxes shaded and without title are not used.

1. Airport of Departure

The IATA three-letter code of the Airport of Departure (or City when the airport is unknown) is inserted and it shall correspond to information in box 9.

IA-IB. Air Waybill Number

When not pre-printed, the IATA three-digit airline code number and Air Waybill serial number is inserted as described hereafter:

(a) the Air Waybill number placed in the upper left corner, in the upper right corner and in the lower right corner of all parts of the Air Waybill;

(b) the Air Waybill number consists of the issuing carrier's three-digit IATA airline code number and serial number of eight digits including a check digit placed in the extreme right hand position.

(c) the check digit is determined by using the unweighted Modulus 7 system, which divides the first 7 digits of the serial number by seven and uses the remainder for verification and as eight digit;

(d) the serial number is of the same size, similar style of type (font) and of the same boldness as the airline code number;

(e) a separating hyphen placed between the airline code number and the serial number is used for the number shown in the upper right corner and in the lower right corner;

In addition the space may be inserted in the serial number of the Air Waybill in order to show clearly the last four digits.

IC. Issuing Carrier's Name and Address

When not pre-printed, the issuing carrier's name and head office address corresponding to the airline code number shown in box IA is inserted.

ID. This Box Is Not Completed

IE. The space below the reference to the Carrier's Conditions of Contract, may be used to print other related statements as may be necessary to conform to national requirements.

2. Shipper's Name and Address

(*a*) The name, address and country of the shipper is inserted.
(*b*) The telephone or telex number may be inserted below.

3. Shipper's Account Number

This box is reserved for use by the issuing carrier at its option.

4. Consignee's Name and Address

(*a*) The name, address and country of the consignee is inserted.
(*b*) The telephone or telex number may be inserted below.

5. Consignee's Account Number—For Carrier Use Only

This box is reserved for use by the delivering carrier at its option.

6. Issuing Carrier's Agent, Name and City

(*a*) The name and location (Airport of city) of the carrier's IATA Cargo Agent entitled to the commission is inserted.
(*b*) When commission is payable to an IATA Cargo agent in the country of destination, the name and location (Airport or city) of such IATA Cargo Agent is inserted, preceded by the words Commissionable Agent.

7. Agent's IATA Code

The IATA code of the agent indicated in box 6 is inserted as follows:

(a) In non-CASS areas, the IATA seven-digit-code is inserted.
(b) In CASS areas, the IATA eleven-digit code is inserted.

8. Account Number

This box is reserved for use by the issuing carrier at its option.

9. Airport of Departure (Address of First Carrier) and Requested Routing

(a) The name of the airport of departure is inserted as the first entry and shall correspond to information.
(b) Any requested routing is inserted.

10. Accounting Information

Only accounting information required by the participating carriers is inserted such as:

(a) Payment by cash or cheque.
(b) Payment by an MCO is only acceptable in connection with baggage shipped as cargo; the MCO number and value of the Exchange Coupon in the currency of the Air Waybill is shown.
(c) For consignment returned because of non-delivery; the new AWB for the returning carriage shall have the original AWB number inserted in this box.

11A. To (By First Carrier)

The IATA three-letter code of the airport of destination of first transfer point (or city when the airport is unknown because the city is served by more than one airport) may be inserted.

11B. By First Carrier

The name of the first carrier (either full name or two-character code) is inserted.

11C. To (By Second Carrier)

The IATA three-letter code of the airport of destination or second transfer point (or city when the airport is unknown because the city is served by more than one airport) may be inserted.

11D. By (Second Carrier)

The IATA two-character code of the second carrier may be inserted.

11E. To (By Third Carrier)

The IATA three-letter code of the airport of destination or third transfer point (or city when the airport is unknown because the city is served by more than one airport) may be inserted.

11F. By (Third Carrier)

The IATA two-character code of the third carrier may be inserted.

12. Currency

(a) The IATA 3-letter currency code of the currency in which the rates are published is inserted.
(b) All amounts entered on the Air Waybill, other than those entered in the "Collect Charges in Destination Currency" boxes 33A to 33D shall be in the currency specified in this box.

13. Charges Codes—For Carrier Use Only

Only when an Air Waybill is transmitted by electronic means this box shall be completed using the following code:

CA — Partial Collect Credit — Partial
CB — Partial Collect Credit—Partial Cash
CC — All Charges Collect
CG — All Charges Collect by GBL
CP — Destination Collect Cash
CX — Destination Collect Credit

NC	—	Service Rate Prepaid Cash No Charge	
PC	—	Partial Prepaid Prepaid Credit	Cash—Partial Collect
PD	—	Partial Prepaid	Credit—Partial Collect Cash
PG	—	All charges prepaid by	GBL
PP	—	All Charges Prepaid Cash	
PX	—	All Charges Prepaid	Credit.

14A-14B. *Weight/Valuation Charge*

(*a*) The charges, entered into boxes 24A, 25A or 24B, 25B must be wholly prepaid or wholly collect respectively.

(*b*) The shipper or agent shall insert and "X", as appropriate, boxes 14A or 14B.

15A-15B. *Other Charges at Origin*

(*a*) The charges, entered into boxes 27A (if applicable), 26A or 27B, 28B, must be wholly prepaid or wholly collect respectively.

(*b*) The shipper or agent shall insert and "X", as appropriate boxes 15A or 15B.

(*c*) If the information contained in the boxes 14A, 14B, 15A and 15B is in conflict with the information in the boxes 24A, 24B, 25B, 27A (is applicable), 27B, 28A and 28B the latter shall take precedence.

16. *Declared Value for Carriage*

(*a*) The declared value for carriage as specified by the shipper is inserted.

(*b*) Where no value is declared, NVD is inserted.

17. *Declared Value for Customs*

(*a*) When the box is unshaded, the shipper or agent may declare and insert such customs value.

(*b*) When the box is unshaded and the shipper or agent does not declare a value for customs, the box shall remain blank.

18. Airport of Destination

The airport of destination of the last carrier (or city when the airport is unknown because the city is served by more than one airport) is inserted.

19A-19B. Flight/Date—For Carrier Use Only

These boxes are reserved for use by participating carriers at their option.

20. Amount of Insurance

(a) When the box is unshaded and only when and where the issuing carrier offers such a service, the amount to be insured shall be inserted.

(b) When the box is unshaded and the service is not provided by the issuing carrier or no insurance is requested by the shipper, the box shall remain blank.

21. Handling Information

Only handling information required by the participating carriers is inserted. The entry has been as clear and concise as possible.

(a) In the case of dangerous goods, either the words "Dangerous Goods as per Attached Shipper's Declaration" and the words "Cargo Aircraft Only" if applicable or the words "Dangerous Goods—Shipper's Declaration not required is inserted as the first entry. For "excepted" radioactive materials, and for dangerous goods which do not require a Shipper's Declaration see box 22.1 paragraph (d).

(b) Other handling information using Cargo-—IMP codes, where appropriate, may be inserted such as:

(1) marks and numbers which appear on the consignment and method of packing;

(2) name, address, telephone or telex number of any person to be notified of arrival of the consignment in addition to the consignee;

(3) name of documents to accompany the AWB such as "Shipper's certification for live animals;"
(4) special handling instructions that may be required;
(5) when not pre-printed, and when the AWB is issued in the USA, the statement: "These commodities licensed by USA for ultimate destination—Diversion contrary to USA law prohibited."

22A-22J. Number of Pieces/RCP

(a) The number of pieces for the applicable rating entry is inserted in box 22A.
(b) Where it is necessary to designate the point over which the sector rates are combined (RCP-Rate Combination Point), such point(s) is indicated by inserting the IATA three-letter city code as an additional line in entry.
(c) Where there is more than one entry, the total number of pieces is inserted below the "Total" line in box 22J.

22B-22K. Gross Weight

(a) The gross weight of the pieces for the applicable rating entry is inserted in box 22B.
(b) The tare weight of the unit load device, when applicable, is inserted as an additional line entry on the "X" rate class line.
(c) Where there is more than one entry, the total gross weight is inserted below the "Total" line in box 22K.

22C. Kg/Lb

The unit of weight (K or L) is inserted in the first rating line only.

22D. Rate Class

M. Minimum charge
N. Normal under 45 kg. (100lb) rate
Q. Quantity over 45 kg. (100lb) rate
C. Specific Commodity Rate
R. Class Rate (less than Normal Rate)

S. Class Rate (Normal Rate without quantity reduction and rate higher than Normal Rate)
U. Pivot weight and applicable pivot weight charge
E. Weight in excess of pivot weight and applicable rate
X. Unit Load Device (as an additional line entry with one of the above)

22E. *Commodity Item Number*

This box is completed as follows:

(a) When a specific commodity rate applies, the IATA item description number is inserted on the "C" rate class line;
(b) When a class discount rate applies, the percentage is inserted on the "R" rate class line (*e.g.* 50% discount shall be expressed as 50);
(c) When a class surcharge rate applies, the percentage is inserted on the "S" rate class line (*e.g.* 50% surcharge shall be expressed as 150);
(d) When a unit load device rate applies the ULD rate class type used is inserted on the "X" rate class line;

22F. *Chargeable Weight*

This box is completed as follows:

(a) The gross weight or volume weight, whichever is higher (rounded upto the next higher half kilogram or full pound) is inserted, provided that where a lower rate for a higher weight break applies which results in a lower total weight charge, the latter weight is inserted.
(b) When a minimum charge applies, no insertion is made on the 'M' rate class line.
(c) When a ULD rate applies, the applicable pivot weight is inserted on the 'U' rate class line.
(d) When a ULD rate applies, the weight in excess of the pivot weight is inserted on the 'E' rate class line.
(e) When a ULD rate applies, and a tare weight allowance is applicable, it is inserted on the "X" rate class line.

Service Code

A service code is inserted in the shaded column between box 22C and box 22D (where required by the issuing carrier). Such service code is only used to identify cargo products moving solely on the issuing carrier's service unless there is specific agreement with the participating carrier(s) to accept such product.

Codes for general use are as follows:

D — Door to door service
J — Priority service
P — Small package service

22G. Rate/Charge

The applicable rate or charge is inserted as follows:

(a) When a minimum charge applies, this charge in inserted on the "M" rate class line;
(b) When a normal rate applies, the applicable rate per unit of weight is inserted on the "N" rate class line;
(c) When a quantity rate applies, the applicable rate per unit of weight is inserted on the "Q" rate class line;
(d) When a specific commodity rate applies, the applicable rate per unit of weight is inserted on the "C" rate class line;
(e) When a discount rate applies, the discounted rate is inserted on the "R" rate class line;
(f) When a class surcharge applies, the surcharged rate is inserted on the "S" rate class line;
(g) When a ULD rating applies, the pivot weight charge or the rate per unit of weight, as applicable, is inserted on the "U" rate class line;
(h) When a ULD rating applies, the over pivot rate per unit or weight is inserted on the "E" rate class line;
(i) When a ULD discount applies, the applicable discount is inserted on the "X" rate class line. The applicable discount is preceded by a minus (–) symbol to denote a discount.

22H-22L. Total

(*a*) The total charge for each line entry is inserted in box 22H on the same horizontal line.

(*b*) When the entry in box 22G is preceded by a minus (–) symbol to denote a ULD discount, the minus symbol is to precede the applicable discount amount entered in the box.

(*c*) When there is more than one entry, the sum is inserted below the total line in box 22L.

22-1. ***Nature and Quantity of Goods (Incl. Dimensions or Volume)***

(*a*) The description of the goods comprising the consignment is inserted followed by the country of origin of the goods, if required, under the regulations of the country of destination.

(*b*) The measurements of the greatest length, greatest width and greatest depth (or volume), specifying the unit of measurement of any consignment rated under the provisions of "Low Density Cargo" or for any consignment consisting of "Valuable cargo" is inserted.

(*c*) When a ULD is used its identification code is inserted on the "X" rate class line.

(*d*) The shipper or his agent may enter the appropriate Harmonised Commodity Description and Coding System number;

(*e*) For "excepted" radioactive materials and dangerous goods for which as Shipper's Declaration is not required, the entry is as shown in section 6.3 and in accordance with instructions published in the IATA Dangerous Goods Regulations, section 8.

(*f*) For "Live Animals" the entry is as shown in section 6.3 and in accordance with the instructions published in the IATA Live Animal Regulations section 2.

Where the information required in Boxes 22A to 22L cannot be readily and fully shown on the AWB such information is included in an extension list.

Where such a list is prepared, the following information is inserted on the AWB:

— total number of pieces in box 22A
— total gross weight in box 22B
— weight unit in box 22C
— total charge in box 22H

A general description of goods, including total volume of the shipment, followed by the words "See Extension List" in box 22-I.

23. Other Charges

(*a*) Descriptions and amounts of individual charges and fees except weight/volume and valuation charge and tax are inserted, the total of which equals the sum entered in boxes 27A (if applicable), 27B, 28A and 28B. To indicate whether the charges accrue to carrier or agent, the following codes are used following the above codes and preceding the amounts:

A. Due agent C. Due cattier

(*c*) When the AWB data is not transmitted by electronic means, it is recommended that the above procedure is used provided that, when the charge code is not used, the pain language description shall clearly indicate to whom the charge accrues (*e.g.* due Carrier or due Agent).

(*d*) When a consignment is returned because of non-delivery, the new AWB for the returning carriage shall have all charges, which should have been but were not collected from the original consignee, inserted in this box.

24A-24B. Weight Charge (Prepaid/Collect)

(*a*) The weight/volume charge for air carriage is inserted and shall correspond to the total shown in boxes 22H or 22L.

(*b*) The weight/volume charge, the valuation charge and tax is inserted as either wholly prepaid or wholly collect.

25A-25B. Valuation Charge (Prepaid/Collect)

(*a*) The valuation charge for air carriage is inserted and shall correspond to the total shown in boxes 22H or 22L.

(*b*) The weight/volume charge, the valuation charge and tax is inserted as either wholly prepaid or wholly collect.

26A-26B. Tax (Prepaid/Collect)

(*a*) When this box is unshaded, any possible tax imposed by government or other official authority which is related to the weight/volume charge and valuation charge is inserted.

(*b*) The weight/volume and valuation charge and tax is inserted as either wholly prepaid or wholly collect.

(*c*) The details of the tax is not to be entered in box 23.

27A-27A. Total Other Prepaid Charges

"Other Charges" incurred at origin are inserted at origin as either wholly prepaid or wholly collect. Other charges incurred in transit and/or at destination shall be collected only provided that charges collect facilities are available in the country of destination; provided further that fixed government and/or airport authority taxes at transit points, known at origin, may be prepaid.

27A. Due Agent

This box is not to be used unless agreed locally.

28A. Due Carrier

The total of prepaid charges due to carrier specified in box 23 are inserted.

27B-28B. Total Other Collect Charges

"Other Charges" incurred at origin are inserted as either wholly prepaid or wholly collect. All collect charges incurred at origin, which are inserted here, must be treated as disbursements. Other charges incurred in transit and/or at destination shall be collected only; provided that charges collect facilities are available in the country of destination.

27B. Due Agent

The total disbursements due to agent specified in box 23 are inserted.

28B. Due Carrier

The total disbursements due to carrier specified in box 23 are inserted.

29A-29B. These boxes are only to be used to print special services which may be provided and to enter the charges related thereto.

30A. Total Prepaid

The total of all prepaid charges, *i.e.*, weight/volume charge, valuation charge, other charges due carrier and agent, and if applicable, tax(es) are inserted.

30B. Total Collect

The total of all the collect charges, *i.e.* weight/volume charge, valuation charge, other charges due carrier and agent, and if applicable, tax(es) are inserted.

31. Shipper's Certification Box

The signature of the shipper or his agent (printed, signed stamped), is inserted.

32A. Executed On (Date)

The date of execution of the AWB is inserted in the sequence of day, month and year. The month shall be expressed alphabetically, either abbreviated or in full.

32B. At (Place)

The name of the place of execution (airport or city of the AWB is inserted).

32C. Signature of the Issuing Carrier or Its Agents

The signature of the issuing carrier or its agent is inserted.

33. This Box is Not Completed

33A to 33D. Collect charges in destination currency—for carrier use only. The delivering carrier may insert in the appropriate box of Original 2 (for consignee) the currency conversion rate and amounts to be collected in destination currency.

This area shall only be used to include bar coded information.

Precautions as to Air Consignment Note (A.C. Note) Under L/C.

(i) Original A.C. Note should be submitted (marked as: Third original for the shipper).

(ii) A.C. note should be issued by airways companies either signed by them or by their agents.

(iii) A.C. notes should be made out in the name of the bankers of the buyers, as far as possible, unless otherwise called for in the L/C.

(iv) A.C. Note should be dated. It should be presented within 2 or 3 days from the date of shipment or within such time from the date of issue as stipulated in the credit.

(v) Particulars of shipment such as description of the goods, weight, quantity, etc. are to be stated in the A.C. Note.

(vi) A.C. Note should state whether freight has been "prepaid" or "to pay".

(vii) A.C. Note should state airport of discharge.

Postal Parcel Receipt (PPR)

Like the AWB, the Post Parcel Receipt (PPR) evidences merely the receipt of the goods to be exported to the buyer and is not a document of title. Since it is possible for the buyer to take delivery of the goods of those despatched in his name, it is advisable to send the post parcels in the name of a foreign correspondent bank rather than a buyer unless the export is under Letter of Credit calling for the despatch of goods directly in the name of the buyer and the exporter is sure that the other terms of the L/C shall be fulfilled. It shall be, however, noted that the banks in certain countries do not entertain/allow the goods to be despatched in their name without their prior approval. In such cases the necessary permission is required to be obtained in advance from such banks. Since customs facilities are not available at all post offices for smooth exportation of the goods, the postal authorities in India have permitted their officials to accept the goods for delivery to the foreign buyers/correspondent provided the original PP form has been signed by the Authorised Dealer/RBI. For the reasons stated earlier, Authorised Dealer/RBI will be reluctant to countersign the PP form if the goods are required to be despatched directly in the name of the buyer, unless the export documents pertaining to the goods are covered under L/C or the advance payment is received.

The important details as observed from the PPR are: its number and date, receiver's/sender's name and address, short description of the goods and amount of charges etc. The receiver/buyer can identify himself with the postal authorities abroad and obtain the delivery of the relative goods.

Precautions as to Post Parcel Receipts Under L/C

(*i*) They should be issued by Post Office.
(*ii*) They should evidence that parcels have been despatched.
(*iii*) They should evidence date of despatch.
(*iv*) They should evidence postage paid.

Bill of Lading (B/L)

Meaning. The Bill of Lading is a document issued by the shipping company or its agents acknowledging the receipt of goods mentioned in the bill for shipment on board of vessel, and undertaking to deliver the goods in the like order and condition as received, to the consignee or his order of assignee, provided, the freight and other charges specified in the Bill of Lading have been duly paid.

Format. Each shipping company has its own Bill of Lading printed in the new standardised aligned document format and as soon as the exporter obtains the mate receipt, he should prepare the Bill of Lading in the forms obtained from the shipping company. For procedure of preparing of Bill of Lading from Master Document-I please refer to Chapter Aligned Documentation System, A specimen of the Bill of Lading given at next page.

Preparation. The exporter should submit the complete set of Bill of Lading together with the mate receipt to the shipping company which would calculate the freight amount on the basis of measurement or weight as certified by the recognised Chamber of

Commerce. On payment of the freight, the shipping company returns the Bill of Lading duly signed and stamped by 25 paise adhesive stamps. If required the exporter can prepare additional copies of the Bill of Lading.

If the Foreign Trade contract provides for a Bill of Lading marked "Freight Paid", it should be ensured that all the copies of the Bill of Lading are actually marked "Freight Paid".

Number of sets. A Bill of Lading is generally made out in the sets of two or three originals. All the originals are duly signed by the master of the ship or the agent of the steamship company and all the originals are equally valid for taking the delivery of the goods and once one original copy is utilised the other original B/L is obtained by the exporter from the Shipping Company and no original copy goes in the wrong hand. Few extra copies of B/L are also issued, generally marked as "Non-negotiable copy" which cannot be utilised for taking the delivery of the goods.

Type of B/L. The exporter has to decide what type of B/L is required by him. It will also depend upon the terms of the L/C, if the documents have to be drawn under L/C and the requirement of the banker if the documents are drawn under export contract and the same are required to be purchased by the bank. So long as the buyer (Importer) has not paid for the goods/accepted the Bill of Exchange if a usance bill is drawn, it would be in the interest of the exporter to make out a B/L to the order of the bank if he wants the bank to purchase the export bill. In case of export documents drawn under L/C, it should be, of course, as per the requirement of the L/C provided there is no violation of local exchange control regulations.

The important details that appear on a B/L are the name of the shipper/consignee/notify party/ship, voyage number and date, quantity and description of goods, marks, number of originals issued, whether on board, signature of issuing authority, port of shipment and destination port. These details are to be given in aligned Bill of Lading for combined transport and port to port shipment format explained in the Chapter on Aligned Documents.

The following are the various types of Bills of Lading, some of which are not acceptable under L/C unless specifically permitted.

(*a*) Received for Shipment B/L certifying only receipt of goods—not acceptable under L/C unless specifically permitted.

(*b*) On deck B/L containing a remark that goods are shipped on deck—not acceptable unless specifically permitted.

(*c*) On board B/L certifying goods received on board the ship.

(*d*) Combined B/L covering several modes of transport.

(*e*) Custody B/L issued by American warehouses pending arrival of carrying vessel in port—acceptable.

(*f*) Forwarding agent B/L issued by forwarding agents not accepted unless specifically authorised—a single B/L covering a group of several consignments meant for different consignees—delivery achieved by issuing delivery orders relating to specified portions of the whole consignment.

(*g*) House B/L unacceptable as either evidence, title or contract of carriage.

(*h*) Short form B/L one on which the detailed conditions of transportation are not printed—not acceptable unless specifically permitted.

(*i*) Through B/L covering goods being transhipped *en route*. It covers the whole voyage and is acceptable if transhipment is permitted.

(*j*) Charter Party B/L covering shipment on chartered ships—issued subject to charter party agreements which supersede the usual memorandum of conditions of carriage appearing on the reverse of B/L not acceptable unless specifically authorised.

(*k*) Ocean/Liner B/L covering shipment by sea from port of shipment by sea from port of shipment to destination—usually covering shipment made under Letter of Credit.

(*l*) Third party B/L is a B/L containing additional clauses limiting the responsibility of the shipping company and indicating defective conditions of the goods. Such a B/L is not acceptable under L/C unless specifically authorised. A clean B/L is one which does not bear any superimposed clause or annotation which expressly declares a defective condition of the goods and/or the packaging. A stale B/L is one which is tendered to the paying bank at so late a date, that though within validity of Letter of Credit it is impossible for it to be despatched to the consignee in time to reach him before the goods themselves arrive at destination port.

Precautions as to Bill of Lading under Letter of Credit

(i) It should be presented in full set (all the originals as stated in B/L) with as many negotiable and non-negotiable copy as mentioned in the L/C. All the originals should bear stamp duty.

(ii) It should be issued and manually signed by the shipping company or its authorised agents.

(iii) The Bills of Lading should be current Bills of Lading. At the time of presenting, if the normal period, required for the particular voyage calculated from the date of the Bill of Lading has expired, such Bills of Lading are treated as "Stale" Bill of Lading.

(iv) Bills of Lading should evidence that the goods are shipped on board unless the L/C permits "deck shipment."

(v) The following types of Bills of Lading should not be accepted (unless specifically called for in the L/C) unless it is a Combined Transport Document and it satisfies the relative exchange control regulations:

   (a) Bills of Lading issued by forwarding agents.
   (b) Charter Party Bills of Lading.
   (c) Country Craft or Sailing Vessel Bills of Lading.
   (d) Evidencing Shipment on Deck.
   (e) Port of Custody Bills of Lading.

(vi) If the L/C does not specifically prohibit, the following types of Bills of Lading can be accepted:

   (a) 'Through' Bills of Lading.
   (b) 'Short From' Bills of Lading.
   (c) Bills of Lading covering unutilised cargos such as those on pallets or in containers.

(vii) It should not contain any derogatory clauses as to the conditions of the goods and/or packaging.

(viii) It should state the name of the shippers/should be issued in the name of the shipper and blank endorsed or issued to the order of overseas bank, depending on the L/C terms. Bills of Lading should not be made out to the order of buyers.

(ix) It should evidence 'freight prepaid, (C&F of CIF contracts) or 'freight to pay' (FOB contracts) as required by the terms of shipment in the L/C.

(x) Received for shipment Bills of Lading if subsequently stamped as 'ON BOARD,' this stamp should bear the date of shipment "ON BOARD" and signature of the carrier.

(xi) Third party of Bills of Lading can be accepted unless otherwise prohibited in the L/C.

(xii) It should bear a date not later than the one stipulated for shipment in the L/C.

(xiii) Shipping marks, if any, should be as called for in the L/C.

(xiv) Ports of shipment and destination should concur with the L/C terms.

(xv) Gross and net weights should be as per invoice, weight certificate, etc.

(xvi) It should cover the entire voyage where transhipment is involved and is not prohibited in the L/C.

(xvii) It should state 'notify' company's name and address wherever called for in the L/C.

(xviii) Additional condition, *viz.* 'Stored in refrigerated compartment' etc. should be incorporated if called for in the L/C.

(xix) B/L need not contain full description of the goods, a short description will suffice. However, it should not be contradictory to the L/C stipulations.

(xx) The number of days which have elapsed since the issue of Bill of Lading should not exceed the period provided in the L/C.

Mate Receipt

Mate Receipt is issued by the Chief of Vessel after the cargo is loaded, and it contains the name of shipper, place of receipt, vessel and voyage No., port of loading, port of discharge, place of delivery, marks and Nos./container No., description of goods, gross weight and other details as per the new aligned document format reproduced in the next page. The receipt is of a transferable nature and must be presented in due course at the shipping company's office to be exchanged into Bill of Lading.

Combined Transport Document (CTD)

With the introduction of multimodal movement of goods in container on the basis of a single contract from and to the interior of the country, government has established Inland Container Depots (ICDs) at selected centres. These dry depots have made it possible to cover the entire movement of goods from ICD to destination, under one transport document called "Combined Transport Document" (CTD). Rules governing Combined Transport Documents are designed by International Chamber of Commerce (Brochure No. 298) considering the international practices. However, to suit the requirement of the Indian conditions, Foreign Exchange Dealers Association of India (FEDAI) in consultation with RBI and Ministry of Commerce has brought out two different sets of rules. CT Document evidence combined transport of goods by container from ICDs and differ in many respects from the traditional Bill of Lading. CT Documents provide an alternative to establishing a series of separate and non-uniform contacts for each segment of the total transport process. The brochure and formats brought out by FEDAI are arrived to standardise the rules and the practices of multimodal transportation of goods, so that consignor, consignee, the Combined Transport Operator (CTO) the bank and the insurer may have a clear understanding of the various aspects relating to carriage of goods in such a manner. Combined Transport Document (with paramount clause on agreed lines) is accepted for negotiation by banks in India under L/C which specifically calls for a CT Document issued subject to FEDAI rules for a Combined Transport Document (FEDAI Brochures 081 and 082 as the case may be). When the export is not covered by L/C bearing such a stipulation, such 082) to replace the CT Document by an ocean B/L issued soon after the container is loaded on board the ocean going vessel.

II. Preparing Invoices

Proforma Invoice

As the name denotes, it is an invoice in established proforma, payment of which is not intended. These invoices are used for obtaining financial assistance like packing credit from institution as proforma invoice together with an offer and acceptance with from a legal contact.

Commercial Invoice

It is the most widely used invoice in commercial transactions. It is the statement of account of sale rendered by the seller to the buyer and is prepared on new aligned document forma. The invoice is usually made out for the full realisable amount of goods as per trade, the exception being the undrawn balance which is shown as a deduction from the full amount.

If the export documents are drawn under L/C unless otherwise stated in the L/C commercial invoice must be made out in the name of the applicant for the credit and the description of the goods in the commercial invoice must correspond with the description in the credit. Similarly it should be noted that unless otherwise stipulated in the credit, banks may refuse commercial invoice issued for amount in excess of the amount permitted by the credit. The invoice should be strictly according to the contract of sale and should be on the paper of the seller and must be signed by him or by the person acting on his behalf.

Guidelines for Preparing Invoice under L/C

(i) It should be duly dated and manually signed by him and in sufficient copies as per the L/C terms.

(ii) It should be made out in the name of opener of the L/C (buyer) unless otherwise stated.

(iii) The description of the goods must strictly correspond to that stated in the L/C. Invoice may show additional description of the goods which should be in conflict with the description as per the L/C. In all other documents, the goods may be described in general terms, but not inconsistent with the description in the L/C.

(iv) Terms of shipment, *e.g.*, CIF/C&F/FOB etc. should be as called for in the L/C.

(v) Other particular such as shipping marks, quantity measurement details, gross and net weights, port of shipment, destination, name of the vessel, bill of landing, number and date stated in the invoice should strictly match with the details given in other documents especially the shipping documents.

(vi) It should be certified by bodies like Chamber of Commerce, Consulate, buyer's local representative, etc. wherever called for.

(vii) Invoice value should not exceed the L/C amount and should be on the basis of agreed price and quantity. The currency should also be mentioned in the L/C. These particulars of the invoice should also agree with the draft.

(viii) Should quote import licence number, sale contract number, etc. where required as per L/C terms.

(ix) Invoices should quote GR/PP Form number.

(x) Invoices should contain the various certifications from the seller, if the L/C so specifies.

(xi) The invoice should not show any deduction or addition not authorised by the credit.

Consular Invoice

Consular Invoice, is document required mainly by the American countries like, Kenya, Uganda, Tanzania, Mauritius, New Zealand, Burma, Iraq, Australia, Fiji, Cyprus, Ghana, Zanzibar etc. This invoice is most important document which need to be submitted for certification to the Embassy of the country concerned. The exporter has to pay to the Embassy concerned some fees for the certification of this invoice.

A consular invoice is required to be prepared in a prescribed format and it should be signed/certified by the consul of the importing country located in the country of export. The main purpose of a consular invoice is to enable the importer's country to collect accurate and authenticated information about the value, quality, source etc. of the import for assessing import duties and for other statistical purposes. It helps the importer to get cleared the goods though the customers without any undue delay. The consular invoice forms are generally available at the importing country's consuls and is certified against payment of some fees.

Consular invoices should be made in multiple copies as per the buyer's requirements.

Customs Invoice

Countries like USA, Canada etc. need custom's invoice. It is generally made out on a special form presented by the customs authorities of the importing country and helps for allowing entry of goods in the importing country at preferential tariff rates. The invoice forms are generally available at the consular office of the importing country and are required to be signed and witnessed after duly filing the same.

Rules of Origin for Filling Canada Customs Invoice

Country of Origin means the country of which goods are *bona fide* growth, produce or manufacture.

In their present form, ready for export the goods must have been finished in the country specified as the country of origin.

In addition, there is a not less than one-half the cost of production requirements" for the qualification for entry under the British Preferential Tariff and Most-Favoured-Nation-Tariff.

For goods seeking entry under the British Preferential Tariff, not less than one-half the cost of production of each such article must have been incurred through the industry of one or more countries entitled to the British Preferential Tariff.

The British content requirement of "one-half" has been modified in the case of a small number of commodities which are mentioned in Canada Customs Memorandum D-36.

For goods seeking entry under the Most-Favoured-Nation Tariff, not less than one-half the cost of production must have been incurred through the industry of countries entitled to the benefits of the Most-Favoured-Nation-Tariff or the British Preferential Tariff.

In the Calculation of cost of production for determining the qualification for entry under the British Preferential Tariff or Most-Favoured-Nation-Tariff, none of the following items are to be included to be considered, *viz.*:

(i) Outside packages and expenses of packing thereinto.
(ii) Manufacturer's or Export's profit and profit or remuneration of any trader, broker or other person dealing in the article in its finished manufactured condition.
(iii) Royalties.
(iv) Customs or excise duty or tax paid or payable on imported materials.
(v) Carriage, insurance etc., from place of production of manufacture to proof shipment.
(vi) Any other charges incurred or to be incurred subsequent to the completion of the manufacture of the goods.

Different rules apply for goods seeking entry under the General Preferential Tariff and a Certificate of Origin From A required, Information regarding the General Preferential Tariff may be obtained from customs Memorandum D 47-518-3.

Fair Market Value

When like goods are sold in the country of export:

> The value to be placed in the fair market value column shall be the invoiced price at which like goods shipped to Canada plus a percentage advance which is equal to the percentage mark up over production cost included in the fair market value of similar goods when sold for home consumption in the country of export to customers with whom the vendor deals at arms length.

When establishing fair market value on the basis of sales of like or similar goods, the following rules apply:

(1) Except as provided (2) below, the only discounts or deductions allowed are those which are shown, allowed and deducted on invoices covering sales for home consumption in the ordinary course of trade. In particular, subsidies, rebates and exemption from or drawback of any Customs duty may not be used to reduce fair market value.

(2) Commodity taxes levied on like or similar goods within the country of export may be deducted from the fair market value providing the goods shipped to Canada have been or will be exempted or relieved from such taxes.

The amount should be shown as a deduction from the fair market value, with appropriate notation.

(3) Fair market value must reflect sales prices in the country of export to purchasers located at the place of direct shipment to Canada, or as near thereto as possible, who are the same or substantially the same trade level as the importer, or at the next and subsequent trade level. The place of direct shipment is the place where the goods begin their continuous journey to Canada.

(4) Fair market value must reflect sales price in effect at the time of shipment of Canada or those made recently prior thereto, and in the same quantities as shipped to Canada or in smaller quantities.

(5) Cost of production includes all materials, labour and factory overheads. The costs of the exported goods and of goods may not be reduced by any subsidy or by reason of exemption from or drawback of any Customs duty.

(6) Where the fair market value is not based on home market sales of like or similar goods it must be determined under other provisions of the Customs Act.

(7) Where packing is included in the price at which goods are sold to purchasers in the country of export, like of substitute packing must be included in the invoiced fair market value of the goods. Additional packing for the overseas transportation of the goods may be invoiced separately as export packing.

Legalised/Visaed Invoice

These are the invoices sworn for their genuineness by the seller as being correct before the appropriate consulate/chamber of commerce/embassy as the case may be and they bear the stamp and authentication of the consulate chamber of commerce/embassy as being in order. A nominal charge is collected by them from the seller for doing this. These invoices are required by some of the

Latin American countries. There is no prescribed form of this invoice.

Certified Invoice

At times exporter is called upon to certify on the invoice that the goods are of particular origin or manufactured/packed at a particular place and in accordance with specific contract. When certificated as appear on the invoice it is called as a certified invoice.

III. Preparing Bill of Exchange/Draft

Meaning of Bill of Exchange/Draft

According to section 5 of the Negotiable Instruments Act, 1881, a bill of exchange is "an instrument in writing containing an unconditional order, signed by the marker, directing a certain person to pay a certain sum of money only to or to the order of a person or to the bearer of the instrument."

A bill of exchange contains an order from the creditor to the debtor to pay a specified amount to a person mentioned therein. The maker of a bill is called the "drawer," the person who is directed to pay is called the "drawee." The person who is entitled to receive payment is called the "payee."

When it is drawn on a foreign firm it is termed as a foreign draft or bill of exchange. It is prepared either in an international currency or Indian rupees depending on the terms of contract. Accordingly, the bill is known by the name of currency in which it is drawn. For example, a bill drawn in US dollars is known a 'Dollar Bill' and when prepared in rupees, being termed as 'Rupee Bill.'

When the goods are shipped by sea, the bills are drawn in sets and two sets of documents including drafts are mailed to the foreign correspondent through an authorised dealer for presentation to the drawee (importer). Each one bears a reference to the other.

Draft/Bill of Exchange are of two types:

(i) 'Sight Draft' or 'Draft at Sight' and
(ii) Usance Draft or Usance Bill.

When the drawer *i.e.*, exporter expects the drawee *i.e.*, importer to make payment immediately after the draft is presented to him, it is called a 'Sight Draft.' Unless and until this draft is retired, the negotiating/collecting bank does not hand over the shipping documents and the buyer cannot take delivery of goods.

Where the exporter has agreed to give credit to the foreign buyer, he draws a 'Usance Bill' *i.e.* draft is drawn for payment at a date later than the date of presentation. A draft may be drawn according to the period of credit such as 30 days sight, 60 days sight and so on, implying thereby, that the drawee *i.e.*, importer is to retire the draft 30 days or 60 days or as the case may be, after it is presented to the drawee who will retire it by writing upon it 'Accepted' with his signature and date.

Thereafter, the documents are handed over to him for enabling him to take the delivery of goods.

As there is no aligned document for draft, the same can be prepared by the exporter in the usual format.

Clean Bill and Documentary Bill

When the drawer of a bill encloses with it a document of title to goods or any other equivalent document it is called a documentary bill.

In an export transaction the exporter delivers to the banker documents like full set of B/L, AWB, PPR etc. together with documents like drafts invoices, packing list etc. for presentment to the drawee.

Depending upon the tenor of the bill *i.e.*, D/P or D/A the documents are delivered to the drawee against payment or acceptance. If no such document is attached with the bill, it is a clean bill. Personal cheques, drafts and travellers cheques are some of the examples of clean bills.

Stamp Duty

There is no longer any stamp duty on either the sight drafts or usance drafts drawn on or made or in favour of a commercial bank or co-operative bank and such bills of exchange are raised out of *bona fide* commercial or trade transactions.

Specimen of Bill of Exchange

There is no standardised format for bill of exchange. It can be prepared in the casual tradition format.

Guidelines for Drawing Bill of Exchange Under L/C

(i) It should be marked as drawn under L/C quoting the L/C number, date and name of L/C issuing bank.

(ii) It should be drawn on the party/bank as stated in the L/C.

(iii) It should be drawn or endorsed in favour of the negotiating bank.

(iv) Amount in words and of figures should agree and be within the available amount under the L/C except when the credit uses the word "about/circa" before the amount. In such cases drawing can exceed the credit amount by 10%.

(v) It should be dated and signed by an authorised person under the seal of the drawer from company, who should be the beneficiary under the L/C.

(vi) If L/C calls for usance draft, the usance should not exceed six months from the date of shipment as per exchange control regulations. Also ensure that the tenor is as per L/C terms.

(vii) The draft should be drawn in sets as per L/C requirements with a minimum of two are marked "FIRST", "SECOND" etc.

(viii) Amount of the draft should correspond to the net amount of the invoice.

(ix) Corrections/alterations should be properly authenticated.

(x) It should bear interest clause wherever necessary.

Acceptance of Usance Bill of Exchange

A bill of exchange payable on demand or at sight or on a fixed date does not need acceptance and hence presentment for acceptance is unnecessary unless such presentation is specifically desired. A bill of exchange payable after sight must be presented for acceptance since the maturity date of the bill can only be determined after such acceptance.

When the drawee of a bill signifies his consent to the drawer's order in the bill by writing his name across the face of the bill with or without the word "accepted" the bill is said to be "accepted." Acceptance of a bill, therefore, means that the drawee gives his consent to pay the amount mentioned therein on the due date/maturity date. The foreign correspondent usually advise the due date to the exporter through his banker in India. On acceptance of the bill, the drawee shall be known as the acceptor and bears the liability to pay the amount of the bill. Usually in exports an acceptance of the bill is a general acceptance and qualified acceptance cannot be entertained.

Noting/Protesting of Foreign Bills

At the time the bills are forwarded to the exporter's bank it is advisable to provide the bank with clear instructions/ steps to be taken in case the bills are dishonoured on presentation or maturity as the case may be. The drawee/holder for value may cause the dishonoured bill to be noted by a Notary Public on the instrument or upon a paper attached thereto or partly upon each. The Notary formally makes a demand of acceptance or payment upon the acceptor or drawee and on his refusal to do so notes the same on the bill. Thus, 'Noting' means the fact the bill has been dishonoured is recorded on it and puts the drawer/holder for value on a higher pedestal in the eyes of law. This is done within a reasonable time after dishonour. Usually the Notary makes the following observations:

- *(a)* The date of dishonour
- *(b)* The reason, if any, assigned for such dishonour
- *(c)* The Notary's charges

The foreign bills must, thereafter be protested for dishonour for it is to be placed as a documentary evidence in the court of law. In other words the observations made thereon by the Notary will be taken at face value. A "protest" is a certificate issued by the Notary Public attesting that the bill has been dishonoured and will usually contain:

- *(a)* the name of the person for whom and against whom the instrument has been protested;
- *(b)* a statement that acceptance or payment was demanded from the acceptor or drawee by the Notary Public and the reason for dishonour;
- *(c)* the place and time of dishonour of the bill;
- *(d)* the signature of the Notary Public.

IV. Obtaining/Preparing Other Documents

Black List Certificate

This is to certify that the ship/aircraft carrying the goods has not touched a particular country on its journey or that the goods are not of a particular country. This certificate is usually called for where countries have strained political relations with another.

Weight Note

This document is used to confirm that the packets/bales etc. are of a particular weight and not more than the stipulated weight as per contract. It may at times give the gross weight and net weight of the whole consignment.

Packing List

It is a list showing details of goods contained in each parcel/ shipment. It shows item-by-item the contents of the containers or parcels shipped to enable the buyer/receiver of the shipment to check the shipment.

Manufacturer's/Supplier's Quality/Inspection Certificate

This is a certificate to the effect that the goods which have been manufactured/supplied are as per the requirement of the contract of sale.

Certificate of Inspection

Inspection certificate, indicating that goods have been inspected before shipment is needed under some contracts or by some countries. This certificate is generally required to be issued by one of the authorised independent inspection agencies/surveyors in the exporter's country. The certificate is issued in the aligned document from as per guidelines give in Chapter on Aligned Export Documents. For further details refer to Chapter on Complying with Quality Control and Preshipment Inspection Requirements.

Languages Certificate

Importers in the EEC countries require a Languages Certificate along with the GSP Certificate in respect of handloom cotton fabrics classifiable under NEMEX Code 55.09. Indian exporters should apply for this certificate simultaneously or separately with the GSP Certificate and application for pre-shipment inspection. The Languages Certificate is issued in quadruplicate, three copies of which are given to the exporter. He should transmit one copy to his overseas importer, along with documents for realisation of export proceeds.

The Languages Certificate is issued by the Textile Committee against a small fee.

Manufacturer's Certificate

In addition to the Certificate of Origin, some countries require a manufacturer's certificate to the effect that goods shipped have actually been manufactured and are available.

Certificate of Chemical Analysis

To ensure that the quality and grade of items like metallic ores, pigments, etc., is the same as specified in the sale contract, importers may require the exporters to send a certificate of chemical analysis from a recognised analyst.

Certificate of Shipment

Certificate of shipping agent that a certain lot of goods have been shipped.

Health/Veterinary/Sanitary Certificates

When the goods that are imported are foodstuffs, marine products hide, livestock etc., usually depending upon the goods which are being imported a certificate from the health/veterinary/sanitary authorities called for. This is because the importer desires to know if the goods are fit for human consumption.

Certificate of Conditioning

Certificate issued by a competent office in which on the basis of the ascertained humidity factor, the dry weight of wool or silk is reckoned and certified.

GSP Certificate

The EEC Member Countries have adopted the Generalised for Preferences. Under GSP, manufactures and semi-manufacturers from developing countries including India will be entitled to a concessional rate import duty in these countries.

Antiquity Certificate

This certificate is issued by the Archaeological Survey of India in the case of antiques.

Certificate of Measurement

Freight can be charged either on the basis of weight or measurement. When it is charged on weight basis, the weight declared by exporter is accepted. However, certificate of measurement from the Indian Chambers of Commerce or any other approved organisation may be obtained by the exporter and given to the shipping company for calculation of necessary freight. This certificate contains the name of the vessel, the port of destination, description of goods, quantity, lengths, breadth, depth etc. of packages.

Transhipment Bill

This document is used for goods imported into a customs port/ airport intended for transhipment.

Transhipment Permit

The Transhipment Permit is the permission for transhipment of goods from the vessel on which the same are booked originally to another for export.

Shipping Order

Shipping order is issued by the admittance of cargo through the port gate. This is also known as 'Vehicle Ticket or Gate Pass.' This includes the details of export cargo, *i.e.*, Shipper's name, Cart/Lorry number, marks on packages, quantity and description.

Shut Out Advance

It is a statement of packages shut out by a ship and is prepared by the shed concerned and sent to the exporter showing the particulars of packages for disposal arrangement.

Short Shipment Form

Short shipment form is an application to the customs authorities at advising the short shipment of goods and for claiming the return of the duty and/or cess paid on such short shipping goods.

Shipping Advice

A shipping advice is used to inform the overseas customer about the shipment advice is prepared in aligned document. The exporter only advises his importer about the invoice number, Bill of Lading/Airway Bill number and date, name of the vessel with date, the port of export, description of goods and quantity and the date of sailing of the vessel.

Index